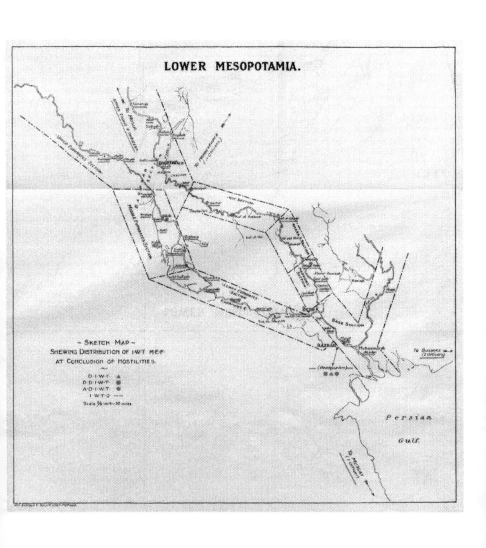

LOWER MESOPOTAMIA.

~ SKETCH MAP ~
SHEWING DISTRIBUTION OF I.W.T. M.E.F.
AT CONCLUSION OF HOSTILITIES.

D·I·W·T
D·D·I·W·T
A·D·I·W·T
I·W·T·O

Scale ½ inch = 32 miles.

Persian

Gulf.

THE INLAND WATER TRANSPORT
IN MESOPOTAMIA

THE INLAND
WATER TRANSPORT
IN MESOPOTAMIA

COMPILED BY

LIEUT.-COL. L. J. HALL O.B.E., R.E.

ASST. DIRECTOR I.W.T.

UNDER THE DIRECTION OF

BRIGADIER-GENERAL R. H. W. HUGHES

C.S.I., C.M.G., D.S.O., R.D.

OFFICIER DE LEGION D'HONNEUR
DIRECTOR OF INLAND WATER TRANSPORT
MESOPOTAMIAN EXPEDITIONARY FORCE

The Naval & Military Press Ltd

published in association with

FIREPOWER
The Royal Artillery Museum
Woolwich

Published by
The Naval & Military Press Ltd
Unit 10 Ridgewood Industrial Park,
Uckfield, East Sussex,
TN22 5QE England
Tel: +44 (0) 1825 749494
Fax: +44 (0) 1825 765701
www.naval–military-press.com

in association with

FIREPOWER
The Royal Artillery Museum, Woolwich
www.firepower.org.uk

*In reprinting in facsimile from the original, any imperfections are inevitably reproduced
and the quality may fall short of modern type and cartographic standards.*

MAJOR-GENERAL SIR G. F. MacMUNN, K.C.B., K.C.S.I., D.S.O., Inspector-General of Communications, Mesopotamian Expeditionary Force, under whose orders the Inland Water Transport operated.

FOREWORD

I HAVE much pleasure in writing a foreword to Lieut.-Colonel Hall's excellent summary of the work done by the Inland Water Transport in Mesopotamia.

In April, 1916, just before the fall of Kut, I took over the duty of Inspector-General of Communications in Mesopotamia, with control of all the services behind the Field Army. At that time, and for long after, the rivers were the only ways by which an army of any size could be maintained. We had a large army and a very inadequate river service, with the result that the army received neither food nor munitions in adequate quantities, and the organisation of a really efficient river service was far beyond any of the resources and personnel that India could make available.

The War Office came to our rescue by sending out a man with a first-class organising head—Brigadier-General (afterwards Major-General) Grey, C.B.—with adequate assistance, followed up by first-class men from the various professions and trades connected with a river service. There was built up almost from the beginning a really first-class river service, with adequate dockyards behind, repair yards up the river, and every sort of installation that would increase speed and power of delivery. In spite of the concurrent railway working part of the way, the river service had to perform the bulk of the work for a long time. It was necessary for the needs of the army to form a river organisation larger than any other in the world, till eventually the combined rail and river service was delivering close on 3000 tons per diem at 500 miles from the port at Basrah.

This result was not attained without the most devoted work of all ranks, and it must be remembered that while some of the winter months are bitterly cold, the heat on the river from May to September is that of a fiery furnace. I would specially dwell on the support that we received from the Directorate of Docks and Inland Waterways at the War Office, who sent us all that we asked for, and on the large number of marine personnel, and the supplies of workshop machinery sent from India. With a fleet of close on 2000 units, it will be realised that the slipways, machinery, and labour required for repairs was a very large item, in addition to erecting yards where barges and smaller craft were put together. This fleet came to us from all over the world for the I.W.T. to organise. Many craft were erected at Basra, while a large number had been already put in hand by the India Office after the inadequacy of the service had been realised.

The report by Lieut.-Colonel Hughes (afterwards Brig.-General and Director of Inland Water Transport) of the work of the vessels accompanying the army during the advance on Baghdad, describes the apotheosis of effort. That advance to Baghdad came before the effects of organisation had matured, and my assurances of maintenance to General Maude were on the very margin of sufficiency. He decided to make the dash, and as the news of the advance brought the sick crawling from the hospitals, so steamers emerged from docks and slipways, and, by a great effort, the victorious army was supplied and reinforced, at a time of heaviest flood, and through a hot weather of unusual severity.

The organisation of this huge river fleet, in an undeveloped country in the midst of war, has been the largest thing of its kind ever seen, and is a lasting example of the value of thoroughness, and of " going large " from the start. Had the Inland Water Transport been run on an inadequate groundwork, or had the War Office or the authorities in India cavilled at our demands, we could neither have maintained the victorious army to its ultimate destination—the Turkish Army from Kut to Mosul—nor could the troops have been kept in the remarkable state of health and efficiency eventually obtained.

The record of the Inland Water Transport, R.E., should remain as a textbook and a pattern for many generations to come.

Signed : G. F. MacMUNN,

Major-General,

Offg. Commander-in-Chief,

Mesopotamian Expeditionary Force.

BAGHDAD, 7–8–1919.

A 2

Brigadier-General R. H. W. Hughes, C.S.I., C.M.G., D.S.O., Director of Inland Water Transport in Mesopotamia from May 1917 till the end of the War.

PREFACE

In order to obtain a clear impression of the difficulties to be encountered and to appreciate subsequent developments, a brief review of the conditions regarding River Transport in Mesopotamia previous to August, 1916, would, in the first instance, appear desirable.

It would be difficult to convey a better idea of the state of affairs existing generally at that time than that expressed in the Report of the Mesopotamian Commission, some extracts from which are given below.

It is necessary to quote somewhat at length to obtain a more correct perspective of the sequence of events leading up to and the reasons for establishing an Inland Water Transport organisation in Mesopotamia.

Extracts from Chapter IX (Transport).—1. River Transport was, from the beginning of the campaign, a dominant factor, as its sufficiency or insufficiency regulated the movements of the expedition.

2. Evidence is overwhelming that a shortage of River Transport existed from the time of the occupation of Kurna in December, 1914, and became serious from and after May, 1915. Despite additions that were made, the shortage had become relatively even greater in April, 1916, than at any earlier period of the campaign, owing to the increased numbers of the Force. Practically at no time after the advance above Kurna was River Transport adequate to requirements. It greatly delayed military operations, in which celerity was an important factor for success ; it affected the comfort and feeding of the troops, and it was a direct cause of suffering to the sick and wounded. As evidence of the shortage, we have been told that it took nearly two months to concentrate troops and supplies for

the advance from Amara to Kut-el-Amara, and that again the advance from Kut and Aziziyeh towards Baghdad was fatally delayed from the same cause. It seems almost certain that, but for the shortage of River Transport, the Turkish Army would have been destroyed between Amara and Ctesiphon. The want was most acutely felt during the strenuous time when every day counted in the attempt to relieve the siege of Kut ; here, in view of the straits in which General Townshend reported his force to be, time was of the utmost importance.

3. General Lake, at that time General Officer Commanding in Mesopotamia, telegraphed to the Chief of the General Staff, Delhi, on March 22nd, 1916, as follows :—

" I doubt firstly whether the paralysing effect which the inadequacy and late supply of River Craft has had on the operations up the Tigris is fully realised by the General Staff at home, and, secondly, why our forecasts as to what it will be possible to convey up-river have varied, and of late have considerably developed. On January 21st, 1916, when Aylmer fought his action at Hannah, there were 10,000 Infantry and 12 Guns in the country available as reinforcements, but which, owing to this cause, could not be sent up to him in time.

" On March 8th, the date of his last operations, I had, approximately, 12,000 Infantry and 26 Guns which, for similar reasons, could not be forwarded."

The evidence shows conclusively that shortage of River Transport was the chief cause of the failure to relieve Kut.

4. The evidence before us tends to show that improved control and administration of the river craft available would have mitigated the evils arising from the shortage, although at no time could such improvement have entirely overcome them. In this connection it should be noted that the work of controlling and managing a miscellaneous fleet of river steamers, tugs, and barges, with their crews, their upkeep, and their traffic, was not in the usual line of Army or Royal Indian Marine experience. It is, we think, unfortunate that someone with experience of the management of such flotillas, on one of the rivers of India or Burma, was not at an early date appointed to assist in this work.

5. In November, 1914, when General Barrett took possession of Basrah, the River Transport available consisted of three steamers, viz. : the *Medjidieh*, which was the most serviceable ; the *Julnar*, which required new engines, and the *Salimi*, which was used as a ferry-boat between Basrah and Kurna. Besides these, there were four lighters of 60 tons, two of 110 tons, and ten of 200 tons, making sixteen in all, and some country sailing boats or mahailas, with a capacity of from 25 to 35 tons.

6. On November 23rd, 1914, after Basrah was occupied, at a conference held at Army Headquarters, Commander A. Hamilton, R.I.M., recommended to the General Staff that they should at once ask for twelve river steamers of the *Medjidieh* class. Commander Hamilton had previously been on the Tigris for two years, and had surveyed the river from Basrah to Baghdad. He was, therefore, competent to speak with exceptional knowledge both of the river and of the class of steamer most suitable to its navigation. He urged the necessity of giving orders early, and, owing to the necessary delay in building the vessels, which he estimated at twelve months, he suggested that they should be got from India ready-built. Nothing, however, was done until January 2nd, 1915, when, in reply to an enquiry as to the steamers available for use above Kurna, General Barrett telegraphed to India that, in order to carry a force of one brigade, one squadron, one battery, and one company of sappers and miners, with five hundred mules and supplies for ten days, seven steamers and one or two lighters would be required in addition to the existing flotilla. These seven steamers and two lighters were purchased in India during February, 1915. They arrived at Basrah in May of the same year. On February 17th, 1915, General Barrett asked for four river tugs, which were purchased in India early in March, 1915, and arrived at Basrah shortly after the seven steamers.

7. On May 27th, 1915, General Nixon, who had in April taken command, informed India that the paddle-steamers and tugs sent could not be relied upon to work above Kurna,

owing to their comparatively deep draught and to the low-ness of the river at certain seasons, and asked for six more tugs of certain power, and with a draught not to exceed 3 feet, subsequently modified to 3 feet 6 inches. There were difficulties in finding in India tugs conforming to the specification, and the order was ultimately passed on to England and merged in the August demand, for river craft to be built there. On July 8th, 1915, a comprehensive memorandum was drawn up by General Kemball and forwarded to India by General Nixon. In this memorandum the shortage of River Craft, and the urgent need for further supplies of craft of a suitable type, were urgently emphasised, and warnings given that if steps were not taken in good time to meet these requirements grave risks were being run of a breakdown at possibly a serious moment.

It was pointed out that the most effective use of the troops available could not be made owing to want of River Transport, and that in any crisis aid by reinforcements would be limited, while a breakdown of steamers might have still more serious consequences. With the memorandum came a pressing request for the building in England of :

Six paddle-steamers of the *Medjidieh* class.
Three stern-wheelers of lighter draught.
Eight tugs of the *Sumana* class.
Forty-three barges to specifications given.

The purport of these requirements was telegraphed to London on August 4th, 1915.

8. Eventually, orders for the six paddle-steamers, three stern-wheel steamers, and eight tugs were placed on November 3rd, 1915, orders for the barges being placed a few days later. The first of these tugs reached Abadan in April, 1916, the first paddlers and stern-wheelers in June, 1916, and the forty-three barges arrived at different dates between April, 1916, and end of the year. All except the six paddle-steamers were shipped either in sections or in the form of plates, and had to be erected after arrival in Meso-potamia, so that a considerable period elapsed after their

arrival before they were available for use. Some were not ready in January, 1917.

Arrangements for their erection in Mesopotamia were made by the India Office, with little prevision of what would be required. The arrangements proved to be quite inadequate. It was a work of no little magnitude to discharge, assemble, erect and fit up complete eleven steamers and forty-three barges, with insufficient plant and mechanics and under trying local conditions. Much loss of valuable time occurred, and vessels expected to be ready for use a few weeks after arrival were not available for many months. Some of the craft were sent in very large and heavy sections. Means of handling them in Mesopotamia proved inadequate, and when an attempt was made to put them together in the river it was found almost impossible, and some sections sank in thirty feet of water. Part of the remaining sections were then ordered to be sent to Bombay for erection there, and thereafter to be towed back to Basrah, involving much cost, risk, and delay. Material for the erection of the barges and other craft was sent out in large shipments. No descriptive note of contents of packages accompanied the first shipments, and no drawings or erection plans were sent with them. The latter were only received in September, 1916, for vessels, the materials for which had arrived four or five months previously. The confusion which arose from this unbusinesslike proceeding was almost unbelievable, and must have been heart-breaking, in view of the urgent need for vessels. Cases were discharged up and down the bank of the river, and stretched a long distance. To find a particular piece required for the completion of any particular barge, tug, or steamer was almost hopeless.

9. Finding that the order from England meant at least twelve months' delay, and in view of the supreme importance of meantime obtaining more River Transport without delay, General Nixon telegraphed to India on October 9th, 1915, as follows :—

"Please procure quickly some powerful light draught tugs or stern-wheelers in India, which will serve present needs and thereby greatly strengthen military operations which are very seriously impeded. This is very urgent need."

and again on October 13th, 1915 :—

" If anything of suitable draught and approximating to other requirements can be sent here soon they will serve as useful stopgaps till new craft arrives. Please, therefore, do whatever is possible to meet our urgent difficulties meanwhile."

In response to these pressing messages, the Indian Government eventually secured in India a large number of steamers and barges which did not, however, arrive till January to April, 1916.

10. The workshops and slips which existed in Mesopotamia on the outbreak of war were naturally of small size, and quite unfitted to cope with the erection and repair of the large fleet of river craft required by the Expeditionary Force. So far as normal conditions were concerned, and even with the outlook of greater trade after the War, there was nothing in prospect to induce the local firms largely to increase their workshops. In consequence, with the arrangements with the Admiralty and India Office, some extensions were undoubtedly made, but these were far short of the needs.

11. After the War Office took control, during 1916, the matter was comprehensively taken in hand. Since that time over 7000 tons of plant for workshops have been sent from England, India, and elsewhere.

Conclusions.—Amongst the conclusions arrived at by the Commission, the following are quoted regarding River Transport :—

A deficiency of River Transport existed from the time the Army left tidal water and advanced up-river from Kurna. This deficiency became very serious as the Lines of Communication lengthened and the numbers of the Forces increased.

Up to the end of 1915 the efforts made to rectify the deficiency of River Transport were wholly inadequate.

During the four months of 1916 the shortage of Transport was fatal to the operations undertaken for the relief of Kut. Large reinforcements could not be moved to the front in time to take part in critical battles.

Bhoosa Pier. Taken from Lookout Tower on Headquarters Buildings.

CONTENTS

PART III

APPENDICES

LIST OF PLATES

xix

The Inland Water Transport in Mesopotamia

PART I

THE WATERWAYS OF MESOPOTAMIA

IT will be convenient to give a brief description of the waterways operated by the Inland Water Transport, and their physical conditions, before proceeding further.

Tigris and Shatt-el-Arab.—Between Abadan and Basrah the only impediment to navigation is the Mohammerah Bar, which is situated below its junction with the Karun River, extends for over half a mile, and consists of a series of sandy lumps in the middle of the river. A good channel lies towards the right bank and this bar cannot be considered as presenting any serious obstruction, being easily removed by dredging to a navigable depth of 20 feet.

The distance from Basrah to Baghdad is approximately 498 miles by water, though only 346 by land route, an indication of the tortuous nature of the navigable channel.

The bar at Gurmat Ali, with a depth of 15 feet L.W.O.S. during the low-water season, is the principal obstruction for shipping to Nahr Umar, but vessels drawing up to 19 feet are able to proceed to Nahr Umar at high-water spring-tides with safety. Difficulty in turning in the narrow channel at Nahr Umar limits their length to about 450 feet.

Shipping to Kurna is limited by the Kurna Bar, which carries a maximum depth of 10 feet during the low-water

B

season in September–November, and a maximum depth of 15 feet during the high-water season in April–May. A tidal range of 2 feet with ebb and flow is felt at Kurna during the low-water season, but during the high-water season the fluctuation is very little and no actual flood-tide is experienced. The average width of the Shatt-el-Arab between Basrah and Kurna is 450 yards during the low-water season, contracting to about 500 feet just above the Shwaiyib Canal. Kurna is situated at the confluence of the Tigris with the old channel of the Euphrates.

Although Kurna forms the limit of ocean navigation, sloops of the *Odin* and *Espiegle* class ascended the Tigris to Ezra's Tomb during the operations of 1915, some difficulty being experienced owing to the tortuous course of the river and sharp bends.

Proceeding up the Tigris from Kurna to Amara, the river soon assumes the aspect of a canal flowing between low banks, with a minimum depth of 8 to 9 feet during the high-river but varying from year to year.

At Ghumaijah Sharghi, 4 miles above Ezra's Tomb, a large accession of water from the marshes on the left bank is received into the Tigris. Above this again a large amount of water is drawn off for irrigation purposes by the following canals : Abu Tamr on the right bank above the Central Control Station, Saiyid Canal on the right bank at Qualet Saleh, Michriya Canal on the left bank 26 miles below Amara, and the Majar Kebir Canal on the right bank 10 miles below Amara.

The average width of the river in the Narrows is about 300 feet, and a complete description of this section is given on page 179 under this sectional heading.

Qualet Saleh on the left bank is the principal town between Kurna and Amara.

Amara, situated on the left bank, is a town of considerable size and importance. The northern terminus of the Basrah-Amara Railway was on the right bank, also large repair shops, stocks of coal and oil fuel, supply dumps and hospitals. The Chahala Canal takes off from the Tigris left

Front of Headquarters Building, Busrah, decorated on occasion of Peace Celebrations.

bank immediately above Amara. Before it was partially bunded, it diverted about 50 per cent of the Tigris water into the marshes. Above Amara the Tigris again increases in width, averaging from 600 to 800 yards, decreasing to narrow necks at places, but with good channels as far as Ali-ash-Shargi on the left bank and 36 miles beyond Amara. The river-banks gradually increase in height, reaching 20 to 25 feet during the low-water season.

From Ali-ash-Shargi upwards, navigation during the low-water season is much impeded by shifting shoals and sandbanks, although during the low-water season of 1917 traffic between Amara and Kut ran with practically no interruption. The minimum depth was 5 feet for short periods between these two points, and the average minimum depth 6 feet.

Kut Port, on the left bank, is distinct from the native town of Kut. This is the southern terminus of the Kut-Baghdad Railway, and, like Amara, is the site of large repair workshops, coal and oil depots and supply dumps. Kut town, also on the left bank opposite the Hai River, is a place of considerable and growing commercial importance.

From Kut upwards, navigation presents greater difficulties throughout the entire stretch of river to Baghdad, the minimum depth having fallen as low as 4 to 5 feet in several reaches during the low-water season of 1917.

From Baghdad to Sinijah, the general physical conditions are similar to the section below, namely, mud, sand, and silt, with stiff clay banks, though navigable conditions are not so favourable. Vessels of 3 feet draught or over are unable to proceed beyond Khan Jadidah during the low-river.

Above Sinijah the river spreads out into wide expanses, dotted with islands, at places contracting to narrow necks. The river-banks and bottom consist of gravel conglomerate rock and boulders. Holding ground is very bad, currents swift over shoals and fords, and there are many sharp and awkward bends to negotiate. Bitumen and gypsum in places bind stones and gravel together with almost the consistency of concrete, and vessels swept against such banks are liable to severe damage.

The Tigris has its source in the Armenian highlands, which also give rise to the Euphrates. The Tigris is peculiar, in that in all its long course to the sea it has few tributaries. The Greater and Lesser Zab, Shat-al-Adhaim, Dialah, and the Wadi, all on the left bank, are the only streams of importance that flow into it. Of these, the Shat-al-Adhaim is practically dry in the summer and autumn, whilst the volume of water discharged from the Dialah and Wadi is very small during the same period.

High- and Low-Water Season.—The high-water season extends from January to June-July. During the earlier part of high-water season, due to the winter rains, sudden fluctuations occur in the river levels, but they generally maintain a slight upward tendency. The first snow-rise occurs during the earlier half of March as a rule, and is due to the melting of the snow in the Push-ti-Ku Hills. From the end of March or middle of April, after the first fluctuation of river level has taken place, the high-level is fairly well maintained for some weeks.

About the middle or end of May the decline sets in, and, although the later snow-rise assists to maintain the level, as a rule the fall is steady and continuous. The low-water season extends from July to December; it is normally at its lowest during September, October, and November, when the curve of levels becomes practically flat, rising usually about the middle of November, when the first rains are experienced.

During the fall of August–September navigable conditions are at their worst, as the channels have not become defined and a large quantity of water runs over shoals carrying from 1 to 2 feet of water only.

As the river continues to fall the water becomes confined between shoals and sand-banks, and scouring begins to take place. By strict control of all shipping into fixed channels this scouring action is materially assisted, and under these conditions, as the river-level falls so does the bottom scour out, the actual depth of water in the channels remaining practically constant.

This scouring action is due to the bed of the river being

River Front elevation of Seraji House.

P.S. 50 type steamer. with two barges in tow,

composed of sand and silt, and being thus susceptible to the action of water. A particular illustration of this occurred in the reaches between Ali Gharbi and Kut during 1917, when, although the river-level at Ali Gharbi was 2 to 3 feet lower than during the same period of 1916, an average least depth of 6 feet was maintained (falling to 5 feet in Mandalayih Reach on one or two occasions) against an average of only 5 feet in 1916.

River transport between Amara and Kut, which carried all supplies and communications, and might be described as the spinal cord of the whole line of communications to the Field Army, ran during 1917 and 1918 with practically no delays or interruptions due to groundings, although during 1916, before any buoying was started, these reaches were frequently congested with stranded vessels. Delays in 1917 were only of short duration and occurred principally during September, when the lowest water was experienced. In 1918 there were practically none. Where clay or other equally hard substance is encountered scouring does not take place, and dredging would have to be resorted to to increase the depth of the channels. Fortunately, these conditions are non-existent on the Tigris below Sinijah, 76 miles by river above Baghdad, where the physical conditions of the country become radically changed.

While recognising that a low low-river level may not imply less actual depth of water in the channels, it should not be assumed that a high low-river level means an increase of the actual depth of water in the channels. At present no records are available on this point, but judging by reports of officers commanding river steamers prior to the War, the same navigable difficulties were encountered during the low-water seasons year after year, irrespective of the actual river level as compared with M.S.L.

It may safely be assumed that navigable conditions in pre-War days were much worse than during 1917 or 1918, due to the lack of buoyage and efficient navigable control of shipping. Each ship then attempted to find her own channel, with the result that no stable channel was formed.

The channels having once become scoured out, a period of some weeks may be expected during which navigable conditions will remain fairly constant.

From the foregoing it will be seen that the periods of worst navigable conditions are August–September, November–December, and part of January.

Floods.—On an average a flood occupies about three days to travel from Mosul to Baghdad and three days from Baghdad to Ali Gharbi. The greatest effect in rise of river level is experienced above Ali Gharbi ; below that point a large quantity of water is drawn off by canals before reaching Amara, where the rise is much less than at Ali Gharbi.

Baghdad.—The largest range recorded during recent years (1907–10) was 20 feet 11 inches. Mean range (1907–11) was 16 feet 4 inches. Greatest rise in twenty-four hours recently recorded was 5·02 feet on the 6th–7th January, 1918. The river level at Baghdad was over 6 feet higher on the 28th April, 1918, than last year's record, and nearly 3 feet higher than Willcock's average level between 1907–11.

Ali Gharbi.—The largest range recorded here in 1917–18 up to March, 1918, was 17·9 feet. The greatest rise in twenty-four hours recently recorded was 5·82 feet on 9th–10th January, 1918.

The Narrows.—The largest range recorded here in 1917 was 4 feet. The greatest rise in twenty-four hours recently recorded was 8·4 inches on 9th–10th January, 1918.

The approximate height above sea-level of the principal points between Fao and Baghdad are as follows :—

	Feet.
Mohammerah	6·88
Basrah	7·54
Qurna	10·49
Ezra's Tomb	13·77
Amara	27·19
Fillaifillah	36·08
Ali Gharbi	40·60
Sheikh Sa'ad	50·18
Kut	55·43
Ctesiphon	102·99
Baghdad	112·50

CONTENTS

The strength of the current varies according to season
and locality, the average strength during the low-water
season varying from 1½ to 2¼ knots to from 2½ to 4 knots
during freshets and floods, increasing to over 5 knots in
sharp bends and narrow channels. Beyond Sinijah a
current up to 7 knots has been reported over the fords and
in narrow necks.

TRIBUTARIES

The Diyalah discharges into the Tigris 19 miles below
Baghdad, and is navigable by sailing craft as far as Ba'qubah,
50 miles above its junction with the Tigris ; shallow draft
steamers have ascended to this point in the high-river
season, but above this the river becomes shallow, with a
wide gravelly channel, and is not navigable.

The Shatt-al-Hai is a distributary of the Tigris, leaving
that river at Kut-al-Amara and joining the Euphrates
near Suq-ash-Shuyukh. It is navigable from February to
June, and is much used by native craft for the export of
corn grown in the rich district through which it flows. At
other seasons the Shatt-al-Hai is not navigable, and from
July to November the bed is in many places dry. There
are no bridges over this stream. It is said to be the old
channel of the Tigris.

The Karun.—From Mohammerah to Ahwaz, a distance
of 110 miles, the Karun averages a quarter of a mile in width
and flows through open uncultivated country, the banks
being generally low and bare. The average slope of the river
over this section is about 5 inches to the mile, and the
current varies from 4 to 5 knots per hour in the season of the
floods to 2 knots between August and November. It is
subject to violent and irregular changes of level. In most
places the difference between high and low river is
ordinarily from 12 to 14 feet, but there is a difference of
24 feet between the lowest recorded reading in October, 1901,

and the highest in February, 1903. The river is at its lowest from the middle of October to the end of November, and highest floods occur in March and April, though occasionally earlier. A weekly ferry-service of stern-wheelers is maintained all the year round between Basrah and Ahwaz, supplemented by additional craft as required. A short distance above Ahwaz rapids are encountered which are a serious obstacle to further navigation. It is possible, however, for light draught vessels to negotiate them at certain seasons of the year, and vessels drawing up to 2 feet 6 inches can then navigate to within 7 miles of Shushtar.

A table of distance on the Tigris and its tributaries is given in Appendix A1.

EUPHRATES RIVER

In considering the Euphrates as a navigable fairway, it is convenient to divide the river into sections, viz. :

(a) Lower Euphrates—Kurna to Shenafiyah.
(b) Middle Euphrates—Shenafiyah so Museyib.
(c) Upper Euphrates—Museyib to Sahaliyah.
(d) Upper Euphrates—Sahaliyah to Jerablus.

(a) With the completion of dredging operations on Hammar Lake, a navigable channel for vessels drawing 6 feet is now available from Kurna to Nasiriyah, the draft varying slightly according to the season of the year. From Nasiriyah to Durraji, a distance of 38 miles, navigable conditions are good all the year round, the least draft in the low-water season being from 4 feet 6 inches to 5 feet.

From Durraji to Shenafiyah vessels drawing from 4 to 5 feet may proceed during the high water, but their draft is restricted during the low-river season to from 2 to 3 feet, owing to the many shoals and banks forming at this time. The beam of vessels navigating this section is also limited to the width of the opening span of the WA'AR railway bridge (viz. 40 feet). Navigable conditions between Nasiriyah and Shenafiyah in the low-water season also largely depends upon the Hindiyah Barrage, the opening or closing of which diverts large quantities of water down either the Hindiyah or Hillah branches respectively. The depth of water in Shenafiyah Lake restricts water transport during the low-water season to the smallest bellums, drawing a few inches only ; during the high-water season, vessels with a draft of 3 feet may be passed through the lake. To improve on these conditions a large amount of bunding and dredging would be required.

(b) The Euphrates practically loses its identity between the Hindiyah Barrage and Sammawah, splitting up into countless irrigation canals and ditches, many of which discharge their water into the vast swamps of the district and are thus wasted, others filtering back into the main river again in the vicinity of Sammawah. The route presenting the best possibilities for navigation and the one therefore selected for that purpose is via the Hindiyah branch part Kufah and down the Mishkab Channel into the lower portion of Shenafiyah Lake, thence into the main river again above Shenafiyah town.

Once across Shenafiyah Lake, the hamels in the Mishkab Channel hamper shipping to a certain degree, also the narrowness and sharp turns in the channel until Abu Sukhair is reached. From Abu Sukhair to the Hindiyah Barrage the river is navigable for vessels with a draft up to 5 feet during the high-water season, but during the low-water season the draft is severely restricted, whilst during such times as the barrage is closed this section of the Euphrates is not navigable except by bellums drawing a few inches.

(c) Immediately above the Hindiyah Barrage the Euphrates forks into its two great branches (the Hindiyah and Hillah), the Hindiyah branch again forking at Kifl, thereby forming the Kufa and Shamiyah channels, which reunite in the vicinity of Shenafiyah. The greater portion of the Hillah branch water is, however, lost in the marshes.

Navigable conditions on the Hindiyah branch have been detailed above. Small steam and motor craft with a draft of from 3 to 4 feet can navigate the Hillah branch from the

Barrage to Rumeitha, although in the low-water season navigation naturally depends upon whether the Hindiyah Barrage is open or closed. The effect of closing this is to render the Euphrates from the Barrage to Durraji practically useless for river transport during this period.

Above the Barrage, where the Euphrates is confined to one channel, vessels drawing from 3 to 4 feet are able to navigate to Sahaliyah during the low-water season, increasing to a draft of 5 feet to 5 feet 6 inches during the high-water.

(d) From Hit upwards to Deir-ez-zor navigation of the river is much impeded by stone weirs carrying water-wheels. In the high-water season navigation may be possible by powerful shallow draft stern-wheelers or motor bellums working single-handed, but the greatest care and judgment is necessary on the downward voyage to prevent stranding and wreckage on these weirs or on other obstructions.

In the low-water season, it is not navigable except to craft drawing less than 2 feet.

A table of distances on this river is given in Appendix A2.

Major-General A. S. Collard, C.B., C.V.O., Director of Inland Waterways and Docks at the War Office when the Inland Water Transport was first organised in Mesopotamia.

SUMMARY OF EVENTS FROM SEPTEMBER 6TH, 1916, TO THE DATE OF THE ARMISTICE

HAVING gained some knowledge of conditions existing previous to September, 1916, it will now be convenient to briefly review subsequent developments, illustrating the progress made by the Inland Water Transport.

1. Shortly following the Report of the Commission, a Committee consisting of three Officers was appointed by the Director of Movements at the War Office and instructed to proceed to Mesopotamia without delay, to report to the I.S.C. and to advise on the question of River Transport generally.

The Officers selected were Colonel W. H. Grey, Major R. H. W. Hughes, D.S.O., and Captain H. E. Ratsey, and they arrived in Mesopotamia on July 31st, 1916. The following day instructions were received by the Army Commander from London that Colonel Grey should take over control of the whole River Transport as soon as he felt in a position to do so.

After a period of preliminary investigation, this was finally done on September 6th, 1916, and the history of the Inland Water Transport in Mesopotamia may be said to properly commence with the publication of Force Routine Order, No. 1454, dated September 8th, 1916.

(1) " In accordance with Orders from the War Office the Mesopotamian Marine has been placed under the Inland Water Transport Service of the Royal Engineers. Colonel Grey, R.E., Deputy Director of Inland Water Transport, therefore, will assume control forthwith of the Service, including all Dockyards and Construction. The principal Marine Transport Officers, Commander Jones and Commander Bingham, will hand over to Colonel Grey, and the former will return to India to report to the Director of the Royal Indian Marine.

11

(2) Other permanent and temporary Officers of the Royal Indian Marine will be placed by the Viceroy under the orders of Colonel Grey.

(3) In giving effect to the War Office Orders, the Army Commander wishes to thank Commander Jones and the Officers of the Royal Indian Marine associated with him, for their service in controlling the Marine in the past, and to bear witness to the very real difficulties they have had to contend with in sustaining the Forces engaged in Mesopotamia."

2. Early Organisation.—The first action taken on assuming control was to initiate a complete reorganisation of methods and redistribution of officers, with the object in view of providing a fully equipped and self-contained Transport Service on the departmental system.

In this connection, new departments were formed, others were taken over as needs arose, whilst existing ones were reorganised, the staff being supplemented where necessary by Royal Engineer Officers who were now arriving from England. These changes resulted in the following departments being included within the Directorate :

Transport.—Movements of all vessels up or down the river ; the supply and distribution of coal and oil fuel, etc.

Dockyards.—Repairs to vessels.

Construction.—Constructional work at the Base : buildings, quarters, etc.

Up-River Works.—Constructional work : wharves, oil tanks, and running of repair workshops up river.

Personnel.—Records and supply of all Eastern races employed, rations, clothing, etc.

Vessels.—Examination and upkeep of vessels other than engine room or machinery, also administration of deck personnel.

Marine Engineering.—Inspection and report on engine-room conditions, and to indicate to dockyards what repairs were to be undertaken. Formerly, the Superintendent of the Dockyards carried out these duties, in addition to his own ; but it was realised that with a prospective fleet of such magnitude as had been ordered for the Tigris the responsibility should be divided.

Accounts.—Finance of all departments, and all payments.

Stores.—Maintenance of supply and issue of all stores.

Buoyage and Pilotage.—Instituted in October, 1916, responsible for the marking of the river. Previous to this time there had been no aids to navigation whatever beyond the primitive system of control in the Narrows.

Native Craft.—This department was formerly directly under the L. of C., but was incorporated in the Inland Water Transport Directorate in November, 1916.

The scope of these departments will be dealt with at greater length subsequently.

3. Personnel.—At the end of September, 1916, the number of officers and men in the River Transport Service was as follows :—

Military officers	32
R.I.M. officers	192
British N.C.O.'s and men	212
Eastern races	6735
Total	7171

When Colonel Grey first assumed control the Senior R.I.M. Officers vacated their posts, but Junior Permanent Officers of that Service were given the option of either remaining or returning to India. With one or two exceptions they elected to place their services at the disposal of the Inland Water Transport. Temporary R.I.M. officers were invited to transfer to the Army, their services in the meantime being retained under their R.I.M. rank. A certain number of these officers agreed to transfer at once, and eventually practically all of them accepted Army commissions. It would have been quite impossible to have carried on the Transport Service without the assistance of these permanent and temporary officers at that time.

Meanwhile officers were arriving slowly from England during the latter part of 1916, and in December a draft of sixty-seven considerably strengthened the position and allowed further developments to be proceeded with.

On assuming control, the Principal Marine Transport

Officer stated that he had had great difficulty in getting crews for ships from India, and that he thought it would not be possible to man all the ships that were then on order. A cable was therefore sent to the War Office asking for assistance from the Colonial Office in this respect, by recruiting crews from West Africa or the West Indies ; the result of this being the despatch of the West African contingent and the reinforcement of the B.W.I. Regiment by seafaring men.

As a similar shortage of other labour, both skilled and unskilled, had been experienced from India, the War Office was asked to send labour from Egypt ; Colonel Grey had arranged the preliminaries of this on his way out, the result being that in October, 1916, the first Egyptian Labour Corps, consisting of six officers and 2512 men, arrived in the country and reported to the Director of Inland Water Transport for duty.

The question was also taken up of obtaining skilled Chinese labour, and recruiting was commenced at Singapore, Hong Kong, and Shanghai, an I.W.T. officer being despatched to the latter place to assist.

It was not, however, until November, 1917, that the complement was brought up to the original establishment approved by the Army Commander in March of that year, and by this time the I.W.T. had developed to such an extent that a further increased establishment had been drawn up, for which sanction had been requested, so that the Department was still actually a long way below the strength required.

4. River Fleet.—The strength of the River Fleet, when it was transferred from the Royal Indian Marine to the Inland Water Transport, consisted of :

> 138 self-propelled vessels, of which only four were
> hospital ships,
> 134 barges,
> 95 motor-boats.

Details of these vessels are given in Appendix B1.

Practically all the paddlers were old vessels which had been brought from England, Egypt, India, or Burma, and no less than twenty others had been lost *en route* up to this time. Exceptions to the former were P.S. 50 and 51, then recently arrived. These vessels had been specially constructed in England on the plans of Messrs. Lynch Bros.' *Mejidieh*, which was at that time considered the ideal type of vessel for the Tigris. Owing to the lack of hospital ships all vessels, with sufficient deck space, had to carry sick and wounded when required.

There was also a considerable shortage of barges in proportion to towing vessels. Steamers arriving at river-head with two barges in tow had, after disembarking their troops, to wait for their barges to be discharged, a process involving obvious delay.

Every effort was made to remedy this state of affairs, and all sources capable of supplying river craft were investigated, arrangements being made to transfer them to Mesopotamia at the earliest possible moment.

5. Dockyards.—It was evident from the beginning that dockyard facilities were inadequate to cope with an increased fleet. The only means of sighting a vessel's bottom up to this time had been to place her on the mud and then to excavate a hole beneath her. The Basrah Dockyard Scheme was therefore revised and put into operation on a more ambitious scale ; slipways capable of dealing with all probable requirements were included, the material for building up the foundation of which was obtained by excavating a wet basin in rear of the Dockyard. Originally started as a borrow pit to provide spoil on which to extend the old Dockyard, the idea was evolved of converting it into a dock where vessels under repair could be berthed alongside, instead of lying in the stream, as had been the practice hitherto. This dock took thirteen months to excavate, an average of a thousand men being employed daily. It occupied $12\frac{1}{2}$ acres of water area and had 6000 feet of frontage for berthing vessels, which could enter or leave at any state of the tide. It was estimated that repairs to vessels would be expedited at least 25 per cent by having them in close proximity to the workshops, instead of having to ferry men and materials to and fro to them in the stream.

Extensive reclamation had also to be carried out in connection with this scheme, and quarters built for the large personnel requisite for the Dockyard.

The S.S. *Abydos*, a 4600-ton cargo steamer, fitted up as a repair ship, arrived in November. It was considered that greater use could be made of her fittings by removing them ashore to be distributed among the workshops. It was also decided to fit up P.S. 34 as a repair ship capable of proceeding up-river with the advance when required, thus freeing the S.S. *Abydos* for other purposes, this vessel being an ocean steamer drawing 18 feet and totally unsuitable for the service intended.

6. Re-erection of Craft.—In addition to the vessels already on order, and which were arriving freely during the latter part of 1916, the Inland Water Transport Commission had ordered a number of vessels of specially selected types, which were to be shipped in plates and angles and were to be re-erected on arrival in Mesopotamia. For this purpose a site was chosen at Margil and a fully equipped ship-building yard laid out there. Previous to this all such work had been carried out by contract, either at Abadan or Mohammerah, under most unsatisfactory conditions, as the firms employed were quite unable to fulfil their contracts, and delays and losses were so frequent that early in September the Inland Water Transport were obliged to send their own officers and men to both of these places to take over the work themselves. In this connection, the arrival at Basrah about this time of the S.S. *Hunnie*, with over 4000 tons of marine and engineers' stores of every possible description, proved of inestimable value. The imperative need for such stores had been realised in England, and they had been shipped direct to Basrah without waiting for any indents. The foresight and energy on the part of Brig.-General A. S. Collard, the newly appointed D.I.W. and D. at the W.O., was of the very greatest help to the I.W.T. in Mesopotamia.

7. River Conditions.—Navigable conditions on the rivers of Mesopotamia differ very much from those in other parts of the world, and special navigation rules had to be drawn to meet the peculiar circumstances of the country. These were drawn up, and put into force when the Inland Water Transport assumed control, and the surprisingly small number of collisions or accidents that have occurred on the river, and the fact that the rules have never needed revision, testify to their success.

One of the most serious difficulties to be overcome, in operating on the Tigris, was that in that portion of the river between Amara and Kurna, known as the "Narrows." The river here is so narrow that two steamers with barges cannot pass one another when both are moving. It is therefore necessary to have a control system, similar to that in the Suez Canal, and for one vessel to tie up to the bank to permit another to pass. As the length of the river where these conditions obtain is twenty-nine miles, it can be easily realised that there is a limit to the number of ships that it is possible to pass through daily even with a most efficient control.

8. Preparation for the Advance on Baghdad.—Every effort was now concentrated on preparing for the expected advance, but before an offensive could be launched, in addition to reinforcements, large reserve dumps of supplies and ammunition had to be accumulated at Amara, Sheikh Sa'ad, and river-head at Arab village. Every available vessel was pressed into service to meet this emergency ; S.T. boats, and even sea-going steamers, being utilised to tow barges as far as Ezra's Tomb and Kurna respectively, which places represented the limit of safe navigation for such vessels. Their barges were taken on to Amara by *Sumana* class tugs, where they were again transferred to the larger paddlers. Meanwhile, the organisation of the Department was developing apace. Steamers and barges were in course of erection ; the despatch of others from overseas was expedited ; workshops, both at the Base and Amara, were extended, resulting in the speeding-up of

c

repairs ; jetties, wharves, and quarters were being erected ; Dockyard facilities improved, and the construction of fuel oil storage tanks at various points on the L. of C. was being undertaken. The results obtained are best illustrated by the improvement shown in tonnage despatched up-river. In August, 1916, this tonnage approximated 300 tons per day, the troops at the Front being then on half rations. This had increased to 1000 tons per day in November, 1916, and 3200 tons per day in February, 1917, shortly before the advance subsequent to the fall of Kut commenced. The appreciation of the Army Commander was expressed to the I.G.C., in the following terms :—

" Nothing could be better than the way Men, Supplies, and Stores have been forwarded recently. Please accept for yourself and convey to those who have assisted, including Directors at the Base, my warm appreciation of their successful efforts."

9. The Advance.—A comprehensive description of the part played by the Inland Water Transport during the strenuous period of the Advance is contained in the Report of Lieut.-Colonel Hughes, D.S.O., who was in immediate command of the Forward Transport, some extracts from which are quoted below :—

" On the 25th the forward movement of the River Transport commenced. Five Motor Lighters with Ammunition, P.S. 17, P.S. 21, P.S. 53, and P.S. 18, each with two barges, left Arab Village during the afternoon and evening. T. 5, with a mahela of coal, and a small barge which had been filled with gangways, trestles, flare-lamps, ropes, mooring pegs, and all other necessary gear for banking-in and unloading ships, also left up with two embarkation and two I.W.T. officers on board.

The vessels proceeded until 11 p.m., when they anchored below Kut, as it was uncertain what obstacles might have been left by the enemy, and it was not considered safe to pass this point in the dark. Next morning at daybreak the ships proceeded, the first ones arriving at the New Advanced Base Depot at Shumran shortly after 6 a.m.

The site chosen was an unsuitable one from an off-loading point of view, the bank being a shelving one, and as the water had recently fallen the foreshore was soft mud. Barges could not be got closer than fifteen to twenty feet from the bank, which did not facilitate rapid discharge. It was well that we had the barge loaded with trestles and gangways available.

The Army Commander and Advanced G.H.Q. arrived at Shumran this day (the 26th instant), having embarked on P.S. 53 at Megasis, and made that vessel their headquarters.

The river at this time was falling after the flood rise of the 18th to 21st. Sub-Lieut. J. H. Brown, R.N.V.R., one of Messrs. Lynch's masters, whom I had taken from P.S. 51, was detailed to buoy the new stretch of river above Arab Village, and to write sailing directions for the benefit of other officers commanding ships, who did not possess local knowledge.

The 26th was spent in organising and reorganising ' formation ' units—that is, ships and barges specially loaded with complete rations for men and animals for one Division or Brigade for so many days. These Units were detailed for each Division, and though very necessary from a military point of view, they resulted in a great loss of tonnage, and in many cases considerable delay in the turn-round of vessels. Three *Sumana* Class tugs had been detailed to the Royal Flying Corps, and three more to the Bridging Train. This also was a great loss to the transport at such a time.

The same day orders were received to send vessels on to Imam Mahdi and Baghaila ; two tugs with barges of supplies left up at midday, followed by all ships arriving from Arab Village and Sheikh Sa'ad, which were sent right through to Imam Mahdi.

The site chosen at Imam Mahdi was quite suitable from an off-loading point of view, as there was deep water close alongside the bank. There was no labour available, however, and the unloading by fatigue parties was slow. However, before much cargo had been put on shore, orders were received that another forward move was to be made and several ships were pushed right through at once with orders to proceed until signalled in, to feed the troops at any point where they might find them.

Advanced G.H.Q. left Shumran at 1 p.m. on March 1st, in P.S. 53, and orders were issued that Azizieh was now to be made the Advanced Base and Shumran evacuated. 1200 tons of supplies had already been landed there and at the Dumps south of the river on the Shatt-el-Hai.

The Army Commander remained at Sheikh Jahd during the 2nd, and supplies were still being landed there and at Imam Mahdi two miles below. The first supply ships sent through reached Azizieh on the evening of the 4th, where the troops were anxiously awaiting them.

A site had been selected at Azizieh, on the upper side of the bend, which, though suitable for discharging during the high-river season, was not so for the low, on account of the narrowness of the channel at this point. I represented this to the Advance Base Commandant when he arrived on the morning of the 5th, but was told that a further advance was contemplated, so that it did not matter for the time being.

At this time we began to have trouble with the navigation, in spite of the efforts of Sub-Lieut. Brown, R.N.V.R. Captains of vessels, eager to do their best, often steamed all night, and in the darkness some cases of groundings occurred. On the 14th, P.S. 20, P.S. 80, and P.S. 2 were all aground; fortunately both the former got off, but P.S. 2, with one barge, remained hard and fast till the water rose again on the 15th. This, however, was the only serious case of grounding during the whole advance to Baghdad.

Numerous prizes in the shape of tugs and barges had been taken in the stretch of river between Baghaila and Azizieh, and on the 2nd instant Lieut. Bayfield, R.I.M., was detailed with T. 64 to take the salvage of these vessels in hand. In addition to the Turkish paddler *Basrah*, which was captured full of prisoners and with three barges, these consisted of the following, and have all now been sent down-stream :—

1 large tug	3 guns.
1 *Sumana* tug	2 guns recaptured.
4 Baghdad Railway barges .	
1 R.F.C. barge	recaptured.
1 barge workshop . . .	
2 large launches . . .	recaptured.

The tugs and launches and the workshop barge had all been set on fire, and were more or less damaged.

The Advanced Base being now established at Azizieh, and labour having been brought up, the discharge of all ships commenced at once. " Formation " ships were again required and were immediately loaded, and as early as the 5th two of them left up for Zeur, or possibly Bustan.

At this time, the lengthening of the line began to be felt in the shortage of Coal and Oil Fuel, particularly the latter. The Navy had almost emptied the one oil barge at Imam Mahdi, and for a time things looked serious. Fortunately, no actual delay or stoppage to the transport occurred, and the arrival of an oil barge at Azizieh (though with a depleted stock due to feeding vessels on the way) on the evening of the 7th just saved the situation. The Coal question, which would have been more serious still, was saved by using S. and T. ration wood, of which a large stock had been landed by this time.

On the 5th and 6th the first ' formation ' ships started up for Zeur ; but before all of them had reached that place they were again ordered on the Bustan, and from there again to Bawi, which for a brief time became river-head.

I left Azizieh on the night of the 8th, leaving Lieut. Bayfield, R.I.M., in charge there. Bawi was reached on the afternoon of the 9th. Coal and oil barges arrived at the same time, and the tugs and gunboats were able to take what they required, though the issue had to be strictly watched as the supply was very limited.

On the morning of the 11th orders were given for all the ships to proceed up to Baghdad. P.S. 53 left at 8 a.m. with the Army Commander and G.H.Q., the remainder following as soon as the Bridge was opened again. The remnants of supplies and stores that had been disembarked at Bawi were re-embarked, and all ships had left that place by nightfall. Eighteen hundred tons had been discharged and re-loaded at Bawi.

During the whole advance the shortage of motor-boats or steam launches was very seriously felt by I.W.T. officers. Launches or tugs had to be temporarily borrowed back from the Bridging Train, Flying Corps, Mine-sweepers, or anyone possible, to board the steamers arriving and give them their orders. The work of supervising the whole line was also rendered difficult by having no fast launch to get about rapidly.

Owing to the rapidity of the Advance, the constant changing of orders to meet new developments, the frequency with which the river-head was moved, being successively Shumran, Imam Mahdi, Azizieh, Zeur, Bustan, Bawi, and Baghdad, all within fourteen days, it was impossible to keep a record of the tonnage and mileage of the numerous vessels. It was as much as we could do to keep pace with the Advance and place officers at the various posts *en route*. Ships would start for one place and discharge a few tons there only, when they would be ordered on, probably two or three times before they were finally emptied. The needs of the Army were met by the ships in every case, both as regards sick and wounded, stores, supplies, ammunition, and reinforcements. We were fortunate in having plenty of water in the river, without having the strong current to contend with that usually prevails on a rising river. Four thousand three hundred and twenty-five tons of supplies had been landed at Azizieh between the 4th and 11th. A proportion of these are being kept there for the present, the remainder being reloaded for Baghdad. The motor lighters ran very well during the fortnight under review and did good service conveying ammunition and rations.

P.S. 53 entered Baghdad at 2.30 p.m. on the 11th, closely followed by S. 2. Sub-Lieut. Brown, R.N.V.R. had been with or in advance of the ships the whole way up, laying buoys and erecting leading marks and writing sailing directions as he progressed. Six Arab pilots were obtained at Baghaila and distributed amongst the ships. There were one or two minor groundings above Azizieh, but beyond the case of P.S. 2 mentioned above there were no serious accidents or delays from this cause during the whole advance.

I arrived at Baghdad at 6 p.m. on the day of occupation, and immediately arranged with the D.Q.M.G. regarding the off-loading of the ships then actually arriving, so as to turn them round as rapidly as possible and also to evacuate sick and wounded. No facilities in the shape of wharves or jetties were found in Baghdad beyond one ramp at the railway terminus capable of taking one barge. There were two steam cranes on this, but both had been blown up by the enemy. P.S. 27 and S. 2 were ordered to unload at the railway wharf at once ; and P.S. 20, P.S. 4, *Mejidieh*, and the other early arrivals, were stopped below Baghdad and banked in and discharged on the right bank opposite Karradah Island.

Military operations were still in progress, and until the 14th ships were loading ' formation ' supplies for above Baghdad, where others were being held in readiness for similar duties. On this date, however, they were released, and a regular routine may be said to have commenced.

The following Turkish craft were found in Baghdad or just above it, and have been sent down river or are in use in Baghdad :—

2 barges (80 tons),
1 large steel motor-launch (minus engines),
1 motor launch (engines damaged, but repairable),
2 anchor boats,
10 dingheys,
1 steam launch (shallow draft).

Two boat bridges have been thrown across the Tigris, one at the site of the old Turkish bridge in the middle of the town and one between Baghdad and Karradah. These are both above the Advanced Base, so do not interfere with shipping from down river, making that place its terminus ; but they undoubtedly cause delay to vessels working above, and the bridge-opening times are now being arranged so as to fit in as well as possible with the regular services of ferry and supply steamers.

The mine-sweeping carried out for the R.N. by the I.W.T. resulted in the finding of six mines in the vicinity of Kut. These were destroyed by rifle-fire. No others were found above this place."

MAJOR-GENERAL the HON. SIR A. R. M. STUART WORTLEY, K.C.M.G., C.B., D.S.O. who, when Director of Movements at the War Office raised and formed the Inland Water Transport. Subsequently D.Q.M.G. in Mesopotamia.

10. Further Operations.—Within a few days of the occupation of Baghdad, a further advance was made up the Tigris, and river communication had to be maintained as far as Sinijah, 76 miles above Baghdad. Beyond this point it was unsafe for navigation by water at this season of the year owing to a falling river and also to a rocky bar situated a short distance above. Further operations resulted in the occupation of Baqubah on the Diala and Feluja on the Euphrates, necessitating the provision of water transport on these two rivers. The length of rivers (Tigris, Shatt-el-Arab, Karoon, and Euphrates) operated by the Inland Water Transport had increased from about 450 miles in September, 1916, to 865 miles on April 1st, 1917. The requirements of these rapidly extending lines of communication could only be met by running ships incessantly and neglecting all but the absolutely necessary repairs required to avert total breakdowns. Fortunately, by this time reinforcements in officers, men, and ships were arriving, and all demands for transport were successfully met.

11. The following extract from a despatch by Lieut.-General Sir Stanley Maude, dealing with the Advance includes, among other items of interest, references to the Inland Water Transport :—

" 44. One of the features peculiar to the Campaign is the length of the Lines of Communications which we have necessarily had to adopt. In consequence, the difficulties by which the Administrative Services and Departments, both in the Field and on the Lines of Communications, have been confronted, have been exceptional. The success or failure of the operations has so largely depended on their efficiency that a substantial measure of credit is due to the Directors and their Assistants, and all Ranks of those Services and Departments, who by capable methods and unwearied energy have surmounted all obstacles and regularly met the needs of the fighting troops with ample supplies, munitions and stores, and have been the means of providing every comfort obtainable for the sick and wounded.

As in the case of fighting troops, the interdependence of these Services and Departments has necessitated the closest co-operation, and equally successful has been the result. We have relied upon three classes of transport—river, rail, and road—the latter being further subdivided into motor and animal transport. The work in all cases has been peculiarly heavy. *The newly formed Inland Water Transport Directorate had first to fill its ranks and then develop its organisation and provide for its many indispensable requirements ; but the personnel, making light of these very real obstacles to rapid progress, worked unceasingly, with the result that night and day an endless chain of river craft passed up and down the river, thereby assuring the maintenance of the troops at the front."*

12. Strength of Fleet.—The strength of the River Transport Fleet at the end of March had increased to :

> 242 self-propelled vessels,
> 315 barges,
> 187 motor-boats.

Details of these will be found in Appendix B2.

In spite of this large increase, however, it soon became evident that, during the low-water season, the fleet would be unable to maintain the army in the field. It was therefore decided to construct an emergency railway line from Kut to Baghdad.

Colonel Ratsey (Chief Engineer) was also despatched to India early in April to select more towing vessels and barges, as, owing to unavoidable delays, craft ordered from England were not arriving to scheduled time. The result of his efforts was the purchase of nine large river steamers which, though too large to ply regularly through the Narrows, were admirably adapted to running above Amara in the wider river. Though late in the season for the sea voyage to Basrah, the risk was taken, and six of them arrived safely before the end of June, the remaining three being held up in Bombay till after the monsoon.

13. Reorganisation.—Consequent upon the occupation of Baghdad and the ever-increasing scope of operations, the organisation of the Inland Water Transport needed further revision and elaboration, and with this end in view many changes were instituted.

Brig.-General Grey was recalled for service in Europe towards the end of May, and was succeeded as Director by

Lieut.-Colonel Hughes, D.S.O., who was at the same time promoted to the rank of Brigadier-General.

Major Ward was promoted to Lieut.-Colonel and Deputy-Director, and relieved Lieut.-Colonel Hughes at Baghdad, representing the Inland Water Transport at G.H.Q., dealing with all matters affecting River Transport in the Forward Area and outside the Lines of Communications.

In February, 1917, the Port Traffic Department, formerly under the Port Administration and Conservancy, had been absorbed into the Inland Water Transport Directorate, its Director, Lieut.-Colonel Brown, being retained and appointed A.D.I.W.T. (Port Traffic).

A Department of River Conservancy was inaugurated, taking over certain work which had also previously been carried out by the Port Administration and Conservancy. The A.D. (Conservancy) was in addition made responsible for Irrigation. To meet the increased needs of the Directorate a new establishment was made out allowing for a total personnel of :

855 Officers,

3,650 British other ratings,

29,485 Eastern races.

Details of these are shown in Appendix C1.

14. Progress.—The summer of 1917 was a period of steady development. The temporary cessation of hostilities during the very hot weather gave no respite to the Inland Water Transport, as large reserve stocks of supplies and material had to be accumulated in the Forward Area, ready for the resumption of operations.

Steamers and barges continued to arrive from Overseas, and both Dockyard and Re-erection Yard were kept working at high pressure in order to cope with the ever-increasing demands of the fleet.

Three new workshops were completed at Basrah Dockyard, and a considerable quantity of new machinery installed. New workshops were also opened at Ezra's Tomb, Kut, and Baghdad, whilst those at Amara were greatly enlarged.

The slipway at the Margil Yard was completed.

The MacMunn Bridge at Amara, built by the Construction Department, I.W.T., was opened for traffic, and the control and maintenance of all bridges on the L.O.C., including those at Qualet Saleh, Sheikh Sa'ad, Kut, and Baghdad, were undertaken by the Inland Water Transport.

The following works were also completed by the Department during this time :—

A pier for ocean-going ships at Engineer Field Park.

The naval pier at Tanooma, Nos. 9 and 10 wharves at Margil, and several smaller jetties in Basrah.

A 1000-ton oil tank at Khora Creek.

A 1000-ton oil tank at Amara.

Slipways for native craft at the Mahaila Depot.

In addition, accommodation of all descriptions for officers, B.O.R.'s and Eastern races was expedited at all stations ; installations of ice-making and filtration plant and electric fans were proceeded with, these measures materially assisting in promoting the health, comfort, and efficiency of all concerned.

The first of a fleet of twenty refrigerating barges ordered, was placed in commission in June.

The whole system of river pilotage was revised in May and June, and 272 Arab pilots were stationed at various points in the river to assist vessels in navigating their various sections.

Three new control stations were opened in the Narrows section, and electric lights were placed round all the difficult bends, thus enabling vessels to navigate this difficult part of the river by night.

To relieve the congestion of shipping at Basrah a new Port at Nahr Umar was opened, and a scheme of wharfage and railway connections prepared.

New I.W.T. stations were opened at Nahr Umar, Baghaila, Azizieh, Zeur, Hinaidi, and Feluja, and the necessary staff appointed.

15. Early Operations on Upper Euphrates.—The Turks

in retreating after they had evacuated Feluja breached the dam across the Saklawayah Canal, with the idea of flooding the surrounding country and thus hindering pursuit. It was therefore necessary before the projected railway to Feluja could be proceeded with to reconstruct this dam and drain the flooded area. This task was entrusted to the Construction Department of the Inland Water Transport, and was successfully carried out.

The only craft in our possession at this time and available for river transport on the Upper Euphrates were a steam barge of 100 tons capacity, a large motor launch minus engines, and a small hurriedly collected fleet of bellums and mahailas. Early in September, 1917, the Native Craft Department of the I.W.T. took over control of all such vessels on the Middle and Upper Euphrates, and these were largely employed in the preparations for the offensive ending with the capture of Ramadie on October 1st, 1917. This added three more steam launches and several gun barges to the fleet, besides several mahailas and bellums. Subsequent operations in this area rendered a considerable reinforcement of the flotilla necessary. Besides, therefore, largely augmenting the fleet of native craft, arrangements were made to lighten steam vessels of their engines and boilers at Advanced Base, and on completion of the railway these were placed on trucks and railed across to Feluja, where they were again launched and placed in commission on the Euphrates. Barges, Red Cross launches, diving boats, and buoyage launches were sent across in a similar manner, and, in addition, other vessels were sent up via Hamar and Shenafiyah Lakes as soon as conditions permitted.

16. River Conditions, 1917.—The low-water season of 1917 was an exceptionally bad one, and the river generally was giving trouble and causing endless delays to navigation. Towards the end of July, reach after reach above Kut had shoaled up, and a redistribution of the fleet became necessary in order to meet these altered conditions. This was put into effect on August 1st, and by this arrangement twelve paddlers and fifteen tugs were based on Kut for the run to Baghdad. Twenty-three of the largest paddlers were based on Amara for the run to Kut, and the remainder of the fleet was based on Basrah, to run through to Kut or as required. The opening of the Kut-Hinaidi Railway about this time, all construction materials and stock for which had been sent up by river transport, somewhat eased the situation on this section of the river. In pre-War days the maximum draft for steam vessels proceeding above Kut at this season of the year had been 3 feet, but, thanks to the efforts of the Buoyage Department, a least draft of 4 feet was maintained throughout for such vessels. Experiments were made for the first time in bandalling, i.e. making retaining walls of bamboos and matsso, so as to divert or concentrate the flow of the current and thus cause the river to scour out its own channel. This subject is dealt with more fully under " Buoyage and Pilotage " (see page 93).

An endeavour was made to improve conditions in the Narrows by the Conservancy Department, by partially closing the Chahala and Majar Kebir Canals, two of the most important distributaries of the Tigris in this vicinity. The result of this was to almost entirely eliminate the difficulties experienced in 1916 (see under " Conservancy and Reclamation ").

17. Upper Tigris.—Operations in this area resulted in the capture of Tekrit (144 miles above Baghdad) on November 5th, 1917. Inland Water Transport officers were stationed at Sadiyah and Akab.

18. Diala.—The Diala bridges were taken over in December, 1917. Inland Water Transport officers were stationed at Baqubah and Diala Mouth to supervise these bridges and to control native craft traffic in this area.

19. Wet Basin.—The wet basin at Basrah Dockyard was opened for working purposes, by the Inspector-General of Communications, on December 22nd, 1917, being then sufficiently advanced for use, though a certain amount of dredging at the entrance remained to be completed.

20. Mohammerah Re-erection Yard.—Towards the end

of 1917 this yard was closed down, all plant, etc., being removed to Margil.

21. Strength of the Fleet.—The strength of the fleet at the end of December, 1917, had increased to :

> 358 self-propelled vessels,
> 585 barges,
> 356 motor-boats.

Details are shown in Appendix B3.

22. Transport.—The following comparative statement will serve to illustrate the progress made regarding the tonnage handled and mileage operated, from the occupation of Baghdad to end of 1917 :—

	Tonnage.	Mileage.
For the quarter ending April 30th, 1917	255,959	60,324,683
„ „ June 30th, 1917	310,780	58,645,842
„ „ Dec. 31st, 1917	452,218	73,445,574

The mileage operated had increased from 865 miles on April 1st, 1917, to 1160 miles on December 31st, 1917.

23. Administration.—For the purpose of better control, the River Tigris, the main line of transportation, was now divided into sections, each section being directly controlled by a responsible officer with headquarters at the principal station on the section (see Frontispiece). Bearing on this subject, the following appeared in Inland Water Transport Orders for the 31st December, 1917 :—

" For the purpose of Inland Water Transport organisation, the River Tigris is divided as follows :—

Base Section.—Up to and including Kurna.

Narrows Section.—From Kurna to Majar Kebir, including Ezra's Tomb, Qualet Saleh, and Majar Kebir.

Amara Section.—From Majar Kebir to Ali Gharbi, including Ali Gharbi.

Kut Section.—From Ali Gharbi to Azizieh, including Sheik Sa'ad, Baghaila, and Azizieh.

Baghdad Section.—From Azizieh upwards, including Hinaidi, Advanced Base, Sadiyeh and river-head, and all stations on Diala River."

The River Euphrates was at first divided into two sections,

viz. Lower and Upper ; but later, owing to developments due to crop raising and collecting, this was altered to three stations, viz. :

> Lower—from Hamar Lake to Shenafiyah.
> Middle—from Shenafiyah to Museyib.
> Upper—from Museyib upwards.

The Middle and Upper sections being outside the Lines of Communication were controlled from Baghdad, the Lower from headquarters at Basrah.

New stations were opened at Ramadie, Madhij, Mufraz, Museyib, and Hillah, on the Euphrates, and at Baqubah on the Diala.

24. Oil Fuel.—The question of the supply and distribution of oil fuel, kerosene, and petrol now began to assume large proportions, and this, in conjunction with the projected substitution of oil fuel for coal on both river steamers and railways, caused a shortage in oil-carrying vessels to be anticipated. Steps were taken to augment the existing fleet, and whilst as many bulk oil barges were obtained from India as possible, suitable transport barges were selected and converted locally for the carriage of both bulk and cased oils. Meanwhile, the erection of storage tanks at various stations up-country was pressed forward in order to release barges which up to that time had been used as stationary depots.

It also became evident at this time that the Anglo-Persian Oil Company was quite unable to cope with the increased demands for cased oils. It was arranged by the Inspector-General of Communication, therefore, that the Inland Water Transport should take over the working of the Tinning Sheds at Abadan, as from January 1st, 1918, with the result that within a short time of assuming control the output had increased by 30 per cent.

Arrangements were made later to take over two of the A.P.O.C. storage tanks at Abadan, also a barge loading wharf, and to construct an additional wharf for loading bulk fuel oil, with the idea of providing a complete and independent loading organisation and of facilitating matters generally.

25. Lower Euphrates.—Troops advancing from Nasiriyah in December, 1917, occupied Durraji, Samawa, and Shenafiyah. Inland Water Transport officers were established at these stations in January, 1918. A buoyage unit was shortly afterwards despatched to Shenafiyah Lake to open up and maintain communications with the Upper Euphrates, thus completing a chain of I.W.T. stations throughout the whole Euphrates Valley from Kurna to beyond Ramadie.

26. Contemporary Works in Progress.—Bhoosa Pier was reconstructed, wharves at Margil, Nahr Umar, and bulk oil storage tanks at various stations up-river were under construction ; the Headquarters building was being extended, and quarters, offices, and stores were in course of erection at many points.

27. Freeland Commission.—The War Office Commission on Transportation, under Major-General Freeland, arrived at Basrah on December 24th, 1917. The purpose of the Mission was to enquire into and report on the methods and facilities of Railway and Water Transport throughout the occupied territories of Mesopotamia. After a period of preliminary investigation at the Base, the Mission proceeded up-country, pursuing its enquiries at Kurna, Amara, Kut, and Baghdad. The conclusions of the Mission were subsequently issued in a confidential Report, which resulted in several changes and rearrangements being effected. Complimentary references are made therein to the efficiency of the I.W.T. Dockyards, the successful and substantial work carried out by the Buoyage and Construction Departments, whilst the dredging work carried out by the Conservancy and Reclamation Department was appreciated.

28. " Fly " Boats.—Eight " Fly " boats were taken over from the Royal Navy in January, and the remaining eight in March, 1918. Four of these were retained as gunboats, R.A. gunners being attached to the Inland Water Transport to replace the naval ratings, whilst the remaining twelve were transferred to the Euphrates for transport purposes.

29. High-water Season, 1918.—A redistribution of the fleet came into operation on January 9th, 1918, to meet the requirements of the high-water season. For this purpose, thirty-two of the large paddlers were based on Amara, and the remainder of the fleet on Basrah, with the exception of twelve tugs and three stern-wheelers which were based on Baghdad for local purposes.

This season was remarkable for the rapidity with which the river rose, the violent fluctuations accompanying the rise, and the maximum height attained, which was only ·8 of a foot below the highest recorded level, and was 4 feet 6 inches higher than the average flood level up to this date. In April the river overflowed its banks, inundating the country over a wide area, and creating an exceptionally strong current. Landmarks were obliterated, and the ordinary difficulties attending navigation were greatly intensified under these conditions. Several serious strandings occurred, mostly caused by the absence of any defined channel over certain areas. In one case a vessel which had grounded on the brink of a ledge capsized and sank in deep water as the river fell.

An additional severe strain thrown on the River Transport was caused by washouts on the Kut-Hinaidi Railway, which for some time was out of action altogether. In spite of such handicaps all previous records were broken, both as regards tonnage handled and ton mileage attained. The actual figures for the quarters concerned are as follows :—

				Tonnage.	Ton mileage.
March 31st	.	.	.	464,196	91,226,221
June 30th	.	.	.	448,505	101,460,969

The record tonnage handled in any one week was 43,012 tons for the week ending March 23rd, 1918, and the record ton mileage in any one week was 9,513,986 ton miles for the week ending May 25th, 1918.

At the commencement of the high-water season most of the Arab pilots were withdrawn, owing to the general improvement in navigational facilities, a few only being retained on special sections.

In June, 1918, a British Officers' Pilot Service for both upward- and downward-bound vessels through the Narrows was introduced, a system which was instrumental in considerably reducing delays and accidents.

30. Slipway.—The Dockyard Slipway was opened by General Freeland on February 18th, 1918, P.S. 53 being the first vessel slipped. On February 28th, H.M.S. *Mantis*, weighing 628 tons, was successfully slipped.

31. Further Reorganisation.—The enormous expansion which had taken place in certain Departments now rendered a certain amount of readjustment advisable, and with this end in view the following changes were brought into effect :

In February, 1918, the Port Traffic Department was separated from the Inland Water Transport and placed under a Port Director directly responsible to the Inspector-General of Communications, the Port of Basrah having now reached a sufficiently advanced degree of development to justify an independent directorate.

In March, 1918, Irrigation, which had become a subject of vastly increased importance to Mesopotamia, was separated from the Inland Water Transport and an independent Directorate formed, to which Lieut.-Colonel Garrow, and nine other I.W.T. officers, were transferred.

As an off-set to this, the dredgers, formerly under the control of the Port Administration and Conservancy, were transferred to the Inland Water Transport and placed under the River Conservancy Department, which now adopted the title of Conservancy and Reclamation, and was made responsible for dredging operations, reclamation, earthworks, and excavations of all kinds.

The Construction and Up-River Works Department were amalgamated, being made responsible for construction work both at the Base and Up-river.

The Dockyard Department took over control of all up-river workshops as they were completed by the Construction Department, being made responsible for their maintenance and efficiency, in addition to that of the Basrah Dockyard,

D

thus separating the Civil and Mechanical Engineering branches into two Departments.

In view of these changes, an amended War Establishment was prepared and subsequently sanctioned, comprising a total personnel of :

> 799 British officers,
> 3,337 British other ranks,
> 38,832 Eastern races.

Their disposition is shown in Appendix C2.

32. Further Operations in the Euphrates.—River transport was an imperative necessity before operations could be resumed on the Euphrates on an extensive scale. Dhibban had now become rail-head and the most important transhipping station. The arrival from Basrah of the flotilla consisting of towing vessels, motor bellums, a hospital ship, and a floating repair shop was, owing to the exceptionally low-water conditions prevailing in Hamar and Shenafiyah Lakes, unavoidably delayed until May. From the beginning of the year, Inland Water Transport officers had been engaged throughout the whole Euphrates area, collecting native craft of all descriptions, and their efforts were attended with such success that operations were commenced with such craft as were then available and without waiting for the arrival of the above-mentioned flotilla. Hit, 71 miles from Dhibban, was captured on March 9th, and several vessels were captured there which were subsequently utilised. The river was surveyed to Khan Baghdadi, 31 miles above Hit, and though 5 feet of water was carried practically all the way, the many weirs and strong current rendered navigation difficult. The arrival of the flotilla, and other reinforcements, materially contributed to the success of further operations in this area. On the cessation of hostilities the Euphrates fleet had increased to :

> 49 steam vessels,
> 74 barges,
> 54 motor-boats ;   besides native craft.

Details of these vessels are given in Appendix B5.

33. Hamar Lake. Dredging Operations.—In March, 1918, surveys and preparations were commenced with a view to completing the navigable cut across Hamar Lake. In all about 24 miles had to be dredged. Of this 6½ miles had been partly dredged by the Port Administration and Conservancy in 1916 and 1917, when the scheme was abandoned for the time. This work was carried on at full pressure day and night through the heat of the summer, and was eventually completed in February, 1919, over 7½ million cubic yards of spoil having been then excavated and deposited to form a bank on the south side of the Channel. This subject is more fully dealt with under "Conservancy and Reclamation" (see page 135).

34. Director.—Brig.-General R. H. W. Hughes, C.S.I., C.M.G., D.S.O., Director I.W.T., left Mesopotamia for duty in Egypt on May 4th, 1918. Colonel J. C. Ward, D.S.O., R.E., Deputy-Director I.W.T., assumed duty as Officiating Director on that date, Lieut.-Colonel G. B. Barton, R.E., Deputy-Director I.W.T., meanwhile replacing him as Deputy-Director I.W.T., Baghdad.

35. Middle Euphrates.—At the beginning of May, 1918, preparations on a large scale were made for the collection of the harvest in the Euphrates Valley, and it became necessary to increase the Inland Water Transport personnel in this area. An Assistant Director of Inland Water Transport was appointed, with headquarters at Hillah, and new stations were opened up at:

Tuarij,	Kifil,	Jerboyia,
Hindiyah,	Kufa,	Afaj,
Dewaniyah,	Shenafiyah,	Abu Sukair.

Native craft were brought from all parts of the occupied territories, and based on these stations, in quantities sufficient to meet estimated requirements.

In connection with Agricultural development in this area, kerosene storage tanks were erected at Hillah, Kufa, Kifil, Dewaniyah, and many other places to supply the needs of cultivators.

A list of these is given in Appendix E1.

36. Fisheries.—The general Food situation, early in 1918, was such that it became necessary to investigate every possible source of local supply. In this connection, it was suggested that the Sea Fisheries of the Persian Gulf might receive more attention.

Previous to this date, a small and uncertain quantity of fish had been obtained through local resources from riverside Arabs, and was mostly issued to hospitals.

In April the Inland Water Transport was deputed to go into the matter and submit proposals for exploiting these Fisheries on as large a scale as possible. An experienced officer was therefore despatched to study the question on the spot, and report on the prospects of such an undertaking.

As a result of his investigations a small Fisheries Sub-Department was instituted, with headquarters at Fao. A specially fitted ice-making barge, with cold storage accommodation, was stationed there and operations commenced forthwith. To supplement the fish caught by the Inland Water Transport staff, which consisted of two British officers, eleven British other ranks, and nineteen Indians, contracts were made with local Arab fishermen for their catches also. The fish were gutted and cleaned by Arab labour under European supervision, then packed in crushed ice, and every alternate day cargoes were despatched to Basrah in specially insulated barges. Operations were carried on for about three months, and during this time a total of 133 tons of fish were so despatched.

As an experiment, a small quantity of fish was smoked ; but, unfortunately, this branch could not be extended, owing to lack of facilities.

The fish were all caught by means of river and longshore fishing. Trawling had been advocated, and a complete trawling outfit was actually made by the staff, with which experiments were made in a vessel improvised for the purpose ; but as the question of a special vessel was never satisfactorily settled, trawling was discontinued.

37. Mine-sweeping.—In May, 1918, the mine-sweeping defences of the Shatt-el-Arab were taken over from the

Royal Navy. The sweeps and kites handed over were not considered suitable for serious work, though they proved very useful for training personnel. Two tugs were fitted with the necessary appliances for this purpose, and practice sweeping was periodically carried out.

Proposals were submitted relative to obtaining a complete outfit of gear sufficient to deal with all eventualities, and to equip a self-contained mine-sweeping unit ; but before the resulting indent could be executed, the cessation of hostilities rendered further action unnecessary.

38. The Caspian.—In July, 1918, in accordance with instructions received from the War Office, a small detachment, consisting of four officers and four British other ranks, was despatched to Northern Persia with orders to assist in selecting and arming vessels for service on the Caspian Sea. These orders were subsequently modified on the Royal Navy assuming these duties, the control of merchant shipping, port administration, and the carrying out of all repair work for the Royal Navy being deputed to the Inland Water Transport, which was considerably reinforced for this purpose. The 4-inch guns from the defence vessels were transported overland for the purpose of arming ships on the Caspian.

After the cessation of hostilities this detachment was transferred to the Mediterranean Command.

39. Bridges.—In addition to the bridges on the Diala and Tigris referred to in pars. 18 and 14 respectively, bridges on the Euphrates were maintained by the Inland Water Transport at the following places :—

Nasiriyah,	Rumetha,
Dewaniyah,	Tuerij,
Hillah,	Kufa,
Kala Abu Sayah,	Museyib,
Dhibban,	Ramadie.

40. Low-water Season, 1918.—Navigable conditions on the Tigris were generally good, though frequent surveys had to be made during this period.

The draft of barges maintained was generally one foot more than at a corresponding date last year. The principal improvement was shown in the Narrows, which section was devoid of groundings throughout the low-water season. This fact may be attributed to the efforts of the Conservancy and Reclamation Department in carefully regulating the amount of water escaping down the Chahala and Majar Kebir branches. In the Upper River, bandalling kept channels open and improved the depth of water generally, though in some places, where the current was insufficient to set up a scour, and also perhaps owing to the amount of silt deposited after the floods having formed a hard crust over the sand in the bed of the river, they failed to have any appreciable result. In such places, the small dredgers, which had recently arrived in the country, were most successfully utilised.

41. Director.—Brig.-General R. H. W. Hughes, C.S.I., C.M.G., D.S.O., returned from leave on September 25th, 1918, and resumed duties as Director of Inland Water Transport.

42. Co-ordination of Transport Services.—One of the results of the Report of the Freeland Commission (see par. 27) was the appointment of a Director-General of Transportation in Mesopotamia, his duties being closer co-ordination of the respective transport services by rail, road, and river.

Major-General R. De Candolle, C.B., the officer selected for this post, arrived in this country at the end of September, 1918, and immediately commenced the collection of the requisite information.

Certain anomalies had existed under the old system, one of them being that the D.I.W.T., with headquarters at Basrah, worked directly under the I.G.C., whilst approximately one-third of the work of his department was outside the Lines of Communication and administered under the orders of the D.Q.M.G. at Baghdad. It was therefore decided that the D.I.W.T. should have his headquarters at Baghdad, so as to be in closer touch with the D.G.T., whilst the latter's deputy would be stationed at Basrah, in order to attend to matters at the Base, including those of the Port. Before any actual changes had been made, however, the Armistice was signed, and it was not considered necessary to proceed further in the circumstances. The appointment of D.G.T. was therefore abolished, so far as Mesopotamia was concerned.

43. Further Operations on Tigris above Baghdad.— During the Advance in October and November, 1918, the steamers *Baghdad, Khalifa, Hamidieh,* and *Bahrinieh* were captured from the Turks at Shergat ; the two former were in fair condition, and a working party was sent up-river to put in hand the necessary repairs, so that they could be floated down on the next high river. The two latter were so damaged that they were not considered worth salving. It was during this Advance that a service of " killicks," or rafts made of inflated skins, was instituted and maintained by the Inland Water Transport, for the purpose of conveying casualties down to Tekrit. A survey of this part of river was also completed by the Buoyage Department as far as Mosul.

44. The Maude Bridge.—Amongst the more important works nearing completion at the conclusion of hostilities was the MAUDE BRIDGE at Baghdad, though this was not actually opened for traffic till December 7th, 1918. A complete description of this bridge is given under " Construction."

45. Personnel.—The comparative strength of the Inland Water Transport in Mesopotamia on the dates indicated consisted of :—

	Dec. 31st, 1916.	Dec. 31st, 1917.	Nov. 11th, 1918.
B.O.'s	292	703	804
W.O.'s	19	51	99
B.O.R.'s	1445	2277	2596
B.W.I.'s	427	382	392
African (or Eastern races) .	16,338	42,640	41,940
	18,521	46,053	45,813

The decline in the figures for November 11th, 1918, was due to the transfer of personnel to the Port Directorate.

A list of the Administrative Staff at the conclusion of hostilities is given on page 209.

46. Fleet.—The strength of the fleet at the conclusion of hostilities had increased to :

> 446 self-propelled vessels,
> 774 barges,
> 414 motor-boats.
>
> Total . 1634

Details of these are given in Appendix B4.

The total value of this fleet approximated £9,204,954.

47. Conclusion.—In conclusion, it may perhaps be permissible to quote here the following Extract from a Report by Sir John Hewitt's Commission (February, 1919), in referring to the work of the Inland Water Transport :—

" A very large sum of money has been invested in the Fleet, the working of which deserves to be regarded as one *of our chief successes in Mesopotamia.* By the aid of the Railway and the Fleet it has been possible to secure the health, comfort, and efficiency of the Troops who have had to serve during a large part of the year in very trying surroundings. At one time, when the needs of the Forward Army were greatest, and the condition of the Tigris most favourable, 2400 *Tons of Stores were landed daily at Baghdad,* 1500 *by Rail and* 900 *by River. The whole amount had to be carried by River from Amara to Kut. . . ."*

Again, Colonel Willcox, C.B., C.M.G. (Consulting Physician to the Force), who conducted a close inquiry into the prevalence of certain diseases amongst the troops, in writing of the conditions existing up to July, 1916, observes with regard to delay in the regular supply of suitable rations at that time :—

" The main cause of the deficiency was really due to the absence of sufficient River Transport. . . ."

He subsequently remarks in the same Report :—

" *The improvement in the condition of the Force owes much to the organisation of the River Transport to its present high state of efficiency. . . ."*

In these circumstances, it may be stated, without fear of contradiction, that the Inland Water Transport has played no inconsiderable part in the successful prosecution of the Mesopotamian Campaign, and though, at times, the resources of the Department have been strained to their utmost, it has never failed to meet emergencies. The reputation of the motto of the Royal Engineers, " UBIQUE," has certainly not suffered, as regards achievement, from its association with the Inland Water Transport in Mesopotamia.

PART II

DEPARTMENTAL ORGANISATION

THE Inland Water Transport in Mesopotamia is administered on the usual Departmental System of similar commercial organisations. It is controlled by the Headquarters' Staff, which consists of a Director, Deputy-Director (Chief Engineer), Assistant Director in charge of administration, and certain Staff Officers, all Departments reporting to the Director as they would to the Board of a Company, and all policy being controlled and appointments made by the Director through his personal staff.

On the Headquarters' Staff also is the D.A.D.I.W.T. troops, who is the Officer Commanding I.W.T. troops in Mesopotamia, and in charge of all discipline of both Europeans and natives.

The actual disposition of officers at the date of the Armistice is shown in Appendix C3.

The various departments comprising the Directorate will now be dealt with separately.

The Director and Officers of the Directorate of the Inland Water Transport R.E.
Mesopotamian Expeditionary Force at the Base on the cessation of hostilities.
November 20th. 1918

DEPARTMENT OF TRANSPORT

On the assumption of control by the Inland Water Transport in September, 1916, a certain amount of re-organisation took place in the Transport Department, the Superintendent of which was made responsible for the following duties :—

(1) To control the movements of all vessels up or down the river.

(2) The maintenance of supply and distribution of coal, oil-fuel, kerosene, and petrol to all departments and all stations on the river.

(3) Upkeep and repair of all barges.

(4) Port towing.

(5) Fleet registration.

These items will be considered separately :

Headquarters' Office.—(1) The control of the movements of vessels—in other words, the economic handling of the fleet—in such a manner as to deliver the maximum amount of troops and military stores at river-head in the minimum time was a matter of outstanding importance; in fact it was the primary objective of the whole Directorate, and all other departments were subordinated to this end. This was dealt with by the Headquarters' Staff of the Transport Department in consultation with the Embarkation Authorities.

The procedure adopted being as follows :

A list of barges ready for service was submitted daily by the Barge Depot. These were then allotted to the various departments and interests concerned, according to their respective tonnage requirements, a daily report being received regarding the loading progress of each barge. A list of vessels under repair, with their probable date of completion, was also submitted daily by the Marine Engineering Department. With the information thus available, a towing programme was arranged in advance.

All vessels were given sailing orders on the day previous to their departure. On completing with fuel and embarking such details as had been arranged for, they picked up the barges which had been allotted to them and proceeded in execution of their orders. A record of the whereabouts of every vessel from day to day was maintained in the Headquarters' Office, both by means of a position board and also by a system of card-indexing, telegraphic advice being received from all up-river stations daily reporting all passing vessels.

The strength of the river fleet handed over by the R.I.M. to the Inland Water Transport is shown in Appendix B1. This fleet was augmented by native craft employed in carrying supplies and coal between Basrah and Amara.

The length of river then operated was :

On the Tigris from Abadan to Sheikh Sa'ad.	273	miles.
,, Karun—Mohammerah to Ahwaz	. 114	,,
,, Euphrates—Kurna to Nasariyah	. 88	,,
	475	,,

The tonnage handled at this time approximated 300 tons per day. This had increased to 1000 tons per day in November, 1916, and 3200 tons per day in February, 1917, shortly before the advance subsequent to the recapture of Kut commenced.

Towing vessels and barges were steadily arriving in this country during this period, and the fleet which had at last become capable of dealing with the requirements of the army in the field opposite Kut, could only cope with the altered conditions brought about by the occupation of Baghdad and subsequent developments, involving the maintenance of ever-lengthening Lines of Communications, by running ships incessantly night and day at high pressure and neglecting all but absolutely essential repairs in order to avert total breakdowns. It therefore became necessary to largely augment the fleet and, with this end in view, all sources at home and abroad capable of supplying river craft were investigated, new vessels were ordered and arrangements made to transfer them to Mesopotamia with all despatch. The respective increase in the strength of the fleet on the dates indicated will be seen by reference to Appendices B1, B2, B3, and B4. The mileage operated had increased to 865 miles on April 1st, 1917, to 1160 miles at December 31st, 1917, and to 1278 miles at the conclusion of hostilities.

The following comparative statement will serve to illustrate the progress made regarding tonnage handled and ton mileage obtaining from the occupation of Baghdad to the date of the Armistice.

For the quarter ending.	Tonnage.	Ton mileage.
June 30th, 1917 . . .	255,959	60,324,683
September 30th, 1917 . .	310,780	58,645,842
December 31st, 1917 . .	452,218	73,445,574
March 31st, 1918 . .	464,196	91,226,221
June 30th, 1918 . . .	448,505	101,460,969
September 30th, 1918 . .	447,141	73,489,771
November 11th, 1918 . .	198,695*	29,400,573*

Accidents.—Despite the hurried conditions under which River Transport has been operated, and the large number of vessels engaged, there has been a remarkable dearth of accidents. The following may be mentioned as being amongst the more serious :

1916. *October 27th.*—Tug *Shirin* caught fire about midnight, due to bricks in furnace falling out on to the floor-plates. The vessel was completely gutted out.

November 26th.—P.S. 30 was completely gutted out by fire at No. 7 Marching Post. Fire was caused by the explosion of a lamp.

1917. *March 23rd.*—P.S. 56, one of the finest paddlers on the river, was seriously damaged by fire which broke out on board, putting her out of service for some weeks.

April 28th.—T. 27 reported badly ashore above Sanijah on hard shingle bottom in two feet of water. All efforts to refloat her failed at first, but she floated off on a subsequent rise in the river.

June 2nd.—H.S. 2 was completely gutted out by fire, six miles above Baghaila. There were no casualties and the

* The last-named figures are for a period of six weeks only.

wreck was salved on 4th June ; the boilers and machinery were not seriously damaged.

August 30*th*.—P.S. 20 grounded in Jamshal Reach in the Narrows, and completely blocked the channel. She was floated off and hauled up-stream, but a bar with two feet of water over it had been formed right across the river. Owing to this block certain ships above and below the bar had to exchange their barges.

September 11*th*.—Barge C. 37, loaded with petrol, was burnt out completely at Abadan.

October 24*th*.—Petrol Barge O.C. 41, which had just been specially fitted for carrying petrol, caught fire at Abadan with about three thousand cases of petrol on board. Barge was beached and fire burnt itself out—slight repairs were carried out, and the barge was towed to Basrah for a thorough overhaul.

1918. *January* 13*th*.—P.T. 40 grounded badly out of channel at Sawerah. Attempts to float her were unavailing and she listed over, slid off the ledge and sank in ten feet of water on 16th of January. Was salved later.

January 15*th*.—Red Cross Motor Launch No. 397 was in collision with S.T. 18 after dark at Basrah. Launch was cut down and sank immediately. Five lives were lost.

May 18*th*.—A storm of great intensity was reported from the Lower Euphrates, principally Shenafiyah Lake. F. 2 was dismasted, a dredger blown ashore, and several mahailas sunk or dismasted. As a result of this storm the lake silted up to as little as one foot in depth.

June 8*th*.—Barge O.C. 56, loaded with cased petrol, caught fire at Basrah. Holds were flooded with water until barge was immersed as deep as possible with safety. Cable was veered and barge hove in towards the bank. She was then allowed to burn out.

Personnel.—The Staff employed in the Headquarters' Office of the Transport Department on the dates indicated consisted of :—

	Sept., 1916.	Dec., 1916.	Dec., 1917.	Nov. 11th, 1918.
B.O.'s .	5	5	4	6
W.O.'s .	2	2	2	1
B.O.R.'s	1	1	2	3
Eastern races	16	15	9	9

COAL AND OIL FUEL

(2) The maintenance of the supply of and distribution of oil fuel was directly administered in the Headquarters Transport Office by the D.A.D. (Coal and Oil Fuel). The Coal Depot at Muftieh was taken over as a going concern from the R.I.M. in September, 1916. Storage accommodation was then available for about 10,000 tons of coal, an average of about 8000 tons being consumed monthly.

Adjoining the Depot was an Oil Fuel Storage Tank of 1000 tons capacity, belonging to Messrs. Strick Scott & Co., who also carried a stock of about 50,000 gallons of cased oils. This firm at first managed the distribution of these oils, under the direction of the Inland Water Transport, but on January 1st, 1918, the whole of the plant and distribution was taken over and directly administered by the Inland Water Transport.

A considerable amount of reclamation work has been undertaken from time to time, protective bunds built and the storage accommodation increased in accordance with the requirements of the fleet. In the early days suitable appliances for dealing with the heavy demands of the campaign were limited, but as circumstances permitted improvements were introduced, jetties erected on the foreshore and Deacauville tracks laid, which greatly facilitated the handling of coal.

Coal.—The coal supply was maintained from India by a fleet of China coast steamers which had been specially requisitioned for this purpose. Originally a certain amount of Welsh coal was imported, more particularly for H.M. ships, but latterly supplies have been entirely confined to Indian coal. Coal was supplied to H.M. Navy, transports, river steamers, railways, shore stations and plants, whilst sub-depots were opened up-river as the Army moved forward. A fleet of motor lighters and steam barges was maintained to keep these depots supplied, in addition to the very large quantity sent up-river by ordinary transport barges. A list of these fleet auxiliaries is given in Appendix B6.

The tonnage dealt with at the Depot reached its maximum in the summer of 1918, when approximately 40,000 tons of coal were handled monthly. A metre gauge railway track was subsequently laid into the Depot from Makina, which proved of great value for supplying both distant stations and inland depots in the vicinity of the Base. A branch of the Basrah Light Railway was also laid up to the southern boundary of the coal-yard, which greatly facilitated the supply of coal to otherwise awkwardly placed units. The labour employed consisted at first of Arab coolies, but owing to their unreliability they were replaced in turn by Lascars, Egyptian Labour Corps, Indian Jail Porter Corps, and finally by Madras coolies and Kurdish labourers.

Oil.—The introduction of oil-burning steamers and the conversion of coal burners to oil necessitated special provision for oil transport and storage. A fleet of specially constructed barges for carrying oil fuel in bulk was gradually obtained from various sources, while suitable transport barges were specially converted for the carriage of cased oils. Two self-propelled tank vessels were also fitted out for this purpose. The composition of this fleet at the time of the Armistice is shown in Appendix B7.

To relieve the strain on Muftieh an additional depot was opened at Khora Creek in August, 1917. A 1000-ton oil fuel tank was erected there and provision made for the storage of kerosene either in bulk or tins and for petrol in tins.

Bulk storage tanks were also erected at various points on the Lines of Communication for both oil fuel and kerosene. A list of these, with their respective capacities and plans, is shown in Appendix E1.

A feature of the Depot at Muftieh is the erection of two 1000-ton ferro-concrete tanks for fuel oil which have been completed since the Armistice. In connection with this scheme a deep-water wharf for bunkering vessels and a comprehensive pumping plant and pipe-line system has been installed, supplying both the central power-house and rail-

ways at Makina. This subject is more fully dealt with under
"Construction." It was at one time projected to lay a
pipe-line from Abadan to Basrah, but this scheme had to
be abandoned owing to lack of material.

A comparative statement, showing the average monthly
consumption of both coal and oil fuel during 1918, is shown
in Appendix E2.

Personnel.—The staff employed in the Coal and Oil Fuel
Department at the Base, including the Headquarters' Office,
Muftieh,* Khora Creek depots, on the dates indicated,
consisted of :—

	Sept., 1916.	Dec., 1916.	Dec., 1917.	Nov. 11th, 1918.
B.O.'s . .	5	6	11	12
B.O.R.'s .	17	14	22	26
Eastern races	20	30	560	685

UPKEEP AND REPAIR OF BARGES

(3) **General Progress.**—During the second week in
September, 1916, and shortly following the assumption of
control by the Inland Water Transport, the barge establishment was transferred from the old repair workshop below
Messrs. Lynch Bros.' wharf to the new depot at Muftieh.
The personnel then consisted of 2 officers, 2 warrant officers,
24 skilled and 71 Marine ratings—a total of 121 in all. The
barge fleet, including special purpose, such as port and oil
barges, consisted at that time of about a hundred craft all
told, whilst an average of about twenty per week passed
through the Depot. Machinery of any kind was conspicuous
by its absence.

Some lack of foresight seems to have been shown when
the new Depot was originally laid out, and apparently no
estimate can have been formed of the amount of work that
would eventually have to be undertaken. The huts were
erected by the Works Directorate and were placed far too

---

* Labour at the Muftieh Coal Depot consisted of locally engaged Arab
coolies in 1916, whose number varied from time to time. These are not
included in the above figures. They were replaced in 1917 by Indians.

E

near the foreshore to allow of sufficient room for the work-shops and stores, whilst material for filling this area was taken from the immediate rear of the huts, with the result that considerable trouble from inundation has always been experienced during the high-water season.

Barges were arriving rapidly from overseas during the latter part of 1916, and the work of preparing them for service necessitated a large increase in the personnel of the Depot. A small machine shop and blacksmith's shop were erected and such machines as could be obtained were installed. These consisted of a drilling machine, a punching and shearing machine, a circular saw and a grindstone, power being supplied to them by a four-cylinder Osler petrol engine.

During 1917, the machine and blacksmith's shops were replaced by the present buildings, and more machines, including a lathe, screwing machine, emery wheel, hacksaw and blower for blacksmith's forge, were added. A large oil engine, obtained from a captured Turkish workshop barge, was repaired and utilised to provide power. The galvanised superstructures from two of the large Indian jute barges were removed and re-erected ashore, providing a carpenter's shop, a sail loft, and a store. New huts to accommodate the increased personnel were built and many of the older ones were rebuilt.

The number of barges passing through the Depot during 1917 averaged nearly eight per day, the total being 2790 ; new barges were arriving from overseas throughout the whole period, necessitating a further steady increase in the personnel.

The establishment continued to develop during 1918, and many improvements were introduced, one of the most important being the substitution of two 18-kilowatt lighting sets for the small $4\frac{1}{2}$-kilowatt set which had been laid down in the previous year. Materials, tools and plant were added as occasion arose.

Early in 1917 a detachment of the B.W.I. Regiment was detailed to the Depot for guard duties. A certain number of these men were tradesmen, and were employed as fitters, etc., whilst others were employed as clerical assistants. Special lines were constructed for these ratings.

Canteens.—Both British and Indian Canteens were maintained in the Depot. The profit from the former enabled a Sports Club to be run and many articles for the amusement and recreation of the men of the Depot to be purchased.

Outside Work.—A large amount of outside work for other departments of the Inland Water Transport was undertaken from time to time by the Depot. For several months the whole of the blacksmiths' work of the Port Traffic Department was carried out here, whilst the Construction and Native Craft departments were assisted very considerably at various times.

Fleet.—The following table shows the types of barges and actual strength of the fleet at the time indicated :—

CLASS.	Number in Commission on			
	Sept. 16	Dec. 31, 1916	Dec. 31, 1917	Nov. 1918
Transport . . .	86	172	*366	*424
Port	11	48	95	167
Oil	7	12	34	73
Hospital . . .	6	3	3	3
Refrigeration . .	—	—	4	14
Water . . .	—	—	4	11
Ice	—	—	3	8
Tractor . . .	—	—	4	4
Hopper . . .	—	—	1	2
Cold storage . .	—	—	—	1
Filtration . . .	—	—	—	4
Miscellaneous special purposes . . .	—	—	—	24
Totals . . .	110	235	514	735

* Includes several Turkish barges captured during the advance These were all sent to the Depot for overhaul preparatory to being added to the fleet.

Work.—The following table shows the comparative increase in the number of barges passing through the Depot and work accomplished at the times indicated :—

	End of 1916.	1917.	Jan. to Nov. 11th, 1918.
Number of days . .	46	365	315
Total number of barges	251	2790	2722
Average per day . .	5·4	7·6	8·6

Personnel.—

	Sept., 1916.	Dec., 1916.	Dec., 1917.	Nov., 1918.
British officers .	2	6	7	7
British other ranks	2	128*	108†	102‡
Civilian clerks .	—	2	3	4
Skilled Eastern labour . .	24	102	244	219
Miscellaneous Eastern races . .	93	247	321	384
	121	485	683	716

TOWING OFFICE

(4) This Office was already in existence on a small scale when the Inland Water Transport assumed control in September, 1916, but the number of towing craft available at that time was quite inadequate to cope with requirements.

Immediate steps were taken to remedy this state of affairs, and a large number of tugs and launches were obtained from India very shortly afterwards, and others were taken over from the Port Administration.

Extensions at Margil threw a very large amount of additional work on this department, and necessitated the establishment of a branch office there.

The staff, which consisted at the time of taking over of one officer in charge, one warrant officer and one clerk, was augmented by two B.O.'s and a number of B.O.R.'s, with

* Include 119 B.W.I. Regiment.
† ,, 80 ,, ,,
‡ ,, 69 ,, ,,

necessary clerical assistance, whilst the officer in charge was promoted to be a D.A.D.I.W.T.

The scope of the Department steadily increased, and with the growth of first Kurna as a railway terminus, and later the development of Nahr Umar as a subsidiary port to Basrah, long-distance towing became a special feature of its work, which extended from Ezra's Tomb to Abadan. This reached its maximum in the quarter ending 31st March, 1918, for which the figures were as follows :—

Average number of tugs employed.	Mileage steamed.	Tonnage handled.
3	13,141	26,862

The figures for the towing work carried out actually within the port area covering the same period were :—

Average number of tugs employed.	Total number of tows.	Total working hours.
15	5356	11,693

A certain amount of deep-sea towing to and from Aden Muscat, Henjam, Bushire, etc., was also undertaken at various times. In addition to ordinary towing work this department was responsible for many other duties, such as the organisation of Ferry services, the supply of fresh water to H.M. ships, ration services and the tending of sheerlegs, whilst discharging heavy lifts from ocean steamers and the multitudinous duties in connection with river and harbour transport in the base area.

Ferries.—The two principal ferry services were the Margil and Tanooma ferries. The former was worked by two creek steamers and soon assumed large proportions, the highest number of passengers carried in any one week reaching a total of 18,118, whilst the latter, which was run by a motor tug, carried as many as 1619 passengers in the same period.

Motor-boat Pool.—This Office was also responsible for the running of the Motor-boat Pool, an institution which resulted in effecting very considerable economy in the use of motor-boats. An average number of from 12 to 15 working boats was maintained in the pool, and during 1918 an average number of about 450 applications per week from officers or departments requiring boats was filled, involving about 500 working hours.

Craft.—The approximate number of craft attached to the Towing Office on the dates specified were :—

	Dec., 1916.	Dec., 1917.	Nov. 11th, 1918
S.T. Class . . .	4	12	13
T. Class . . .	Nil	Nil	4
T.L. Class . . .	2	2	1
L. Class . . .	1	3	7
Motor Tugs . . .	Nil	Nil	3

Personnel.—The staff of this department on the dates indicated consisted of :—

	Dec., 1916.	Dec., 1917.	Nov., 11th, 1918.
Eastern races . .	4	3	10
B.O.'s	2	4	4
B.O.R.'s . . .	4	10	16

FLEET REGISTRATION OFFICE

(5) Though this was at first intended to be an independent department, it was found more convenient in practice that this office should work in close collaboration with the Headquarters' Transport Office, and it has latterly been included as a branch of this department. It was initiated in September, 1916, and was made responsible for :

(1) The technical registration of the fleet.

(2) The checking of all specifications, plans, measurements, etc., of craft.

(3) Recording the allocation of all vessels of the fleet, including barges and motor-boats (the latter being done in consultation with Headquarters, Lines of Communication).

(4) Recording the position of all craft *en route* or on order.

(5) All business in connection with the hiring or chartering of vessels.

(6) The storage and registration of all I.W.T. drawings.

A Drawing Office was included, in which all drawings in connection with changes in structural alterations to craft were prepared as well as a considerable amount of drawing and tracing work being carried out for other departments.

A photographer and complete set of apparatus was also borne on the strength of this establishment.

The work of this office (i.e. maintaining an efficient fleet register) though not directly productive was as necessary to the Inland Water Transport organisation as time-tables are to a railway company, which it closely resembles in that, though both are very simple things to look at, they require an infinite amount of care and patience to produce and maintain accurately.

The staff of this department on the dates indicated consisted of :—

	Dec., 1916.	Dec., 1917.	Nov. 11th, 1918.
B.O.'s .	2	4	4
B.O.R.'s	2	3	7
Eastern races	4	4	4

OUTSTATIONS

The following outstations are included within the Base section, and are directly administered by the A.D.I.W.T.

Margil.—An I.W.T. officer was stationed at Lower Margil to supervise the berthing of ocean transports, the loading and discharging of all river craft, and to control the movements of river traffic in this area generally.

On 1st December, 1918, all work in connection with ocean transports was taken over by the Port Directorate.

The staff maintained at Margil on the dates indicated consisted of :—

	Dec., 1916.	Dec., 1917.	Nov. 11th, 1918.
B.O.'s .	2	3	4
W.O.'s .	2	—	—
B.O.R.'s	—	5	6
Eastern races	30	43	41

Abadan is on the left bank of the Shatt-el-Arab, thirty miles below Basrah, and is the site of the A.P.O.C. refinery.

An I.W.T. representative was stationed here whose duties were to ensure that demands for oils of every description were promptly executed, to check measurements of bulk oil supplied, to tally and supervise the loading of cased oils, to grant receipts in respect of all quantities delivered, and to expedite despatch of barges generally. Regarding the latter item, it soon became evident that the A.P.O.C. were unable to provide sufficient local labour to keep things going. To remedy this labour gangs were supplied by the I.W.T., the cost of whose wages were debited to the A.P.O.C. This resulted in materially speeding-up loading. A camp was laid out and quarters erected by the Construction Department for the I.W.T. personnel. An additional barge-loading wharf was also constructed by this department, and at the end of 1918 two of the storage tanks belonging to the A.P.O.C. were taken over entirely for I.W.T. use. The tinning-sheds are dealt with under "Marine Engineering."

The I.W.T. staff at Abadan on the dates specified consisted of :—

	Dec., 1916.	Dec., 1917.	Nov. 11th, 1918.
B.O.'s	1	1	2
B.O.R.'s . . .	—	—	8
Eastern races . .	16	8	25

Naur Umar is situated on the right bank of the river, twenty-two miles above Basrah. It was developed as a port in June, 1917, to relieve congestion in Basrah, and was particularly useful as such whilst trouble was being experienced with the Gurmat Ali Railway bridge.

Two deep-sea wharves and eighteen barge jetties were constructed by the I.W.T., in addition to quarters for the I.W.T. and port traffic personnel and tanks for the storage of oil fuel. The tonnage discharged reached its maximum in April, 1918, when 43,658 tons were landed there. A large amount of railway and S. and T. material was loaded for up-river at this place, but it gradually declined in importance as facilities at Margil improved and was closed down at the end of April, 1919.

The I.W.T. staff maintained there on the dates specified
consisted of :—

	Dec., 1917.	Nov., 1918.
B.O.'s	7	5
B.O.R.'s	8	6
Eastern races	85	65

Kurna is situated at the junction of the Euphrates and
Tigris and, on completion of the railway from Amara, became
of some importance as a transhipping station. It fell off
considerably on completion of the line through to Basrah,
since which time it has only been used as supply base for
the dredgers working in Hamar Lake and as a medical
examination station for native craft.

Substantial jetties, and a number of sheds, offices, and
stores were built by the I.W.T., and a large amount of
labour expended in filling and levelling.

The I.W.T. staff on the dates specified consisted of :—

	Dec., 1916.	Dec., 1917.	Nov. 1918.
B.O.'s	2	2	1
B.O.R.'s	4	7	4
Eastern races	82	187	19

Ahwaz is river-head on the Karun River and headquarters
of the Karun front. A stern-wheeler is stationed there to
facilitate the rapid transport of troops. A weekly ferry
service between Basrah and Ahwaz is maintained, supplemented by additional craft as required.

The I.W.T. staff there has consisted throughout of :

1 British officer,
4 British other ranks,
10 Eastern races.

EUPHRATES AREA

Transport work on the Euphrates is controlled by the
officers commanding sections, and does not come under this
department. The subject is therefore fully dealt with under
sectional headings.

Previous to 1918 river transport in this area was almost entirely operated by native craft, but early in this year a fleet of " F " Class steamers with small barges was sent there to supplement the few launches and stern-wheelers which had either been railed there via Baghdad and Feluja or had been captured from the Turks. The tonnage handled reached its maximum during the collection of the 1918 harvest, when an average of 25,000 tons per month was handled, corresponding to 220,000 ton miles. The fleet on the Euphrates at the date of the Armistice consisted of :—

> 49 steam vessels,
> 74 barges,
> 54 motor-boats,
> in addition to native craft.

For details, see Appendix B5.

Grey Bridge, entrance to I.W.T. Marine Dockyard, Basrah.
March 18th, 1919

Entrance to Ashar wet Basin.
September 17th, 1917

DEPARTMENT OF DOCKYARDS

THE Dockyard Department of the Inland Water Transport comprises, in addition to Basrah Dockyard, the workshops at Amara, Kut, Karradah, Nasiriyah, and Hillah, the floating workshops *Vulcan*, P.S. 34, and *Ngawun*, and the motor dockyards at Basrah and Baghdad.

Basrah Dockyard.—From the date of the British occupation of Basrah until July, 1916, all repairs to river craft were carried out at the old Turkish dockyard situated about 600 yards from the entrance to Ashar Creek. The yard was small, badly laid out, and at low water was only accessible to launches of less than 3 feet in draught, whilst the personnel and tools therein were hopelessly inadequate to cope with the requirements of the fleet, even at that date. It was therefore decided to build a new dockyard, and for this purpose a site was selected on the right bank of the Shatt-el-Arab between Ashar and Khandaq Creeks, covering an area of about 5½ acres. It was commenced in December, 1915, and by the end of April, 1916, was in running order. All repairs to steam craft were undertaken at this yard, whilst the old Turkish yard was utilised for repairs to motor-boats only. The new yard at that time contained machine, boiler, and carpenter's shops, a smithy, foundry, and the usual offices, but although a great improvement on the old yard, it was early realised that the area would have to be enlarged, new shops added and slipways built. Suggestions regarding this were at once put forward, but little was done until September, 1916, when the Inland Water Transport assumed control, and preparations for improvements and additions on a very large scale were initiated. As a result new shops were erected, the existing ones added to, and more machinery was laid down. A tidal basin was

decided upon so that vessels could be brought right into
the dockyard for repairs and thus obviate the delays occasioned by ferrying workmen to and fro to vessels moored
in the stream. The construction of slipways was undertaken so that efficient repairs might be executed to the
under-water parts of vessels, which had previously been
carried out on the mud at low water.

The area was increased to approximately 40 acres, and
this required a very large amount of reclamation and filling
work to be undertaken. This, and the construction of the
bank for the slipway was carried out by Egyptian labour,
from the spoil excavated from the wet basin and the slipway approach. Arrangements were made for the construction of wharves and jetties, and orders were placed in
England and India for plant and materials of all kinds
which would equip the dockyard in a thoroughly up-to-date
manner, rendering it capable of expeditiously and efficiently
dealing with repairs of any kind.

The area of the tidal basin or dock (the inwater dock) is
approximately 14 acres at highest water, and 10 at lowest ;
the depth at the most shallow part being 10 feet at low
tide in the high-water season, and 5 feet in the low. The
banks have a slope of 1 in 2, and willows have been planted
to consolidate them.

Of the seven slipways laid down, three are of 700 feet in
length with a gradient of 1 in 19, and capable of carrying
a deadweight on the carriages of 700 tons in the case of two,
and 250 in the third. The other four are intended for small
steam and motor craft and are 245 feet long with a gradient
of 1 in 10. To the end of 1918, 330 vessels of a total dis-
placement of 65,544 tons have been slipped on the main
slips, and 197 on the motor-boat slips. They were opened
by Major-General Freeland on the 18th February, 1918.

The average daily number of steam vessels (not including
motor-boats) at the dockyard under repair is about forty,
and due to the improved conditions and greater facilities
over one hundred such vessels per week were sometimes
repaired in 1918 as compared to less than thirty in 1916,

The Dockyard Slipway looking down the slope.
October 18th, 1917

General View of Nos. 1, 2, and 3 Slipways, Basrah Dockyard, 700 ton barge
in foreground.

the work also being of a higher standard and more expeditiously carried out.

Since the opening of the new yard in July, 1916, most of the various shops have increased to about four times their previous size, and in addition new shops and buildings such as a time office, post office, guardroom, pump-house, boat-building shed, power house, hospital, heat-stroke station, drinking-water posts, ration store, cookhouse, dining-rooms, canteens, rapid destructor, etc., have been built. The dockyard is self-contained, and for the particular class of work compares favourably with any in India.

In addition to the ordinary running repairs of the fleet, the majority of vessels arriving from overseas were fitted out for service in this yard ; 130 having been prepared in 1917 alone. During the last six months of 1918, 31 craft were converted from coal to oil-burning, and in addition to the work carried out for I.W.T. Departments, a considerable amount is carried out for sea transport, other Government Departments and private firms.

A list of the machines in the dockyard is given in Appendix D2.

Personnel.—The personnel has been considerably increased since 1916 as the following figures will show :—

	Sept. 22nd, 1916.	Dec. 30th, 1916.	Dec. 27th, 1917.	Nov. 11th, 1918
Officers.	18	23	34	39
B.O.R.'s	28	75	201	202
Eastern races	868	1990	3588	3585

Amara.—A small workshop capable of dealing with running repairs to vessels passing through was established on the right bank at Amara in October, 1915. The position of this shop was just below the old bridge and on the best site available within the military perimeter. Sheds, machines, and personnel were imported from India. With the extension of military operations further north and consequent increase in the amount of shipping, the workshop was found inadequate to cope with requirements. A larger one was therefore erected on an adjoining site. When the Kurna-Amara Railway first came into useful being towards the end of 1916 and preparations were being made for the advance, a certain number of the larger vessels were based on Amara, which necessitated a still further increase in repairing facilities. The present site situated just above Pindi Point was then chosen and the erection of a thoroughly up-to-date workshop was commenced, being completed in April, 1917. It covers an area of 372,976 square feet and extensive reclamation, revetting, and bunding work was necessitated. Practically any repairs to hulls or machinery, apart from underwater, can now be undertaken there.

A list of the machines installed is given in Appendix D2.

The personnel employed at the times specified consisted of :—

	April, 1916.	Dec., 1916.	Dec., 1917.	Nov. 11th, 1918.
B.O.'s . .	3	2	9	8
W.O.'s . .	—	1	1	—
B.O.R.'s .	14	25	58	43
Indians, Arabs, Chinese .	41	46	310	270

Kut.—The need for workshops at Kut (153 miles by river from Amara) was occasioned by its central position regarding shipping plying between Amara and Baghdad and as being the terminus of the Kut-Baghdad Railway and the Amara-Kut Ferry.

Immediately following the British occupation the erection of workshops was commenced, and they were in running order by September, 1917. They consisted of the usual shops and machinery suited to the repairs to paddlers, tugs, and motor-boats, and with living quarters covered an area of approximately 140,000 square feet. There is a small slipway suitable for motor-boats. A list of machines is given in Appendix D2.

The personnel employed on the dates indicated consisted of :—

	Dec. 31st, 1917.	Nov. 11th, 1918.
B.O.'s . .	3	3
B.O.R.'s .	1	7
Indians .	128	115
Chinese .	29	71

After the opening ceremony P.S. 53 on the Slipway.

Sea-going tug on No. 1 Slipway. Basrah Dockyard.

Baghdad.—On the fall of Baghdad sufficient plant and machinery were discovered there to put in order and supplement an old Turkish workshop, from which it was subsequently removed either to the new workshops at Karradah or to the motor repair dockyard at Baghdad. The former was opened in November, 1917, and covers an area of about 468,000 square feet. The site needed considerable filling and the level has been raised as much as 8 feet in places. It is well equipped with all necessary machinery to carry out repairs to steam craft, a list of which will be found in Appendix D2. It has also done much useful work for the construction section, I.W.T., and other Government departments.

The number of vessels repaired at this depot was as follows :—

From January, 1917, to March, 1918 (P.S. 34) . 872
From March, 1918, to November 11th, 1918
(Shore Workshops) 768
———
1640

The personnel employed on the dates specified consisted of :—

	Nov. 31st, 1917.	Nov. 11th, 1918.
B.O.'s . .	4	6
B.O.R.'s .	26	28
Indian . .	46	65
Local . .	—	196

Hillah.—At Hillah a small workshop was opened in May, 1918, principally for the repairing of motor-boats, but a good deal of work is also done to the shallow-draft steam vessels, " fly " boats, and similar craft. It covers an area of 5112 square feet. A list of the machines installed is given in Appendix D2.

The personnel employed at the conclusion of hostilities consisted of :—

	Nov. 11th, 1918.
B.O. . .	1
B.O.R.'s .	3
Indians ,	16

Nasiriyah.—The workshop at Nasiriyah was started in February, 1916, two houses on the left bank being utilised for the purpose. It was increased in size in October, 1916, and a substantial jetty built in connection with it. The yard covers an area of about 9620 square feet and is well adapted for repairs to the smaller types of steam craft and motor-boats. A considerable amount of work was also done in the past for Ordnance and R.F.C. A list of machines is given in Appendix D2.

The personnel employed on the dates indicated consisted of :—

	Dec. 31st, 1917.	Nov. 11th, 1918.
B.O.'s .	1	1
B.O.R.'s	12	9
Indians	23	24
Chinese	11	13

"Vulcan."—The floating workshop *Vulcan* is a double-decked barge 76 feet by 16 feet 5 inches of shallow draught. She was fitted out in April, 1918, with all the necessary appliances and machines for repair work to the smaller vessels on the Upper Euphrates, where she has done very useful work.

The personnel employed is as follows :—

	Nov. 11th, 1918.
B.O. .	1
B.O.R.'s	2
Indians	22

"Ngawun."—The floating workshop *Ngawun* is a self-propelled motor-boat of 50 feet in length. She was fitted out in December, 1916, with a few machines and necessary tools for the repair of motor-boats connected principally with the Buoyage Section.

The personnel employed consisted of :

	Nov. 11th, 1918.
B.O.R.'s	1
Indians	5

Workshop Barge Vulcan erected at Margil Re-erection Works.
April 10th, 1918

Portion of Tidal Basin, I.W.T. Marine Dockyard, Basrah, shewing Motor Boat Depot.
March 18th. 1919

P.S. 34.—P.S. 34 (a Nile paddle-steamer, 140 feet by 24 feet) was fitted out in January, 1917, in Basrah, and proceeded to Sheik Sa'ad, where she remained till the advance in which she did much valuable work. Her crew was entirely British, and she was equipped with a searchlight, machine-gun, and the more important machinery necessary for expeditious repairs to river craft. Fitted out originally by the Construction Department, she has been used latterly on construction work at different places.

The workshop personnel maintained, apart from this vessel's crew on the dates indicated, consisted of :

	Dec., 1916.	Dec., 1917.	Nov. 11th, 1918.
B.O.'s	2	1	1
B.O.R.'s . . .	33	10	4
Eastern races . .	—	25	20

MOTOR REPAIR DOCKYARDS

Basrah.—The R.I.M. Dockyard, Basrah, was taken over solely for motor-boat work at the beginning of July, 1916, at the same time the steam section was removed to the new dockyard.

At that time there was no machinery and only one set of rails for slips. A number of machines were obtained and installed in October, 1916. Two new slipways were laid down in December, 1916, and a set of screw chocks for lifting the smaller boats was built in February, 1917. Various machines have been added from time to time.

At the end of 1916 experiments were made in converting native craft into mechanically propelled craft. The first boat was finished the middle of April, 1917, this being a bellum with a length of 54 feet and a beam of 7 feet 6 inches. This was fitted with a Ford engine of about 20 h.p. and gave very satisfactory results. Kelvin and Parson engines

F

were then ordered from England to fit out a fleet of 100 of these boats. Up to the end of 1918, 53 had been completed.

As there was some difficulty in getting spares for motor-boats, these had to be made in the dockyard, and a smithy and brass foundry, in addition to the machine shop, were started early in 1917.

At the time the I.W.T. took over from the R.I.M. the British personnel of the yard was small, the first draft of R.E.'s reporting for duty on the 11th October, 1916, and other drafts on the 6th December, 1916, and the 3rd January, 1917, put the yard in good working order.

Until January, 1918, the men employed in the dockyard were quartered in the Motor Repair Dockyard Camp, but this soon became overcrowded, and most of the Eastern races were transferred to Keshla Camp. Huts for the accommodation of the British personnel were erected in December, 1916, and January, 1917.

The fleet of motor-boats is made up of a large number of different types and sizes, ranging from 18 feet to 70 feet in length, and are powered with engines ranging from 3–4 h.p. to 125 h.p., the make of engine most in use being the Kelvin. A number of boats are fitted with light American engines, and generally speaking these have not stood up to the work. The British engines and the heavier types of American engines have proved satisfactory. One of the chief troubles with engines is the circulating water pump, this is brought about by the large amount of fine sand in the water on several sections of the river.

As the motor-boat drivers sent up from India were insufficient, and a number of those sent were inefficient, a school for motor-boat drivers was started on the 22nd October, 1917, and it has been found necessary to keep this school going since that date.

On the 18th February, 1919, the Motor Repair Dockyard was moved to the new site prepared at the I.W.T. Dockyard.

Fleet.—The following statement shows the strength of

Motor Boat Dockyard Basin. Old Turkish Dockyard Dismantled, 1918.
July 1st, 1917

M. 164 (" URNER ").

Dimensions: length, 40′ 9″; breadth, 6′ 9″; depth, 2′ 10″. Draft, 2′ 4″. Engines, 6 cylinders, Van Blerck; B H.P. 60/85. Speed, 20 knots.

Six launches of this class all built in the United Kingdom.

P S. 53 being hauled up the Slipway after the Slipway being d.clared open.

H.M.S. Mantis and Anglo-Persian Oil Co. Barge on Slipway, I.W.T. Dockyard, Basra, (February 23rd, 1918).

the fleet of motor-boats at various periods since September, 1916 :—

CLASS.	Dec., 1916.	Dec., 1917.	Nov., 1918.
M. (General Service) .	170	263	305
M. Red Cross and Medical	inclusive	66	100
M B. (Native craft) . .	—	5	35
Buoyage	—	—	17
Fire	—	2	8
M.T. (tugs) . . .	—	7	7
	170	343	472

Personnel.—The following statement shows the strength of the personnel employed on the dates indicated :—

	Dec., 1916.	Dec., 1917.	Nov. 1918.
Dockyard :			
British officers . .	6	7	10
R.I.M. W.O.'s . .	6	7	—
R.E.'s and attd. Regts.	22	63	96
B.W.I.'s . . .	29	20	5
Indian Volunteers .	2	14	2
W.A.C. . . .	—	11	—
Eastern races . .	133	423	578
Afloat :			
R.E.'s and attd. Regts.	25	81	100
B.W.I.'s and R.E.			
Coloured Section .	65	85	62
Indian Volunteers .	47	46	14
Eastern races . .	265	609	823
School for Motor-boat			
Drivers :			
Officer . . .	—	1	1
Staff . . .	—	4	3
Pupils . . .	—	39	30

Baghdad.—The Motor-boat Dockyard is situated near G.H.Q., covering an area of about 41,382 square feet, and was opened in January, 1918. It possesses a slipway capable of taking a deadweight on the carriage of 85 tons from which vessels can be side-slipped right into work-

shops, and also a special slipway for Hydro-Colisseurs. It
is well equipped with high-class machinery suitable for all
kinds of motor-boat repair work.*

The personnel on the date indicated consisted of :

	Nov. 11th, 1918:
B.O.'s	4
B.O.R.'s . . .	28
Indians . . .	16
Local mechanics . .	129

* At the conclusion of hostilities there were over a hundred motor-boats
based on Baghdad, and an average of twenty-five passed through this
depot.

M.T. 8.

f Dimensions: length, 54' 1"; extreme breadth, 10' 10"; depth. 4' 6". Service draft. 3'5".
Engines, Gardner; 4 cylinders; S/S., B.H.P. 50. Speed, light, 10 knots. Towing 3 knots.
Fuel capacity, 115 gallons paraffin. Consumption, 120 gallons per 24 hours.
Seven vessels of this class all built in the United Kingdom.

M. 4 (" Captured Motor Launch ").

Dimensions: length, 70'; breadth, 9'; depth, 4' 9". Service draft, 3' 0", driven by two
sets of 4 cylinders Yarrow petrol engines; B.H.P. 80, Speed, 14 knots.

DEPARTMENT OF CONSTRUCTION

An article dealing with the work of this department would hardly be complete without some reference to its history previous to inclusion within the Inland Water Transport Directorate.

The Marine Repair Workshops Unit was originally recruited from the staff of the then recently completed Sara Bridge in Bengal and from that of various Indian railways. This unit, a small but efficient one, arrived in Mesopotamia in November, 1915, under the command of Captain R. T. D. Alexander, who transferred to the I.W.T. when they took over in September, 1916, as O.C. Up-River Works, subsequently being promoted to A.D.I.W.T. Construction. Amongst the earlier works undertaken were the laying out and construction of Basrah Dockyard, and the establishment of repair workshops at Amara and Nasiriyah.

Organisation.—On arrival in Mesopotamia, the Inland Water Transport, as a completely self-contained unit, formed its own construction department, a staff of engineers having been sent from England for the purpose. This department took charge of all constructional work at the Base. At the same time the Marine Repair Workshops Unit was incorporated within the Inland Water Transport Directorate, and formed the nucleus of another engineering department under the title " Up-River Works." The Up-River Works Department was responsible for all constructional work and the running of all repair workshops on the two rivers, *excluding* the Base, with the exception that they continued the construction of certain work at the Basrah Dockyard which they had already undertaken.

In March, 1918, a further reorganisation of the engineering departments of the Inland Water Transport took place

Under this arrangement all constructional work, both at the Base and Up-River, was merged into one department called the " *Construction* " Department, under an Assistant Director.

The up-river workshops, as running concerns, were amalgamated with Basrah Dockyard and also placed under an Assistant Director of Dockyards, thus putting all mechanical engineering under one head.

Works.—The engineering works carried out by the Inland Water Transport in Mesopotamia extend from Bushire in the Persian Gulf to the various fronts, the furthest points at which work was actually done being at Hit on the Euphrates, Tekrit on the Tigris, and Khanikin to the north-east of Baghdad and near the Persian frontier.

A short account of some of the more important of these works will be of interest.

Bushire.—Three wharves 100 feet long with 50 feet tee heads. All piles shod and driven through hard clay.

Erection of a distilling plant capable of distilling 10 tons of water per day. This plant was taken over from the Works Directorate in an incomplete state and involved considerable renewal.

Koweit.—A wharf 350 feet long, constructed for loading sand. Sand was quarried from tunnels, as the very best quality was required for reinforced concrete work. A total of 5000 tons was shipped to Basrah.

Abadan.—A large camp for I.W.T. personnel with attendant quarters constructed, also a fire-proof wharf 410 feet long, wrought iron pipes being used as piles with angle iron bracings and walings and a reinforced concrete deck. This wharf carried a pipe line laid along it connected to the I.W.T. shore tanks for loading oil tank barges.

Basrah.—The most important work carried out at the Base was the construction of Basrah Dockyard, for which this department was entirely responsible from its earliest beginning. It was handed over for administration and working, bit by bit, as completed, to the Dockyards Department. A description of its inception, growth, and

View of Dockyard Basin excavations, showing Bund across entrance.

Dockyard Basin just previous to letting water in.

Opening ceremony of the Slipways J.W.T. Dockyard, Basrah.

Similar to No. 95, but from a position which shows the arrangement of Cofferdam
strutting.

September 17th, 1917

subsequent development is given under this departmental heading.

Other works of importance at the Base are at :—

Margil.—(1) Laying out and construction of the Craft Re-erection Yard, including slipway, workshop, jetties, etc.

(2) Store sheds, offices, quarters, light railway connections, wharves, and cranes at the I.W.T. Stores Depot (both the latter items are fully described under departmental headings).

Muftieh.—(1) A small workshop, quarters, stores, and power house at the barge depot.

(2) Mahaila slipways constructed of 12 feet by 12 feet piles 10 feet apart with continuous camps, quarters, offices, stores, etc., at the Mahaila Depot.

(3) Fuel depot, comprising two 1000-ton circular reinforced concrete tanks, 60 feet in diameter, 14 feet deep, of which 4 feet is underground. These tanks are the main fuel oil storage at the Base and are filled from tankers through a pipe line running along a fire-proof L-shaped jetty with reinforced concrete deck.

A pump house with two belt-driven force pumps and one steam force pump capable of supplying oil to Makina Railway Station, E. and M. Central Power House, and all other duties necessary for receiving and despatching oil.

A 220-ton high level pressed steel plate oil-tank at Makina Station, connected to the fuel depot by 3½ miles of 4-inch piping, fitted with relief valves and expansion bends at suitable intervals.

Khora Creek.—An oil storage installation comprising a steel 1000-ton fuel oil reservoir, a steel 220-ton overhead kerosine tank and various smaller tanks and sheds for tinned oils. Also a wharf, pipe line, and pumping plant in connection with the above. Quarters, offices, and a large camp for clerks, motor-boat drivers, etc.

The Inland Water Transport headquarters building on the river front, constructed with heavy masonry pillars, light framing and party walls, furnishing both offices and living accommodation.

Several wharves of a permanent nature and otherwise, notably those at Margil (Nos. 9 and 10), Tanooma, Engineer Field Park Headquarters, and the Hospital Pier. Camps at Tanooma, Muftieh, Margil, and Keshla Camp.

To appreciate the difficulty experienced in carrying out work of this kind, it must be borne in mind that practically all unoccupied ground in the vicinity of Basrah, in fact all land near the river front is on an average 2 feet below the flood level so that the preparation of sites for dockyards, camps, stores, etc., entailed raising the ground level some 3 feet, the necessary filling having to be obtained from borrow pits, often dug at a considerable distance from the river front, as in the early days reclaiming by suction dredger was not possible in the limited time available.

This difficulty in the case of the dockyard was in part met by utilising the ground excavated from the wet basin and river approaches, also the ground removed from the lower end of slipways inside the coffer dam to build up the bank necessary to give the proper incline. The bank carrying the winding gear at the top end of the ways was no less than 22 feet above the natural ground level.

Kurna.—Substantial jetties were built, the need for which arose with the rapid development of the Kurna-Amara Railway ; making it possible to berth light draught ocean-going vessels and to discharge their cargo for immediate shipment by rail. A number of sheds, offices, and stores were also built in order to complete the depot. A very large amount of labour was expended on filling and levelling the site.

Ezra's Tomb.—A small workshop erected in February, 1917. A fuel oil depot comprising a steel 450-ton tank and pumping plant and quarters for the staff were erected.

Narrows.—Five small power houses placed at points near the more acute bends where lighting was considered necessary ; altogether a total length of 15 miles was wired and lighted by electricity, making it possible for vessels to navigate by night. A workshop was erected at the central

Dockyard Slipway, shewing pumping plant. The ship funnels beyond the Cofferdam
show roughly the height of water outside.

September 17th, 1917

Entrance to Ashar Wet Basin.

August 2nd, 1917

station for the maintenance of the lighting plant and minor repairs to craft. It was completed in December, 1917.

Qualet Saleh.—Inland Water Transport officers' quarters and buildings, and the floating bridge were commenced in April, 1917, and completed at the end of June. The floating bridge is formed of Arab mashoofs, and sustains a timber superstructure. Its construction is comparatively light, but it is capable of carrying a load of $3\frac{1}{2}$ tons.

Amara.—The whole of the river front of the Inland Water Transport depot was revetted, three large wharves constructed, and several new buildings erected. The I.W.T. area has a river frontage of 300 yards, and this work entailed earth filling to the extent of 260,000 cubic feet. It comprises offices, quarters, store sheds, a large workshop, and a water tower 60 feet high which is also used as a signal station. Also a complete oil storage installation comprising a 1000-ton tank and a 500-ton tank with independent pump houses, but so connected that either pump can work either tank and either tank can deliver oil to the high level railway tank at Amara Station through a pipe line 2 miles long. It is interesting to note that the main offices and officers' quarters (a building of 126 feet long by 30 feet wide and 33 feet height) was moved intact to a distance of 350 feet in order to admit of a point of land on which the building was originally constructed being cut away for the purpose of river conservancy. The building was removed on trollies and sustained no damage in transit.

A new pontoon bridge was constructed, from materials actually in Mesopotamia at the time, being placed about a mile down-stream from the position of the old bridge. It is 708 feet long, and has a width of 20 feet over all. It is approached by a piled way 265 feet long. The bridge opening is 282 feet, and when swung back it offers a clear channel 255 feet wide between the protecting dolphins. The opening section is constructed of steel pontoons placed 30 feet between centres and spanned with steel joists and timber bearers to which the decking is spiked. The rise and fall is taken up by two ramp girders 62 feet long resting on terminal pontoons which are confined between dolphins.

The bridge is opened with the aid of a steam winch, and both operations, i.e. opening it for ships to pass through and closing it again to admit road traffic, can be carried out in under four minutes. It carries a live load of 8 tons. The whole work was completed in less than six months.

Sheik Sa'ad.—Reinforced concrete foundation for 3-ton crane, workshop, quarters, and a bridge or mahailas which was moved up to Kut in February, 1918.

Kut.—An oil pumping plant and storage installation of 1320 tons capacity with a subsidiary overhead railway tank of 16 tons capacity at Kut Station connected by a 4-inch pipe-line 1½ miles long.

Quarters, store sheds, and workshops.

The mahaila bridge referred to above, and a mahaila slipway capable of taking any mahaila on the river.

At this station mud brick quarters were constructed (probably the first mud brick quarters of a permanent nature in Mesopotamia), which have been found extremely cool and comfortable.

Baghaila.—The original Kut bridge was removed to Baghaila for military reasons during October, 1917, and was completed there and ready for the passage of Class II traffic in November, 1917.

Zeur.—Quarters for officers, B.O.R.'s, and Indians, a 220-ton high-level tank for fuel oil storage and a small pumping plant.

Baghdad.—*Baghdad City.*—High-level tank at Baghdad West Railway Station with pipe-line to river one mile long. Floating and masonry ramps at the arsenal and at the railway wharf.

The motor-boat dockyard containing workshops, offices, quarters, and a shed and slipway for Hydro-Glisseurs. Also a slipway capable of lifting vessels of the *Sumana* class.

The north bridge was rebuilt under traffic. The Maude Bridge. This is by far the most important work of its kind yet carried out in Mesopotamia, and a detailed description will be of interest.

It is 1260 feet between abutments and is supported on 31 pontoons, 34 feet 6 inches by 12 feet by 4 feet, moored both up-stream and down to heavy buoys, with two terminal pontoons to take the ramp spans which connect the floating part with the shore. These terminal pontoons are confined between timber dolphins with roller hinges and can only move in a vertical plane. To allow for the difference in the level of the river of approximately 22 feet, there are two 62-feet ramp spans (on roller hinges at one end and rocker bearings on the other) resting on one transome girder on each bank ; these are operated by counterweights and adjusted by geared blocks, and the transome can be raised or lowered in the matter of a few minutes. The transome girder is built up of two 15-inch by 5-inch joists, and when adjusted rests on a support plate fitted to the transome supports, which are built up on trestles of joists and channels and are on reinforced concrete rafts carried on heavy piled foundations. The ramp girders were part of a sinking set used in India and have been suitably strengthened. Ten of these girders were ordered some time ago from India, and have now all been used on various bridges and works.

The main girders of the bridge from pontoon to pontoon, with hinged joints, are light lattice girders salved from the old bridge, considerably strengthened and widened. The cross girders on top of these are 12-inch by 4-inch teak and the floor joists are 9-inch by 3-inch teak carrying a 3-inch decking. The roadway is 10 feet 6 inches wide and is confined between two 6-inch by 6-inch timber curbs, allowing a 3-foot path on either side for pedestrians. The total width of the bridge between hand-rails being 17 feet 6 inches.

On the left bank terminal pontoon there is an out board hinge, carrying a 4½-inch pin which connects the first small pontoon to it. From this pin eleven pontoons of the bridge swing up-stream. On the eleventh pontoon two wire ropes are attached, one of these passes through a snatch block fixed to a buoy 40 feet below the bridge, and then passing under the bridge on to the drum of a winch 700 feet upstream of the bridge on the left bank, the other wire going direct from the pontoon to the second drum of the winch.

The winch is operated by a compound steam engine and an oil-fired Cochran boiler, and can either open or close the " Cut " in three minutes ; when " cut " for shipping there is a clear gap of 270 feet, which is sufficient to admit safe navigation through.

The bridge can carry a rolling load of 15 tons, which is slightly heavier than the heaviest road vehicle in the country—a tractor. For the opening ceremony on December 7th, 1918, a battery of 18-pounder guns crossed the bridge at full gallop.

All the pontoons, girders, and other steel work, the piles, mooring buoys, and cables, the winding engine and which were available in the country and are adapted to suit the work, so that no material has been ordered from either India or home for this bridge, which has taken only four months to complete.

Advanced Base.—The I.W.T. Depot comprising quarters, store sheds, offices, and a complete oil fuel installation with storage capacity for 1160 tons for both fuel oil and kerosine, with pumping plant and pipe lines.

Hinaidi.—Oil fuel installation with storage capacity for 1000 tons, including fuel oil, 220 tons kerosine, and 140 tons bulk petrol storage. Pumping plant, quarters, offices, etc.

Karradah.—Layout and construction of dockyard and workshops (described under " Dockyards ").

Diala River.—Bridges at Diala Mouth, Baquba, and Abu Saida.

Khanikin.—An oil fuel installation for railways, consisting of storage for 250 tons of fuel oil, pumping plant, high level tank, etc.

Euphrates.—*Hit.*—Quarters, small oil storage tanks.

Ramadie.—Floating bridge, small oil storage tanks.

Dhibban.—Quarters, floating bridge, oil storage tanks, etc.

Feluja.—Workshop, oil storage tanks, etc.

Museyib.—Floating bridge.

Kufa.—Floating bridge and small oil storage tank.

Kala Abu Saiya.—Floating bridge.

Hillah.—Quarters, oil fuel depot, mahaila slipway, workshop, and pile bridge, with a steel lifting span giving a clear gap of 30 feet and capable of carrying a load of 8 tons.

Tuerij.—Floating bridge.

Dewaniyah.—Large oil storage installation for railways, consisting of one 500-ton ground tank, one 220-ton high level tank, pump-house, and pipe line ; also a minor bridge and small kerosine oil storage installation.

Rumetha.—Pile bridge with timber lifting span.

Nasiriyah, including Ur.—Quarters, store sheds, a workshop, wharf, and bellum bridge. A large scheme for oil storage for I.W.T. and railways at Nasiriyah and Ur. The storage at Ur comprises a 1000-ton ground tank and a 220-ton high-level tank with pump-house. The storage at Nasiriyah is of 450 tons capacity, with a large pump-house capable of pumping oil through a pipe line 9 miles long from Nasiriyah to Ur.

Many other works both of permanent and temporary nature have been undertaken at various times in addition to those enumerated in the foregoing list. The upkeep and maintenance of all wharves, buildings, bridges, etc., after they have been erected forms no inconsiderable part of the work of this department, whilst its administration with so many works going on at the same time over hundreds of miles of a country like Mesopotamia has been no light task. The supply of men and materials to far distant points such as Hit, Tekrit, Khanikin, and Bushire has often taxed the resources of the department to its utmost, but it has never failed to meet emergencies.

Personnel.—The staff of the Construction and Up-River Works Departments on the dates indicated consisted of :—

Date.	Department.	Strength.				
		B.O.'s.	B.O.R.'s. and B.W.I.'s.	Eastern Races.	Totals.	Grand Total.
Dec. 31st, 1916.	Base Construction Department	12	51	4212	4275	6209
	Up-River Works Department: Construction Section	13 } 18	160 } 185	1015 } 1731	1188 } 1924	
	Repair Workshops Section	5	25	716	746	
Dec. 31st, 1917.	Base Construction Department	17	115	3012	3144	7602
	Up-River Works Department: Construction Section	35 } 51	247 } 347	3452 } 4060	3734 } 4458	
	Repair Workshops Section	16	100	608	725	
Nov. 11th, 1918.	Construction Department (Base and Up-River)	60	347	5246	—	5653

The wreck of T.L. 13, salved by Buoyage & Pilotage Dept. and lying on pontoon on left bank of Shat-al-Arab at Basrah ready to be towed to Dockyard.
October 23rd, 1917

Hammar Lake Dredging Scheme. Dredger "Oswald" cutting junction of Mezlik diversion and Euphrates at Beni Said.
January 29th, 1919

DEPARTMENT ON BUOYAGE AND PILOTAGE

THIS Department is also responsible for bandalling, salvage work, marine surveys, in addition to a certain amount of minor dredging work.

These subjects will be considered separately.

Buoyage.—Previous to September, 1916, no system of buoyage or marking the navigable channels of the Tigris, Euphrates, or Karun Rivers, existed, neither were there any aid to navigation whatever, beyond a primitive system of control in the Narrows.

During the latter part of 1916 a buoyage system on a small scale was introduced on the Tigris, between Amara and Arab Village, also on the Karun River. The department responsible for this work gradually developed as personnel and equipment became available, and conditions required expansion. With the capture of Baghdad, and subsequent operations both on the Tigris and Euphrates, buoyage work increased accordingly, until during the low-water season of 1918 the Tigris, from Basrah to Samarrah, a distance of 600 miles, the Karun from Mohammerah to Ahwaz, a distance of 110 miles, and the Euphrates from Kurna to Sahalyia, a distance of 480 miles, were effectively buoyed, or marked, as the requirements of river transport demanded.

During the low-water season and worst transitional phases each section of the river was daily patrolled, channels were surveyed, sounded, and marked either by buoys or transit marks, officers being continually employed upon these duties. These officers were also responsible for the control of shipping, boarding, and piloting vessels through especially bad channels and reaches, refloating stranded ships, and accelerating the despatch of river transport generally.

The system of buoyage adopted was that all

Red buoys were left to starboard and black buoys to port
when proceeding up-river, irrespective of the shape of
the buoy.
Black and white buoys marked middle grounds, and could
be passed on either side.
Green buoys marked wrecks or other obstructions.

Owing to increased expense and the difficulty experienced
in procuring buoys, bamboo stakes have latterly been
largely used in lieu of buoys, starboard hand stakes being
distinguished by a large tuft of brushwood and port hand
stakes by a cross.

The system of transit marks introduced was designed to
direct vessels from bank to bank, where crossings occur.
Vessels following whichever bank they were directed to until
more transit marks or buoys were encountered.

To illustrate the amount of buoying and marking necessary throughout Mesopotamia during the low-water season
of 1918

214 sets of transit marks, and
583 buoys

were in use at one time between Amara and Baghdad, the
whole necessitating the closest attention to ensure correct
siting and upkeep, as channels and crossings were constantly
altering and buoys were destroyed by passing steamers.
Over five thousand of these buoys were expended annually.

Bandalling.—Bandalling was introduced from India
during the low-water season of 1917, and is a system whereby,
whilst conforming with the actual trend of the channel, the
water flowing down a reach is concentrated within certain
limits, shoals, and sand-banks, where advantageously
situated, being utilised to assist, with the object of forming
one single deep channel where previously perhaps there
existed three or four independent shallower channels.

Bamboos up to 20 feet in length and 3 to 4 inches in
diameter, with mats, are used to construct the training

Alingment of Bandals on Tigris above Kut, shewing formation of silt behind same.
October 8th, 1918

General view of Bandalling Hinaidi Reach.
October 15th, 1918

screen. The bamboos are driven into the sand 18 to 24 inches apart, other bamboos are lashed across these, and the whole is then backed by saplings placed 8 to 10 feet apart. The mats are placed on the weather, or up-stream side, of the bamboos, extending 3 to 4 feet below the surface of the water. The lines of bandals are placed at an angle to the current, each independent line being about 150 to 200 feet long and in echelon with one another. Two series of lines in echelon are placed facing one another, thus forming a kind of funnel down which the water is directed. Water which before was spread over the extreme width of the river, much of it being lost down blind channels, is thus diverted into one channel and scouring commences to take place.

In 1918 bandalling operations on a very much larger scale were carried out, resulting in a draft of 4 feet 9 inches for steamers and 4 feet for barges being maintained from Kut to Baghdad throughout the whole low-water season. To effect this 852 bandalmen specially imported from India were employed, and the expenditure of 35,000 bamboos and a similar quantity of mats was incurred.

Pilotage.—In September, 1916, apart from such European officers as had been employed in locally owned steam vessels in pre-War days, the only pilots available were Arabs, whose experience of the river had been gained in native craft, and as these pilots had usually been permanently allotted to one vessel, regardless of the length of her voyage, this practice resulted, as might be expected, in endless groundings and delays, it obviously being impossible that they could remain acquainted with the changes that were continually taking place throughout the whole length of an unmarked river.

An entire revision in the organisation of the pilot service was therefore instituted, pilot stations were established at Basrah, Amara, Ali Gharbi, Kut, Baghailah, Azizieh, Zeur, and Baghdad, and pilots were only employed on a particular section adjacent to their respective station. By localising pilots in this way their knowledge of their own particular

G

section became enhanced, and by frequently relieving them at each station, a higher state of efficiency was reached and maintained. Their numbers were increased as the fleet expanded from about 100 at the end of 1916 to nearly 300 in June, 1917.

As the system of buoying and marking the river was perfected, pilots were gradually withdrawn, and the establishment reduced in accordance with requirements, until at the end of the low-water season, 1917, only about 40 pilots remained, these being stationed at certain points for special purposes.

In June, 1917, when Nahr Umar was first opened up as a port for ocean-going steamers, vessels were piloted between that place and Margil by pilots belonging to this department, an establishment of four British officers having been sanctioned for this purpose. This system continued until Nahr Umar was included within the port limits of Basrah, when this establishment was transferred to the port officer.

Salvage.—The salvage branch of this department has been extremely successful, and has been instrumental in recovering much valuable property as well as a large amount of specie. The sphere of operations extended from Samarrah in the north, to Henjam in the Persian Gulf, south.

The salvage unit consists of :

> Two submersible pontoon barges, capables of lifting 700 tons each.
> A salvage vessel (S.V. 1), and
> Ten complete diving units,

the latter being stationed at various points such as Amara, Kut, Baghdad, Hillah, Nasiriyah, in readiness for immediate service when required.

Salvage parties followed the advance of the British forces up both the Tigris and Euphrates, salving much valuable material, including guns which had been thrown into the river by the Turks, and abandoned launches and barges.

Hammar Lake Dredging Scheme. Taken from roof of Dredger "Oswald" shewing junction at Beni Said of Mezlik Diversion and Euphrates.

January 29th, 1919

Hammar Lake Dredging Scheme. Junction of Mezlik Diversion and Euphrates at Beni Said.

January 29th, 1919

Salvage operations have since resulted in the recovery of the following craft :—

S. 6,	L. 92,
T. 23,	P.T. 40,
L. 30,	T.L. 29,
T.L. 13,	T.L. 31.

Recaptured tug *Pioneer*,
Armed Thornycroft motor launch,
Steam launch *Mozaffer*,
Barges, A. 598, B. 40, B. 272, A. 223, D. 81, O.B. 20, C. 546, D. 262, Port 51,
A Clayton disinfector barge, also 6 Turkish barges, numerous motor-boats, mahailas, bellums, lorries, and large quantities of Government stores of all descriptions, from alongside wharves and ships.

This is exclusive of the large number of stranded craft which have been refloated from time to time by buoyage officers, and which, in some cases, required digging out and launching on ways.

During April and May, 1917, 769 cases of specie, out of a total of 771 cases lost overboard from a barge alongside H.T. *Ekma* in Basrah Harbour were salved.

A certain amount of under-water demolition work has been undertaken, but diving operations are rendered difficult owing to the muddy nature of the river, making it impossible to see submerged objects distinctly. The strong current also hampered such operations.

In addition to actual salvage work this branch of the department is responsible for the laying and up-keep of all buoys and moorings for the Inland Water Transport Flotilla in the port of Basrah. In this connection it may be remarked that 55 sets of heavy moorings, each capable of accommodating two river steamers, or four barges abreast, as well as 17 sets of buoys for launches and other special purposes, have been laid down within the port limits up to the present time.

Surveys.—A trigonometrical survey of the Shatt-el-Arab

River from Gurmat Ali to a point 4 miles above Kurna was made between July, 1917, and December, 1917, on a scale of 500 yards to the inch, plans of Gurmat Ali Bar, Nahr Umar, West Nahr Umar, Kurna Bar and Kurna being made on a scale of 200 feet to the inch.

The principal value of this survey was to show that ocean-going steamers up to 450 feet in length and 20 foot draught could be navigated to Nahr Umar in safety, and the further possibility of discharging berths for ocean steamers between Nahr Umar and Kurna. Charts and plans have been printed in India and are now available for issue.

In addition, rough surveys have been taken by buoyage officers of all reaches and crossings of the Tigris where constant changes in the direction and locality of the channels are taking place from year to year.

These sketch surveys, in addition to river gauge readings taken daily at various stations, are filed and supply valuable data as to probable changes during future years.

Sailing directions for the Tigris from Basrah to Mosul, Karoon River, Mohammerah to Ahwaz, and Euphrates (Hindiyah Barrage) to Sahalyia have been compiled ; sailing directions for that stretch of the Euphrates from Kurna to Hindiyah Barrage will be taken in hand when an officer is available. Included with these sailing directions are general notes on the river, Mesopotamian Inland Water Navigation Rules, Narrows Control Rules, bridge signals, and other details of value to vessels navigating these waterways.

The I.W.T. Signal Book also including the Mesopotamian Inland Water Navigation Rules, Narrows Control System, bridge signals, and distinguishing signals for the principal vessels of the I.W.T. Flotilla in Mesopotamia has been compiled and published in conjunction with the foregoing.

Dredging.—The dredging flotilla controlled by this department is as follows :—

1. S.V. 1 fitted with Priestman's Crane and grabs, for dredging mud, clay, and rock.

Brig.-Gen. R.H.W. Hughes, C.S.I., C.M.G., D.S.O., Director of I.W.T., M.E.F. with Officers in charge of operations on Hammar Lake Dredging Scheme.

January 29th, 1919

S.V.I. (Salvage Vessel ").

Dimensions: length, 160'; extreme breadth, 31'; depth, 8'. Service draft (maximum), 4' 3". Engines. T/SC., S/C.: 4 cylinders; N.H.P. 33·3. Speed 8·5 knots. Scotch boiler. Fuel capacity, 39·5 tons oil. Consumption, 4·5 tons per 24 hours. Built in the United Kingdom for present service.

2. *Nemotha*, self-propelled suction dredger with 10-inch suction and two 10-inch centrifugal pumps.
3. *Mole*, belt-driven bucket dredger, captured from the Turks.
4. S.D. 1 suction dredger with cutter ⎫
5. S.D. 2 suction dredger   ⎬ 6-inch suction.
6. S.D. 3 suction dredger   ⎭

    Nos. 3, 4, 5, and 6 are non self-propelled.

Dredging operations were undertaken in 1917 to clear away the bars hindering navigation at the entrance of the Ashar and Khora Creeks. The *Mole* and small pontoon barges were used for this purpose to avoid stopping all traffic while dredging was going on, the spoil being used for reclamation work at Khora Creek. Total quantity removed being 4800 cubic yards.

This unit was subsequently despatched in January, 1918, to the Hamar Lake and successfully opened up a channel 900 feet long by 40 feet wide and 4 to 5 feet deep, from the Hamar Lake to the Mezlik Channel, sufficient to permit the passage of craft 150 feet in length by 30 feet beam by 3 feet 6 inches draught. A large flotilla of craft for service on the Upper Euphrates was passed through in March and April, 1918.

On completion of this work, this unit proceeded to the Shenafiyah Lake and was employed dredging away the bars and flats across the lake to permit the passage of craft drawing 3 to 4 feet, until transferred to the C. and R. Department in July, 1918.

The total approximate length of channel dredged in the Shenafiyah Lake was 2000 feet in length by 40 feet wide and 4 feet deep, where previously only 8 to 12 inches of water was to be found.

Valuable dredging work has been carried out by the S.V. 1 clearing away the remains of the coffer dam and increasing the depth of water at the foot of the new slipways built at Basrah.

This vessel has also carried out valuable reclamation

work about the dockyard and dockyard officers' quarters, deepening Khandaq Creek, the entrance to Ashar and Khora Creeks, the spoil being used to fill up borrow pits, full of stagnant water breeding mosquitoes.

The *Nemotha* has been principally employed dredging out a channel down the left bank at Hinaidi opposite the lower end of Hinaidi Station. This channel was dredged to a depth of 8 to 10 feet below low-water level, 60 feet wide and 1500 to 1800 feet long. She has also rendered valuable service dredging off vessels stranded during floods on sand-banks.

The three small suction dredgers S.D. 1, 2, and 3 have rendered valuable service in assisting to refloat stranded vessels by dredging away the sand beneath them, and also by dredging away deposits of silt from slipways and landing stages at Baghdad during the low-water season.

Personnel.—The staff of the whole department on the dates indicated consisted of :

	Dec. 1916.	Dec. 1917.	Nov. 11th, 1918.
B.O.'s	4	36	37
B.O.R.'s and B.W.I.'s .	2	43	51
Eastern races . .	213	*804	†1360

* Includes 267 Arab pilots.   † Includes 41 Arab pilots.

Type B. First vessel on Margil Slipway.

March, 1917.

Margil Re-erection Works, H.S.W 12 in course of re-erection.

June 28th, 1917

DEPARTMENT OF CRAFT RE-ERECTION

Inception.—Amongst other preparations made for a renewed offensive in 1916, a large number of river craft and barges of various types had been ordered in sections and plates and angles from both England and Canada, with a view to having them shipped out and re-erected by Messrs. Lynch Bros. at Margil, or by Messrs. Strick, Scott and Co. at Mohammerah, or in India. Regarding the latter proposition, there was grave doubt whether it would be possible to complete such vessels before the monsoon set in, during which period it is impossible for shallow draft river craft to make the sea voyage without incurring great danger. In these circumstances and in view of the fact that the above-mentioned firms could not effectively deal with the programme, it was decided to establish a re-erection yard on the Shatt-el-Arab.

The Admiralty was already erecting gunboats at Abadan on ground adjoining the Anglo-Persian Oil Co.'s Oil Refinery, and the War Office was in favour of having the re-erection yard established in the vicinity of these works so that such facilities as the company possessed would be available in the early stages for helping forward construction. This ground was carefully examined as well as various other sites in the vicinity, but it was decided that apart from its exposed position, it was generally most unsuitable, whilst the facilities offered by the Anglo-Persian Oil Co. were practically a negligible quantity. A further examination was therefore made along the river-banks, and finally the present site was selected. This is situated at Margil on the right bank of the Shatt-el-Arab about 4 miles above the main dockyard at Ashar, and possesses natural advantages for putting river craft together and completing them afloat.

The ground at this time was covered with date palms and interspersed with irrigation ditches so that a considerable amount of clearing and levelling was necessary before building berths could be prepared or erection work started.

Early Works.—The first craft to be put together were five small stern wheelers and tugs from Singapore which arrived in sections early in September, 1916. The first consignment of barges from England arrived at the end of the same month, but no facilities for assembling them were yet available in the port. The sections had therefore either to be lifted overside by the steamers' derricks on to pontoons, or temporarily made floatable, as they leaked very badly, and then hauled on shore over landing ways. This took considerable time, and unloading was not completed until the end of October, when the work of erection commenced. At this time only a small piece of ground had been cleared and no workshops or sheds of any kind had been erected. The only accommodation for the personnel, which, at this time, consisted of 4 officers, 6 B.O.R.'s, and 600 skilled native workmen, was in tents.

The barges were put together with great difficulty, as the sections were in such large pieces and no cranes were available. After the floating sections were bolted together, the upper sections, weighing over three tons each, had to be placed on pontoons and lifted by temporary derricks and hand labour into their proper positions. In spite of these difficulties the five barges were completed and put into commission by the end of December.

Improvements.—From December, 1916, until April, 1917, as no more barges were arriving, advantage was taken of this interval to complete twelve building berths and to improve workshop facilities generally. The berths occupied a river frontage of 600 yards by 150 yards deep, and were capable of taking six barges in front and six in rear, with a main railway track between carrying four steam cranes for lifting the material into position, whilst boats were being erected. The workshop when completed contained two bays, each 72 feet by 30 feet, fitted with lathes, drilling,

P.T. 5, on the Slipway at Margil.

September 17th, 1917

Barge C. 416. Just before launching at Margil, where re-erected.

June 28th, 1917

punching, and shearing and other smaller machines, the necessary driving power being obtained from a 10-h.p. portable engine. An oil driven air compressor was also installed and pipes laid from it to all parts of the yard so that pneumatic hammers, drills, etc., could be used at the various building berths.

A slipway 500 feet long, built on an incline of 1 in 19, was laid down with approach jetties and powerful steam winding gear, the whole being designed to haul up vessels with a maximum dead weight of 200 tons.

A wharf with 200 feet frontage was built for ocean steamers to come alongside, and was equipped with steam cranes and a 24-inch Decauville rail track. This wharf was handed over to the Stores Department as soon as the main part of the re-erection plant and material was delivered.

A small jetty was also constructed for river craft, fitting out or under repairs, to lay alongside.

An electric power house with a 22-kw. dynamo, driven by an oil engine, giving light to the yard and camp was installed, to that when necessary the work could be carried on day and night and that everything should be ready for the barges due to arrive in April. During this time the steel work and pontoons for the MacMunn Bridge at Amara were prepared. This consisted of 10 pontoons 29 feet 10 inches by 13 feet 10 inches by 4 feet 10 inches and four steel bow-string girders weighing 5 tons each. These pontoons had to be made from steel plates taken from an old oil-tank and any other old plates available. All work was done by hand and pneumatic tools as the workshop was not big enough to take such large work, every part was first erected in the yard, marked for re-erection, and then dismantled for shipping to Amara. Meanwhile barges and river craft which had been towed from India were brought to this depot, to have their temporary sea stiffening dismantled, repaired when necessary, and fitted out in readiness for river service.

Later Works.—At the beginning of April, 1917, the expected consignment of material for barges and river steamers arrived from England, and to cope with this expeditiously, the personnel was increased to 14 officers, 60 B.O.R.'s, and 2000 native ratings. This enabled the material to be quickly discharged and sorted out. Erection commenced as soon as a complete barge had been delivered. The first barge was commenced on 9th May, erected, riveted, and launched in 19 days, finished and put into commission on 1st June, making in all 22 working days for the complete erection. As the work was laid out there was always an average of 12 vessels building at the same time, and the average output of barges and other river craft was 15 per month. At the same time the work of fitting out the *Samana* class of twin-screw tugs and small paddl etugs was handed over to this department. The hulls of these craft came from England on the decks of transports, and the boilers, machinery, deck fittings, etc., had to be fitted on board and trials run. For some months an average of two of these tugs were fitted out per week. The building yard was extended at this time beyond the slipway, sufficient ground being prepared to give four more building berths similar to the original ones. The crane track was also carried along the slipway jetty, which was extended for this purpose also in order to give a fitting out berth for craft sent to this part of the yard for repair, and to keep the building slips and frontage clear.

During 1917, besides 30 barges and 25 tugs, 10 refrigerating barges were erected and fitted out, complete with refrigerating machinery and cold storage chambers for carrying frozen meat up-river, whilst other refrigerating barges were towed out from England and had their machinery fitted on board and tested. Three stern-wheel hospital ships were erected from plates and angles, launched and fitted out complete ; sections of motor lighters brought out from England were put together and the engines fitted on board, and four pontoons for ferrying heavy guns and tractors were made from stock material. Owing to the increased work thrown on to the department the personnel had to be again reinforced and the workshop increased to

Class C. 308. Small Troop Barge ready for Launching, Margil Yard.

Barge C. 416. Just launched at Margil Re-erection Works.
June 28th, 1917

double its size, a 60-h.p. horizontal engine and marine boiler with oil fuel being installed and extra lathes, drilling machines, punching and shearing machines erected and the power station increased by two 26-kw. De Laval steam turbines and dynamos and two 16-kw. paraffin sets designed to light the stores, yard, and jetties as well as the camp.

Special Work.—During 1918 and until the cessation of hostilities the whole yard was going at full pressure, and besides turning out 50 barges and 37 river steamers and tugs, a considerable amount of special work was undertaken, including the sheerlegs pontoon *Goliath*, which arrived in plates and angles from Buenos Aires. This sheerleg pontoon was erected, launched, and had the engine and boiler fitted on board. The sheerlegs are 100 feet in height and capable of lifting 60 tons.

Six barges were fitted up with hydraulic bhoosa presses for pressing hay, the pumps being driven by a portable steam engine.

A floating workshop was also made for the Construction Department, and one large and three small suction dredgers were fitted up and put into commission.

Motor Craft.—In 1917, ten Hydro-Glisseurs arrived from France and were taken over for fitting out and maintenance by this department. This entailed the erection of an additional small workshop and the provision of a special staff.

At the end of 1916, seventeen motor lighters had been taken over from the Royal Navy, these were subsequently based on this depot for repairs, which was a considerable item until such time as they had been put in thorough working order, and necessitated enlarging the glisseur shop and increasing the staff accordingly. Later on, the repair of all motor-boats in the Margil area and of all motor tugs based at Basrah was taken over, which involved laying down a small slipway and increasing still further the size of the motor repair workshop. The upkeep and repair of all steam barges was also subsequently undertaken.

Camp.—For over a year the whole I.W.T. Camp, Margil,

came under this department, including men from the stores, construction, and filtration departments and containing over 5000 native workmen and 400 B.O.R.'s who had all to be rationed, housed, clothed, etc. Owing to the isolated position of this camp, and there being no means of communication, some means of entertaining the men had to be provided, and many kinds of games and sports were instituted both for British and natives. A canteen in which the B.O.R.'s could purchase all kinds of stores, was started and proved a great success ; an entertainment committee was formed, which provided a reading-room, weekly concerts of all kinds, and later on a cinema was purchased and a weekly cinema entertainment was given on different nights to British, Chinese, and Indians. A large filtration plant was erected in 1917 and this supplied pure drinking water to all parts of the camp, largely owing to which the general health of the camp was excellent.

Tonnage.—The total tonnage (measurement) built and commissioned at this yard from September, 1916, to the date of the armistice was approximately 26,200 tons.

Personnel.—The staff employed at the depot on the date specified consisted of :—

	Sept., 1916.	April, 1917.	Dec., 1917.	Nov. 11th, 1918
B.O.'s . .	4	14	27	22
B.O.R.'s .	6	60	97	86
Eastern races	600	2000	3500	3000

M.B. 4 ("MOTOR BELLUM").

Dimensions: length 61'; breadth, 8' 8"; depth, 3' 9". Service draft (maximum), 2' 6".
Engines, 26—30 H.P. Kelvin. Speed, 8·5 knots. Native built hulls.

P.T. 42 ("BRUNEL").

Dimensions: length, 134'; breadth, 35'; depth 7'. Draft maximum, 4' 2". Engines,
D.C., S/C. (C/P.); 2 Cylinders; H.N.P. 41. Speed, light, 8 knots. Towing, 5 knots. Fuel
capacity, 35 tons coal.

Ten vessels originally from the L.C.C. Thames Service.

A. 134 ("MAHAILA").

Native sailing craft, lengths varying from 50' to 70', and carrying capacities from 12
tons upwards.

DEPARTMENT OF NATIVE CRAFT

THE two principal types of native craft utilised for river transport are known as the mahaila and the bellum. The mahaila is of moderate draught, broad in the beam, and particularly noticeable for her high sheer forward and aft. Tonnage carried varies from 5 to 150 tons.

The bellum is a long narrow double-ended shallow-draught canoe-shaped craft, absolutely flat on the bottom and with no keel. Both stem and stern are rounded and finished off with a curve. The sheer is not so exaggerated as in the case of the mahaila. The tonnage carried varies from 1 to 80 tons.

Both types are undoubtedly of very ancient origin and are admirably adapted for the waters in which they have to work. There are numerous variations of these types amongst the smaller classes of craft working on the Tigris and Euphrates, but the larger river craft of from 20 to 100 tons capacity are all built after either one or other of these types.

Given favourable conditions mahailas and bellums can travel very considerable distances; mahailas doing the trip to Amara, a distance of 132 miles, up-stream, in four days, and with a favourable wind the record for the same run down-stream is under twenty hours. When proceeding up-stream against wind and current and unable to sail, a long tow rope led from the stern through a block at the mast-head to the crew on the bank who constitute the motive power is used. This is a method of propulsion peculiar to Mesopotamia.

The first organisation of native craft in Mesopotamia was that of the Bellum Transport Corps, formed in March, 1915, to ferry supplies and troops across the floods between Basrah and Shaiba. These passenger bellums played an important part in the operations at Shaiba in April, 1915. In June, 1915, the attack against the Turkish position at Norfolk Hill above Kurna was made in passenger bellums. This Corps was handed over to the O.C. mahailas in April, 1916, and in June, 1916, it was placed directly under the I.G.C. At that time the most important run on which native craft were employed was that between Basrah and Amara, which continued to increase till it reached its maximum in the four weeks ending 31st March, 1917, during which period 15,463 tons were so transported.

In September, 1916, the Mahaila Repair Depot was opened at Muftieh. On October 5th, 1916, a Controller of Native Craft was appointed, and on November 16th, 1916, the Department was incorporated within the Inland Water Transport Directorate. Native craft officers were also then appointed at Kurna and Amara, and the Small Craft Department at Ashar was opened shortly afterwards. All repairs to native craft were carried out by the Inland Water Transport and the owners were debited with the cost.

In January, 1917, all native craft of over 12 tons capacity were requisitioned by the Army, and placed under the control of the Director of Inland Water Transport. The procedure regarding registration and control is laid down in Lines of Communication Memorandum No. 8 of January 22nd, 1917. See Appendix F1.

A considerable number of craft were captured at Baghdad, and shortly after the occupation by the British an O.C. mahailas was appointed and a repair depot opened there. Native craft were principally employed in this area, between Baghdad and Hinaidi, Baghdad and Baquba, and also between Baghdad and Sindiyah. Whilst the Kut-Hinaidi Railway was under construction native craft were largely employed to carry railway material from Amara to Kut.

On September 6th, 1917, the control of native craft in the Middle and Upper Euphrates was taken over and the native craft which comprised the only river transport available at that time contributed largely to the preparations for the offensive ending in the capture of Ramadie. They were even more employed in the preparations for the Khan Baghdadi offensive.

In March, 1918, it was decided to send all available bellums to the Middle Euphrates to assist in the collection of the harvest there, and in addition to those obtained from the Euphrates area itself over 160 were transferred from the Tigris for this purpose. The amount of grain reported to have been transported in this manner was estimated at 50,000 tons.

In July, 1918, owing to a decreased demand for transport on the Tigris, it was decided to exempt as many native craft as possible from Government service, and at the cessation of hostilities 144 of these craft had already been demobilised.

During the whole period under review large numbers of native craft had been allotted to various departments, two of the principal allotments being to port traffic for discharging ocean steamers and to local resources at Amara for bringing in local produce. The actual distribution of native craft at the time of the armistice was as follows :—

Basrah Section	.	.	.	. 579 of all kinds.
Baghdad ,,	.	.	.	. 212 ,,
Upper Euphrates .	.	.	. 141 ,,
Middle ,,	.	.	.	. 704 ,,
Lower ,,	.	.	.	. 100 ,,
Bridges	.	.	.	. 573 ,,
Telegraphs .	.	.	.	. 6 ,,
Buoyage and pilotage .	.	. 47 ,,
Miscellaneous	.	.	.	. 77 ,,

Total . . 2439

The craft at Basrah included Amara and allotments to all departments at the Base.

Early in 1917 it was proposed to fit some bellums of about 15 tons capacity with old Ford car engines discarded by the mechanical transport, and three were so fitted in the motor dockyard. The experiment proved so successful that a further 50 bellums were fitted with Kelvin and Parsons engines. They were partly used for the harvest collection on the Euphrates and partly allotted to various departments.

Native craft have also been extensively used for constructing floating bridges, practically every type of craft from gufars to the largest mahailas having been utilised as required for this purpose. In addition a certain number of mahailas and bellums have been fitted at various times with tanks to facilitate the distribution of both oil fuel and kerosene, and a regular service has been maintained throughout for the transport of bricks and road-making material, also for the collection of ashes from ocean-going vessels.

The largest tonnage handled by native craft in any one month was 35,141 tons in February, 1918 (ton mileage 2,139,033), a daily average of 1255 tons.

The largest tonnage similarly handled in any one quarter was 95,786 tons in the quarter ending 3rd March, 1918 (ton mileage 5,707,396), a daily average of 1076 tons.

The largest ton mileage performed in a month was 2,900,008 ton miles in April, 1917, and that in a quarter was 7,040,940 ton miles in the quarter ending 26th May, 1917.

The number of craft under control on the dates specified below was as follows :—

Dec. 31st, 1916.	Dec. 31st, 1917.	Nov. 11th, 1918.
310	1796	2439

Floating Bridge at Sk. Saad open for passing steamer.

April, 1917

S T. 15 (" Lord Carmichael.").

Dimensions; length, 106'; extreme breadth, 23'; depth, 8'. Service draft maximum, 7'. Engines, T/S., S/C., C.; 4 cylinders. Speed. 13 knots. Towing, 7'5 knots. Fuel capacity, 73 tons coal. Consumption, 18 tons per 24 hours.
Two vessels of this class from Eastern Bengal State Railway.

Strength of department on dates specified below was as follows :—

	Dec. 31st, 1916.	Dec. 31st, 1917.	Nov. 11th, 1918.
B.O.'s	9	29	14
B.O.R.'s . . .	10	60	42
Other ratings . .	36	6521	6200*

* Figures for craft at Base only. The control of native craft at out-stations having been taken over by the O.C.'s of Sections records for them were not kept at Headquarters.

H

DEPARTMENT OF ACCOUNTS

THE Accounts Office of the Principal Marine Transport officer, as it existed on 7th September, 1916, was taken over by the Inland Water Transport Directorate with a staff of two civilian officers and 14 civilian clerks.

It was realised at the outset that so small a staff could not cope with the work which the growing strength of the Unit would demand, and steps were therefore immediately taken to augment it.

System Introduced.—On 1st October, 1916, a system of accounts was instituted whereby the actual cost of the Directorate could be determined, also what sums had been expended on account of other branches of the service and the civil authorities.

It will be understood that a considerable amount of cash and stores indented for by this Directorate would be expended on behalf of other units, which, although a charge against Government, was certainly not part of the expenses of this Directorate. This has been kept up, but it is regretted that with the fluctuating staff caused by sickness and other reasons it has been, generally speaking, in arrear. At the present moment, however, all that is required is a staff capable of writing up the books from existing records, which are complete, except that prices of stores and cost of their freight from England and India have not yet been received.

It was also found necessary to establish a special section to scrutinise claims for payments for oils, stores, etc., bought by the Directorate, great care having to be exercised in each instance that proper authority had been obtained.

The magnitude of the work dealt with will be realised when it is remembered that this Directorate is the sole purchaser of oils from the Anglo-Persian Oil Company, supplying other units in the field as required.

It is a point of interest perhaps that whereas this department, in the first instance, was almost entirely concerned with expenditure by the Directorate, at the present time the recoveries of stores supplied to outside departments form by far the greater part of its duties, which have increased *pro rata*.

It was soon realised that to ensure the proper conduct of the duties of the department it was necessary that all officers dealing in any manner with Government funds should submit their statements of accounts to the Superintendent, the whole being submitted by him to the audit authorities at the Base.

The only exception to this rule was that the A.D.I.W.T. (Native Craft) remained responsible for payments on account of native craft paid by him, though his accounts were also passed to audit through this office.

The first step taken to co-ordinate the accounts of the Directorate was to place the accounts of the dockyard under the Superintendent of Accounts, and an Accounts Office was opened there with an officer in charge in December, 1916.

The increase in personnel of the Directorate next necessitated a departure from the marine method of maintaining the pay accounts of ratings. The marine system referred to, though admirable for a ship's company, was found too cumbersome for the purpose required.

It was decided, therefore, that ledger accounts should be opened for each member of the Unit, with the exception of B.O.'s and B.O.R.'s whose accounts have been maintained at Poona throughout.

The accounts were first opened on 1st February, 1917, and will be the subject of further comment.

Out-Stations.—Following on the extension of operations it was found necessary to detail officers to other of the more important stations in order to supervise the accounts work there under the direction of this office.

Accounts offices were opened accordingly as follows :—

Amara and Advanced Base (June, 1917), Kut (October, 1917), Hillah (June, 1918), and Nasiriyah (February, 1919).

The opening at the last-named station was necessitated by the return of the mahailas from the Middle Euphrates which required an accounts officer, with special knowledge of the system of payment.

Payments.—It has always been the aim of the Department to pay all ratings at the place where they are working, and every effort has been made to reduce the number of ratings coming to headquarters for pay. Thus, ratings working at depots have always been paid at those depots, and in the same manner those on river craft are paid on their vessels.

The object has been to reduce absence from work to a minimum, and this has been attained to the advantage of the Directorate, though it must be admitted that the conditions are not altogether ideal for those paying.

Messing in River Steamers.—In August, 1917, a system of messing for officers travelling up and down the river on certain classes of vessels was introduced and placed under the administration of this Department.

An officer was specially posted for the work, and various sappers have been taken on the strength from time to time, as it was found preferable to place one on each craft to attend to the messing under the Officer Commanding.

It will perhaps indicate the size of the undertaking that up to the end of March, 1919, the number of officers messed was 114,525, or a daily average of 186·2.

Costing System.—A Costing System for the dockyard was instituted from June, 1917. This Directorate was doing a very considerable amount of work for other branches of the service, even including urgent repairs to sea-going vessels, and the costing system was started in order that the charges debited against them might be as accurate as possible under field conditions.

Time-keeping.—At the same time the time-keeping was taken over by the Accounts Office as it formed an important part of the costing scheme.

This system was also the means of saving considerable sums to Government, for, inasmuch as the essence of good costing is accurate time-keeping, a great deal of attention was given to the latter, with the result that the number of ratings absent from work without authority was reduced to practically nil.

It must be admitted that the final figures were sometimes in arrears owing to the difficulty of obtaining adequate clerical assistance, but the ground work was always prepared from which the desired results could be compiled even at a later date.

Nothing of particular note occurred during 1918, but one of the difficulties of keeping routine work up-to-date was the wave of sickness which again passed over the Department. The number of effective officers at headquarters on one occasion was three out of thirteen.

Native Craft.—In April, 1918, the Department was instructed to prepare and administer a scheme to regulate payments to the native crafts engaged in collecting the harvest upon the Middle Euphrates. Many difficulties were encountered owing to the novel conditions under which the work had to be conducted, but these were overcome in course of time.

Progress.—By September, 1918, the volume of work had increased to so great an extent that it was found necessary to rearrange the working hours of the office.

The ledgers in which the ratings' accounts were kept were in such constant demand that the number of hours during which they could be in use had to be extended.

A double-shift system was accordingly instituted, one from 06.00 hours to 15.00 hours, the other from 15.00 hours to 23.59 hours. The office is consequently open 18 hours out of the 24, and as an officer is always on duty, any urgent matter can be dealt with.

In November, 1918, the mahaila accounts, formerly

administered by the A.D.I.W.T., Native Craft, were transferred to this Department, which thus became responsible for the whole of the financial work of the Directorate.

Conclusions.—It is desired to record certain conclusions which have been arrived at from the experience gained during the campaign.

The maintenance of ratings accounts in the field was the natural outcome of the earlier period of the War when the first of them arrived in this country, and their accounts were administered under " Marine Regulations, India."

It has been mentioned before that as the advance proceeded the procedure had to be modified to suit the exigencies of the situation.

The methods adopted have proved satisfactory, and although they have been criticised, they have answered the purpose for which they were instituted.

Much trouble might have been avoided had the authorities overseas been conversant with the exact particulars required here of each rating arriving in this country, but it has been proved that the maintenance in the field of a very large number of ratings accounts present no difficulties, provided that the primary information of terms of enlistment, nominal rolls, rates of exchange (where necessary), etc., are promptly and correctly forthcoming.

Expenditure.—It will be of interest to note the figures representing the cash expenditure of the department for the periods stated, viz :

October, November, December, 1916 . Rs. 26,78,147–3–7
1917 .   .   .   .   .   .Rs. 228,78,780-11-8
1918 .   .   .   .   .   .Rs. 320,43,027-14-8

Personnel.—The strength of the department has increased steadily, and a table is given below showing the personnel at different dates :—

	Officers.	B.O.R. Clerks.	B.O.R. Ship's St'w'ds.	Civilian Clerks.
7 Sept., 1916.	2	—	—	14
31 Dec., 1916.	4	2	—	24
31 Dec., 1917.	19	19	24	54
31 Dec., 1918.	25	37	27	68

It should be understood that the above figures represent the full strength of the department, which has rarely been the actual effective strength.

Much absence has been caused by sickness, indeed during the summer of 1917, an exceptionally hot one even for this country, the strength varied so considerably that at one time only one officer was actually on duty in the whole department.

DEPARTMENT OF STORES

THE extensive stores now constituting the main supply depot of the Inland Water Transport are situated at Margil, adjoining the Craft Re-erection Yard.

Inception.—This department has developed from a very small beginning in 1915–16, when infinitesimal stocks of engineering material were kept by the R.I.M. in a small godown in the old Turkish Dockyard on Ashar Creek.

In July, 1916, improved accommodation was provided in the present I.W.T. Main Dockyard, but in order to cope with the requirements of the rapidly increasing fleet and expanding workshops, it soon became apparent that a separate department with greater space for extension was necessary.

The prize ship *Hunnie* was the first vessel to be discharged at the new site selected, at Margil, in October, 1916. (See par. 6, " Summary of Events.")

The greater portion of her cargo consisted of tools, cranes, and material for the construction of sheds and jetties, but, as no facilities whatever existed for landing cargo, and the staff then consisted of two officers and six B.O.R.'s only, the initial difficulties were considerable.

There was insufficient water to allow the steamer to berth close alongside the bank and there was no wharf at that time, and most of her cargo had to be brought ashore by the aid of blocks and tackle fixed to tree-trunks ; much of the heavier material being actually dumped into the river and pulled up the bank.

Development.—Meanwhile one wooden shed, 60 feet by 40 feet, had been erected, the remaining storage consisting of unlimited foreshore and palm trees.

By January, 1917, a wharf equipped with steam cranes

for seagoing vessels, a jetty for river craft, and six godowns, each 100 feet by 50 feet, had been completed, all perishable stores were under cover, the original shed had become the office, and the greater portion of the staff from the dock-yard stores with much of their material had been transferred.

Improvements and extensions were carried out at intervals as pressure of other work permitted until about the spring of 1918 the depot had attained its present dimensions.

The covered accommodation now consists of offices, 16 large sheds extending to over 10,000 square yards, 5 huts for special purposes, and about 20 acres of open stacking ground.

The area is served by nearly 3000 yards of narrow gauge railway and a variety of cranes ranging from a 10-ton electric derrick having a jib radius of 85 feet to a 20-cwt. steam traveller.

The number of officers and men required to cope with the work steadily increased, and the stock held became such that it was comparatively seldom any normal demand could not be met.

Stores.—Material is stored in groups, machinery, oils and colours, tools, ropes, deck and engine-room sundries, hospital equipment, and many others each in charge of an expert storekeeper with an Indian staff. Distribution to store sheds is made, after check, by the Receiving Officer, who in turn has taken over from the Stevedoring Section.

Issues are collected in a despatch shed, where they are checked and packed prior to being handed to the Transit Officer for delivery.

Some 350 indents, involving roughly 6000 issues, are dealt with each week.

Consumable stores for the Directorate have been received in approximately equal quantities from England and India —plant and machinery almost entirely from England. Two hundred and eighty-two ships have carried Inland

Water Transport cargo, which has been discharged either alongside or into lighters in mid-stream.

Tonnage.—The average weekly tonnage received in the first half of 1917 amounted to 575 tons only, chiefly timber. Between July, 1917, and November, 1918, the average had risen to 940 tons, the maximum being in the week ending 18th June, 1918, when 2312 tons were landed and passed through the checkers' hands.

The tonnage loaded for local issues or in lighters for despatch up-river averaged about 250 tons per week in the first six months of 1917, but thereafter increased to an average of 685 tons, comprising over 1000 packages, with a maximum week of 1421 tons.

The number of river craft loaded each week averaged 25.

Out-Stations.—In May, 1918, Out-Station Store Depots at Muftieh, Amara, Kut, Baghdad, and Nasiriyah became an integral part of the Stores Department. This was a very necessary development, Up-River Sections of the Directorate having previously had to work from hand to mouth on stores sent up as required.

The Out-Station Depots are equipped to meet all likely demands, and now practically all local issues are made by them, depot stocks being periodically recouped from Margil.

The Stores Department is responsible for the maintenance of an efficient store records system throughout the Unit, and is the source of supply of many important items such as coke, metals, and ropes of the whole of the forces in Mesopotamia.

Personnel.—The staff of the department on the dates indicated consisted of :—

	Dec. 1916.	Dec. 1917.	Nov. 11th, 1918.
B.O.'s	3	7	17
B.O.R.'s	22	71	95
Civilian assistants	10	14	27
Eastern races	—	540	417

DEPARTMENT OF MARINE ENGINEERING

THIS department was formed in September, 1916, the superintendent being then made responsible for the following duties :—

1. Upkeep and repair of hulls and machinery of all self-propelled craft, other than motor-boats.
2. Control of engine-room personnel.
3. The supervision of issue and renewal of all engine-room stores.

Administration.—In September, 1916, the urgency of keeping the river fleet running at full pressure was so important that only absolutely necessary repairs were effected. If, on arrival at the Base, a vessel could possibly be turned round and again despatched up-river, this was done ; in fact the gravest risk of total breakdown was incurred on many occasions in the endeavour to deliver the maximum quantity of troops and military stores at river-head. For example, on one occasion P.S. 53 was kept running for three trips with a badly bent crank shaft, and many other instances could be quoted.

Every vessel on arrival at the Base was boarded by a representative of this department, who decided what hull and machinery repairs, if any, should be put in hand at the dockyard. Arrivals were reported and reports of vessels under repair, giving approximate sailing dates, were submitted daily.

These inspection duties were gradually extended till by November, 1918, the department was responsible for the following further duties :—

1. Boarding and inspecting all vessels arriving at the

Base. Necessary hull and machinery repairs decided, and work put in hand at the dockyard.

2. Similar duties carried out on all yard and harbour craft, i.e. S.T. Class, T.L. Class, L. Class, etc.

3. Inspection of refrigerating machinery afloat.

4. Inspection of the boilers of all vessels, and keeping records of the same.

Inspection.—The following figures show the number of craft inspected and trials run per month :—

Date.	Number of vessels inspected monthly.	Number of steam trials run.
September, 1916 . . .	44	—
October, 1916	79	—
November, 1916 . . .	120	—
December, 1916 . . .	201	14
January, 1917	141	14
February, 1917	178	15
March, 1917	161	16
April–September, 1917 . .	160	55
October, 1917–February, 1918 .	170	46
March, 1918–September, 1918 .	190	40
October and November, 1918 .	150	12

Inspecting Marine Engineers, attached to this department, were appointed to Up-River Stations on the dates shown :—

Amara on the 24th April, 1917.
Dhibban on the 8th May, 1918.
Kut on the 15th July, 1918.
Baghdad on the 18th September, 1917.

Other Work.—In addition to the above regular duties, the following items will serve to illustrate the extent of the work undertaken by this department at various times :—

Trial trips were run, and the performances of new vessels fully reported on.

Reports were submitted on local craft.

Arrangements were made for storing vessels both at the Base and Up-River Stations.

Arrangements were made to supply Basrah City with 10,000 gallons of water per diem.

Lighting plant at the motor dockyard was installed.

The working of the Abadan tin sheds was taken over.

Examinations of engine-room ratings for certificates of competency were regularly held.

The upkeep of and repairs to motor-lighters.

The conversion of coal burning vessels to oil fuel.

Special log book and log registers introduced and issued.

Personnel establishment made out for each type of vessel.

Stores establishment made out for each type of vessel.

Conversion to Oil Fuel.—Investigations were made relative to the conversion of 45 vessels from coal to oil burning. By December, 1918, 35 vessels had been so converted with a very large resultant saving in fuel and personnel.

Stores.—A monthly store list was made out for each class of vessel, and ships' indents were cut down to this list. The control and delivery of engine stores, under supervision of officers of this department, was instrumental in effecting considerable all-round economy, as the figures quoted below in respect of various kinds of oil will show. Other items have been reduced *pro rata*.

Number of vessels stored.	Date.	Stores Supplied.		
		Engine oil.	Mobile oil.	Kerosine.
497	January, 1918 .	3318 galls.	1344 galls.	1350 galls.
530	September, 1918	2528 ,,	432 ,,	604 ,,

In connection with the supply of stores to vessels based on Up-River Stations, arrangements were made, whereby indents were submitted through this office, and stores were despatched monthly on a special barge.

Examinations.—Examinations for native engine-room ratings were inaugurated which included the issuing of 1st and 2nd Class Driver Certificates to successful candidates.

An average of thirty men have been examined monthly, and in this way it has been possible to obtain a supply of native drivers, capable of taking over appointments formerly held by officers and B.O.R.'s.

Motor Lighters.—Seventeen motor lighters were taken over from the Royal Navy in December, 1916, and three more in January, 1918. An officer of this department was appointed in charge of the Motor Lighter Repair Depot, and was responsible for their upkeep and repair. Complete lists of machinery spares, for twelve months were prepared and indented for.

Abadan Tin Sheds.—In view of the urgency of increasing the output at the Anglo-Persian Oil Company's Tin Sheds, Abadan, it was decided that Government should take over working control from the 1st January, 1918.

This department was made responsible for supervision, upkeep of plant, and output of cases, tins, and drums.

The I.W.T. assumed control with the understanding that any additional labour required should be provided by Government. On taking over, it was found that many of the machines were in need of overhaul and adjustment, and that to increase the output more supervision was necessary and more skilled labour required. This labour could not be obtained locally, and although several communications were sent to India, it was not until an I.W.T. officer was sent there to recruit that the men were eventually secured.

At the time of taking over, it was considered that with extra labour and with the I.W.T. in charge, the plant was capable of turning out 8000 tins per day. This figure was subsequently exceeded, and on occasions over 10,000 tins per day were averaged over considerable periods without any increase of plant. For the greater part of the year 1918–1919, it was impossible to secure regular supplies of the necessary tin-making materials, thereby frequently reducing the possible maximum output.

The following comparative figures show the average output for December, 1917, the last month under A.P.O.C.

management and for a representative week's work under
I.W.T. management, when sufficient quantities of materials
had become available ; the maximum output in any one day
being 14,150 tins.

	Total Staff.	Average cans daily.	Cans per hour.	Cans per man per hour.	Hours per day.
Under A.P.O.C. management, December, 1917	545	4392	366	0·67	12
Under I.W.T. management	745	10,671	1123	1·50	9½

Personnel.—After preliminary investigation, a minimum
establishment for every vessel in the fleet was prepared, and
by this means 494 engine-room native ratings were dispensed with.

In this connection the following statement will serve to
show the reduction in personnel coincident with the increase
of fleet :—

DATE.	Ships in com- mission.	In charge of engines.			Eastern races.
		Officers.	B.O.R.'s	Native drivers.	
December, 1916	151	37	42	72	1768
December, 1917	334	93	72	169	3949
November, 1918	364	88	40	236	3182

The total staff of the department ashore and afloat on the
dates indicated consisted of :—

		Dec., 1916.	Dec., 1917.	Dec., 1918.
Officers { afloat	. .	59	131	125
{ ashore	. .	8	14	17
B.O.R.'s { afloat	. .	71	116	88
{ ashore	. .	21	24	13
Eastern { afloat	. .	1768	3949	3182
races { ashore	. .	—	2	2
Total .		1927	4236	3427

I.W.T. Personnel at Abadan Tinsheds :	Dec., 1916.	Dec., 1917.	Dec., 1918.
Officers. . . .	—	—	2
B.O.R.'s . . .	—	—	12
Eastern races . .	—	—	321
Grand total .	1927	4236	3762

DEPARTMENT OF VESSELS

THIS department was instituted in October, 1916, being made responsible for the inspection and upkeep of all deck fittings, awnings, screens, etc., the supervision of issue and renewal of running and consumable deck stores, and the provision and maintenance of deck personnel of all vessels.

Sail Loft.—In November, 1916, a sail and rigging loft was established, to which a carpenter's and painter's shop was subsequently added. Two condemned barges were re-decked, and fitted out for this purpose, accommodation being provided on board for the large personnel necessary to such an establishment. Flag-making and all repairs to ships' boats were also undertaken at this depot.

Stores (Deck).—The system of individual ships drawing their own stores having proved unsatisfactory, it was decided to detail a special officer to the Stores Department to supervise issues to all vessels. A scale was drawn up for each ship of the fleet, this officer being responsible that this was not exceeded. Periodical inspection of each vessel's stores were made to ensure that every economy was being effected, having due regard to efficiency.

The introduction of this scheme resulted in a large reduction in the consumption of deck stores.

Personnel.—In March, 1917, certificated officers were urgently required to bring ships from India to Mesopotamia. To enable a sufficient number of these to be released for this purpose, non-commissioned officers were detailed to relieve officers in command of river craft. This experiment proved so successful that it was proceeded with until practically the entire fleet, with the exception of the large troop carriers, was navigated by non-commissioned officers.

A further development of the scheme took place towards

the end of 1917, when, owing to the increase in the fleet, and the shortage of European personnel, it was decided to run as many vessels as possible with native masters. A system of examinations was introduced, and they were regularly held at the Base, certificates being granted to successful candidates. Suitable men were encouraged to sit for these examinations, and a careful record kept of their service.

In order to cope with the extra clerical work entailed it was found necessary to open a special subsidiary office for this purpose. At the conclusion of hostilities practically all Europeans afloat had been relieved by native masters, or *serangs*, who proved thoroughly efficient and reliable under peace conditions. A School for Seacunnies was established to train intelligent Lascars to take charge of motor launches. This was under the charge of a second class master, and certificates were granted to approved candidates.

Out-Stations.—A branch office was established at **Amara** in April, 1917, and subsequently, as the requirements of the Service demanded, they were extended to Kut, Baghdad, and Dhibban. The officer in charge of each sub-office was responsible for the upkeep of vessels, the issue of stores, and the records of deck personnel for all craft based in his area.

SCHEDULE SHOWING REDUCTION OF PERSONNEL
WITH INCREASE OF FLEET

DATE.	ASHORE.		AFLOAT.			SHIPS IN COMMISSION.			
	Officers.	B.O.R.'s.	Officers.	B.O.R.'s.	I.O.R.'s.	Officers i/c.	B.O.R.'s i/c.	Serangs i/c.	Total
Oct., 1916 .	1	1	73	33	1079	50	2	43	95
Dec., 1916 .	4	7	57	93	1846	49	54	48	151
Dec., 1917 .	10	16	95	217	4057	57	97	180	334
Nov., 1918 .	11	24	31	117	3879	25	43	296	364

DEPARTMENT OF CONSERVANCY AND RECLAMATION

EARLY in the year 1916, a Directorate was formed at Basrah under the title Port Administration and Conservancy, which commenced the collection of data and information with a view to eventually improving navigable conditions on the Tigris.

In February, 1917, River Conservancy above the Port of Basrah was handed over to the Inland Water Transport, but little was actually done until June of that year when Lieut.-Colonel R. G. Garrow, R.E., arrived from England and was placed in charge of the Conservancy Branch of this Directorate. It was then decided that drastic action was an immediate necessity to endeavour to improve the condition of the river, instead of working on the safer lines of recording observations and collecting data over a long period, with a view to ultimately working out a comprehensive scheme, as had been the intention hitherto. At the same time serious attention was being given by G.H.Q. to the general improvement and extension of local irrigation, and as the two sciences of Conservancy and Irrigation are so closely allied, Colonel Garrow was appointed, by the orders of the Army Commander, Assistant Director for Irrigation as well as for Conservancy. This arrangement continued until February, 1918, when in view of the increasing importance of irrigation to Mesopotamia it was decided to form an independent Directorate of Irrigation ; but as the Army in the Field was still dependent upon river transport for its main supply, it was also decided that the conservancy of the rivers should remain under the control of the Inland Water Transport, in order to prevent the interests of navigation suffering from the demands of irrigation. At the same time it was decided to transfer control of the dredgers from the Port Administration and Conservancy to the Inland Water Transport Directorate.

These alterations led to a reorganisation of the River Conservancy and Irrigation Department, which was re-named "Conservancy and Reclamation." In addition to continuing the conservancy of the rivers this department undertook all earthworks and reclamation required by the Inland Water Transport at the Base, besides dredging operations.

Tigris.—To revert to the formation of the department in 1917. The principal effort of the Conservancy Branch was at first directed to improve navigable conditions in the "Narrows."

The Tigris may be said to more or less lose its identity when it reaches Amara, due to the large number of dis-tributaries which take off water in all directions and dissi-pate it into the marshes. The principal of these dis-tributaries are the Bitera on the right bank, 10 miles above Amara ; the Chahala on the left bank at Amara itself, which takes off practically half the volume of the Tigris ; the Majar Kebir on the right bank, 13 miles below Amara, which takes off about 30 per cent of the remaining volume, and the Micherya on the left bank, 15 miles below the Majar Kebir, which under present conditions through its by-pass takes off 10 per cent of the still remaining volume. This much-reduced stream forms what is known as the "Narrows," a detailed description of which is given in Part I. At the lower end of the "Narrows," 29 miles below the Micherya Canal, a certain quantity of water finds its way back into the main river from the marshes at Gumaijah Shargi, and thence downwards the volume gradually increases again until the confluence with the Euphrates at Kurna is reached.

In the latter part of 1916, the Port Administration and Conservancy built a permanent dam across the Micherya Canal, with a by-pass which only allowed a very small quantity of water to pass through for irrigation purposes ; but though this certainly increased the volume of water passing down the "Narrows," the increase was hardly sufficient to create much improvement in navigable conditions. In 1917, it was therefore decided that steps must be taken with some of the other distributaries if open navigation in the "Narrows" was to be maintained throughout the low-water season. An earthen dam was accordingly constructed across the Majar Kebir Canal, which reduced the volume escaping by that channel from 49 cubic metres per second to 17 cubic metres per second. At the same time, a spur was built from the left bank of the Tigris across the entrance to the Chahala, which acting in conjunction with certain dredging operations carried out on the point of land opposite, on the right bank, diverted about 30 per cent of the Chahala water down the Tigris. The effect of these two works was almost immediately felt in the "Narrows," considerable scour taking place, and the level of the bed being lowered by about 9 inches, whilst the width of the channel increased considerably in the narrower portions.

The general water level of the Tigris in the summer of 1917 was exceptionally low, and had the above works not been carried out it is practically certain that navigation through the "Narrows" would have been suspended entirely. As it was there were a large number of groundings, though conditions rapidly improved towards the end of the season, when the scouring effect had time to make itself felt. At the end of the low-water season, when the floods commenced, it was necessary to partially demolish the dams in both the Majar Kebir and the Chahala, in order to allow flood-water to escape. The dams were, however, left to the last possible moment, so as to divert as much water as possible through the "Narrows" with a view to increasing the scour ; but by the end of the high-water season there was practically nothing left of either of these dams, and new works had to be constructed for the low-water season of 1918.

The Majar Kebir was then dealt with in practically the same way as in the previous year, except that the dam was carried completely across the canal, and a by-pass which could be regulated arranged on either side to allow sufficient water to escape for irrigation purposes. In the Chahala a similar dam was constructed about 4 miles below its departure from the Tigris. In the case of Majar Kebir no trouble was experienced whatever. A mat blanket was laid below the dam, and through the by-pass no scour to speak of took place. In the Chahala, however, owing to the looser nature of the soil, and the much greater volume of water to be controlled, serious difficulty was experienced, and it was only with the utmost care and watchfulness that the by-pass was prevented from scouring out and forming a new bed for the river. Other difficulties were caused in 1918 by the Political Department demanding water for local irrigation beyond their estimated requirements, and frequently an ncreased volume of water had to be diverted out of the river for this purpose, to the detriment of navigation in the "Narrows." However, principally due to the fact that the work was taken in hand in sufficient time, a minimum draft of 5 feet 2 inches was maintained in this section throughout the whole low-water season, and there was not one single case of grounding caused by insufficient depth of water. Again, at the end of the low-water season of 1918 the works above-mentioned had to be partially demolished to permit the escape of flood water.

It is pointed out that these works were entirely emergency works undertaken to maintain navigation for the time being. At the same time, they have had a most beneficial effect on navigable conditions in the " Narrows " generally, having widened and deepened it throughout, and the information obtained by watching the results of these experiments should be of the greatest value to any future systematic scheme of conservancy which may be undertaken.

In addition to the above works on the Tigris, a large amount of survey work has been carried out and measurements of silt and river discharge taken which will be of permanent value.

Euphrates.—Early in 1915, it was realised that communication between Basrah and Nasiriyah by water was a matter of some urgency. The River Euphrates losing its identity after its bifurcation at the Hindiyah Barrage, becomes united again in the neighbourhood of Samawah, only to again lose itself in the marshes below Nasiriyah, where a large area of land is permanently inundated, and is now known as the Hamar Lake. The old bed of the Euphrates passed through this present Lake and joined the Tigris at Kurna. The later branch flows through the southern portion of the Lake until it again joins the Shatt-el-Arab at Gurmat Ali, a few miles above Basrah.

The Port Administration and Conservancy had imported a fleet of dredgers to Mesopotamia and commenced work on dredging a channel across Hamar Lake in 1916. For many reasons the scheme was not an unqualified success, and work was abandoned. The following year more dredgers were imported, a revised scheme prepared, and the work restarted. In the meantime a railway had been laid to Nasiriyah, so that the urgency of water communication was not so vital as formerly, and after some discussion, by orders of the War Office, the scheme was abandoned after only 6½ miles of channel had been partially dredged.

In the latter part of 1917, the question was again raised, as owing to the serious shortage of railway material in the country and the difficulty of obtaining further supplies from overseas, due to the continuance of the War, it was considered advisable to utilise a waterway, wherever there was one available which could be made navigable, in preference to building a railway. Moreover, substantial advantages to irrigation were anticipated from the completion of this work, and it was therefore decided to proceed with the scheme. By this time the dredgers had been handed over to the Inland Water Transport, and the scheme was taken up in earnest in February, 1918.

The fleet of dredgers employed consisted of :

(1) *Lees*	.	.	30-inch suction
(2) *Campbell*	.	.	24-inch suction
(3) *Oswald*	.	.	24-inch suction
(4) *Quorra*	.	.	24-inch suction
(5) *Mudlark*	.	.	15-inch suction

all being suction dredgers and fitted with cutters for working in the hard river-bed, and with pipe-line and terminal pontoons for discharging the material ashore.

Surveys and preparations were begun in March, and on October 31st the channel was navigable by the smaller types of river craft. On January 29th, 1919, connection was made with the Euphrates at Beni Said, when through navigation by any of the river craft became practicable. The distance across the lake is 14½ miles. Three and a quarter miles of shoals had to be dredged to the eastward of the lake and a dry cut 6 miles in length to be made from the upper end of the lake to Beni Said, to eliminate the existing tortuous and difficult Mezlik Channel. Thus about 24 miles of channel had to be dredged (including the 6½ miles partially completed by the Port Administration and Conservancy in 1916 and 1917). The whole work was essentially completed by the end of February, 1919, twelve months after surveys were commenced. Over 7½ million cubic yards of excavation (not counting the building of retaining bunds) were made, and the spoil was deposited to form a bank on the south side of the channel. This bank will probably become part of a continuous bund to shut off and reclaim for cultivation a large part of the southern portion of Hamar Lake. Dredging is being continued in the river below the lake in connection with this scheme.

A work of this magnitude in such a country as Mesopotamia called for a great deal of organisation. It was carried on at full pressure day and night all through the summer heat. Fuel and stores had to be transported from the Base, a distance of 90 to 120 miles, and the keeping of the dredgers in working condition, in itself a considerable

Reclamation work at Basrah by Dredger Campbell.

" PAHLWAN "
(Floating Crane self-propelled).
Dimensions: length. 135'; extreme breadth. 44'; depth, 10' 6". Service draft, 7' 9".
Speed, 5 knots. Lifts 30 tons at a radius of 60 ft.
From the Karachi Port Trust.

task, was successfully accomplished by the Inland Water Transport Dockyard. The personnel necessarily occupied very limited quarters, but good health was generally maintained through careful attention to their comforts and wants.

The cost, including all charges, approximated 3 crores of rupees.

For the purposes of reinforcing the Inland Water Transport flotilla on the Upper Euphrates (which had either been railed across from Baghdad and refloated at Feluja or had been taken up through the Shenafiyah Lake, and other channels in the high water of 1918), or withdrawing them in case of disaster, it was considered advisable to attempt the conservancy of a low-water season route between the Lower Euphrates and the Middle Euphrates. That is to say, in the maze of channels extending between Shenafiyah and Hindiyah various routes were surveyed. The needs of irrigation interfered considerably with those of navigation, but it was ultimately decided that the route across the Shenafiyah Lake and through the Mishkab and Kufa Channels should be conserved for navigation. A channel 1500 feet long, 40 feet wide and 3 feet deep, was cut with a small bucket dredger through the Shenafiyah Lake below the entrance to the Mishkab. Six thousand lineal feet of training bunds and bandalls were constructed with a view to creating scour. Before these works could near completion the collapse of the Turks, and extensive modifications in complementary irrigation projects, rendered it inadvisable to spend more time and money on them, and very reluctantly the project was dropped.

It is a matter of interest that owing to the cessation of this work and to the abandonment of the greater part of the irrigation schemes, all the channels in this region have since deteriorated to such an extent that although the rivers are still high there is no navigable connection whatever.

Other Works.—Among the principal other works carried out by this department the following are worthy of particular mention :—

Dredging was done at Amara, to give access to the oil fuel berths and to ease the sharp bend in the river there.

During the retreat of the Turks in March, 1917, a bund 2000 feet long, with a maximum height of 20 feet at Shujair, 20 miles above Baghailah, was breached to delay our advance. This bund closed a depression on the right bank of the Tigris, and the breaching caused great damage to the cultivated areas and threatened to interfere with navigation. It was therefore reconstructed during the next low-water season.

A bund 600 feet long at Musandaq, 11 miles below Sheikh Sa'ad, was similarly reconstructed.

At the Base a great deal of reclamation was done for camps and depots. In this connection, the earth-filling brought by light railway, donkeys, and bellums amounted in the year 1918 alone to 150,000 cubic yards.

At the Base two large dredging and reclamation schemes commenced by the Port Administration and Conservancy were completed, providing 55 acres of raised land for military depots.

Reclamation in the dockyard area was also accomplished by means of a dredger.

The excavation of the south channel into the Inland Water Transport dock was completed in June, 1918.

The flood bunds protecting Inland Water Transport depots were maintained in repair, and a large amount of incidental work of this nature was dealt with.

Some large shoals were dredged in the Euphrates above Beni Said, and at Suq-esh-Shuyukh.

The Euphrates was surveyed and charted from Qurnah to Nasiriyah, a distance of 90 miles, careful levelling being run right through. The river from Nasiriyah to Wa'ar was also surveyed, and stretches, totalling in length 33 miles, which were found to be bad for navigation were carefully charted.

An accurate level was run up the River Tigris from Amara to Baghdad, Basrah to Amara having been previously completed by the Port Administration and Conservancy, and all tide gauges were co-ordinated to mean sea-level.

From January to April, 1919, the dredger *Campbell* was employed improving conditions on Mohammerah Bar.

The protection of roads and buildings from damage by erosion does not constitute conservancy from a navigation point of view, but temporary revetments were constructed in several places as required by the military authorities.

Personnel.—The personnel was at its maximum at the end of 1918, and included :

British officers	38
British other ranks	68
Civilian clerks	13
Civilian dredging masters and engineers .	39
Eastern races	2880

not including men employed by local contractors for earth-filling or bund-making, or Prisoners of War Labour Corps.

DEPARTMENT OF PERSONNEL

THE earliest records of the personnel department date back to about the middle of 1915, when various ratings were sent up from India under Royal Indian Marine Squadron Orders, exclusive of the personnel which was then arriving ex paddle steamers.

In January, 1916, a Registrar and Rations Superintendent was appointed by the Principal Marine Transport Officer, to supervise the arrival of all drafts of Eastern labour ; his duty being to board transports on arrival, make out nominal rolls of all labour ratings and issue identity discs. In February, 1916, a Superintendent of Personnel was appointed, and in September, 1916, the department was transferred to the Inland Water Transport Directorate.

Labour arriving from India was at first accommodated in huts at the back of General Headquarters building (the British Consulate in pre-War days) ; they were subsequently hulked in the prize ship *Franz Ferdinand*, an Austrian liner taken in the Indian Ocean shortly after the outbreak of hostilities and sent to Basrah early in 1915.

The rapidly growing strength of the personnel arriving from India, necessitating more extensive accommodation, a camp site was chosen at Tanooma in May, 1916, and the Military Works Department took in hand the erection of huts and laying out of the camp, which was first occupied in August, 1916, and then contained accommodation for about six hundred ratings. The staff consisted of the Camp Commandant, one non-commissioned officer and four sappers. An experimental bore for the supply of fresh water to the camp was made, but given up after a depth of 157 feet had been reached without results, and tank storage was the only alternative until a pipe-line was subsequently laid.

From December, 1916, and through the early part of 1917, labour drafts for the Inland Water Transport Directorate were arriving from India, often at the rate of two thousand a week, and a light railway had to be laid from the landing stages at Gardilan to the camp, to convey kits and supplies, a distance of approximately two miles. Previous to the laying of this light line by the Inland Water Transport Construction Department transport had been limited to the capacity of two motor lorries and half a dozen bullock carts plus manual labour, over tracks which were at times well-nigh impassable by reason of mud. Among other minor inconveniences of the camp in these earlier days were the frequent cases of night sniping on the part of hostile Arabs from the surrounding desert.

The work of the department consists of the co-ordination with the 3rd Echelon of all records of personnel arriving from overseas, of transfers from and to the various departments within the Directorate, the maintenance of crews on all vessels, the issue and withdrawal of all clothing, and other work incidental to the Quartermaster's Department, which also comes under the Assistant Director of Inland Water Transport (Personnel).

The department is also responsible, through its Camp Commandant, for the vaccination and inoculation of all ratings for small-pox, plague, cholera, and typhus on their first arrival in the country ; for all awards, renewals of contracts, repatriations to India, and final disposal of the effects of men who in the execution of their duty to the Raj were destined to find a resting-place in Mesopotamia : and it is satisfactory to be able to record that in the case of these the most scrupulous care has always been exercised to accord a burial or cremation in strict accordance with the man's creed or caste—Hindu, Mohammedan, Parsee, Egyptian, Chinese, Buddhist, or Christian.

The strength of the personnel of the unit reached its maximum in December, 1917, when the figure stood at

37,857, of all Eastern categories, as against 16,487 on December 31st of the previous year (1916). There was a small decline in figures during 1918, following on the transfer of personnel to the newly formed Port Directorate.

On conclusion of hostilities the Eastern strength was 36,449, which, owing to labour commitments from India, rose to 37,064 on December 31st, 1918. The strength on November 11th, 1918, included 419 Indian and Anglo-Indian clerical ratings, 14,955 Marine ratings employed afloat and ashore, 6425 Indian and 4116 Chinese skilled mechanics, 7042 Indian and 214 Chinese unskilled labourers, and over three thousand locally engaged workmen.

In addition to the foregoing, the department during the years 1916 and 1917 had contingents of the Egyptian Labour Corps and Mauritius Labour Battalion on its strength. Within four months of the cessation of hostilities ten thousand ratings had either been repatriated or were awaiting passage to India. That service with the Inland Water Transport, Mesopotamian Expeditionary Force, has been nothing in the nature of conscription, is eloquently testified to by the fact that no fewer than 2117 re-engagements were made by the department during 1918, and since hostilities have ceased over a thousand applications have been made for extension of agreements ; these are in addition to the hundreds of men who have proceeded to India on expiry of contracts, and after a short holiday re-enrolled for a second and third period of service.

Staff.—The staff of the department on the dates specified consisted of :—

	Sept., 1916.	Dec. 31st, 1916.	Dec. 31st, 1917.	Nov. 11th, 1918.
B.O.'s . .	6	6	9	11
B.O.R.'s .	6	17	30	24
B.W.I. . .	—	36	39	15
Eastern races	138	170	240	193

And 1 civilian assistant throughout.

Tunnel Tug being hauled aboard S.S. "Rheinfels" by "Goliath" for shipment overseas.

Nahr Umar, H.T. "Urlana" discharging railway material.
August 22nd, 1917

DEPARTMENT OF PORT TRAFFIC

DURING the year 1916 a Directorate was formed at Basrah, under the title of " Port Administration and River Conservancy."

This department was charged with responsibility for :

(1) The discharge of ocean transports to quay or port craft and the conveyance of port craft so loaded to quay.

(2) The construction and maintenance of port works.

(3) River conservancy from river-head to the sea.

(4) The control of movements of ships and kindred matters within the area specified in (3) above.

In February, 1917, it ceased to operate as a whole, and responsibilities for its various functions were divided as follows :—

(1) *Under the I.W.T.*

River conservancy from Gurmat Ali to river-head.

Discharge of ocean transports to quay.

Discharge of ocean transports to barge.

Berthing alongside quays of barges loaded ex transports.

Checking of supplies ex transports and barges.

(2) *Under the I.G.C.*

Port construction and conservancy.

Port Officer and pilots.

In order to carry out the latter duties enumerated under I.W.T. the post of Assistant Director, Port Traffic, was created, his duties being those of discharging cargo from vessels to quay direct and the conveyance of loaded barges to the quays. The actual handling of the cargo ex ship or barge berthed alongside the quay was carried out by the consignee services concerned.

At the end of 1917 cargo was distributed from ships in the following proportion :

> 60 per cent to barges.
> 40 per cent to quay berths.

The average rate of discharge being about 3000 tons per day.

The Port of Basrah had developed to such an extent that early in 1918 it was decided to establish an independent Port Directorate, to which the Port Traffic branch of the I.W.T. was transferred in February. The actual monthly tonnage discharged from sea-going ships from early in 1916 to January, 1918, was as follows :—

1916.			1917.		
January	.	. no records	January .	.	79,085
February	.	. no records	February	.	93,699
March 12th	.	. no records	March	.	98,073
13th March to 12th April	.	43,249	April	.	94,673
13th April to 12th May	.	57,540	May	.	90,504
13th May to 12th June	.	44,325	June	.	73,845
13th June to 30th June	.	22,554	July	.	84,559
June Port traffic records	.	30,000	August	.	109,620
July	. . .	. 38,916	September	.	100,136
August	. . .	. 44,183	October	.	108,852
September	. .	. 54,256	November	.	112,503
October	. . .	. 50,792	December	.	104,593
November	. .	. 61,214			
December	. .	. 61,123	January, 1918	.	131,838

The drop in June and July may be attributed to hot weather conditions.

View taken from Signalling Tower shewing I.W.T. Motor Boat Jetty and I.G.C. Motor Boat House and Jetty.

March 18th, 1919

SECTIONAL ORGANISATION

THE rivers are divided into sections for the purpose of better administration, and the organisation of these is carried out, as far as possible, on commercial lines. Each section is controlled according to its relative importance by either a Deputy-Director, Assistant Director, or Deputy Assistant Director of Inland Water Transport.

The heads of these sections act as agents for the Director, and also as agents for each of the departments. The technical departments have their own special officers attached to the head of each section; these officers are responsible to the head of the section for the efficiency of that particular branch of its work, and also to the chief of the department at headquarters for its efficiency as a whole.

There are eight sections (vide par. 23 of "Summary of Events"), viz. :

The Forward Area

1. Baghdad.
2. Upper Euphrates.
3. Middle Euphrates.
4. Amara.
5. Kut.
6. The Narrows.
7. Lower Euphrates.
8. Base.

The latter is directly administered by the A.D.I.W.T. (Transport), and has already been dealt with under that departmental heading. The remainder will be dealt with in the order mentioned.

FORWARD AREA

1. BAGHDAD SECTION
2. UPPER EUPHRATES SECTION
3. MIDDLE EUPHRATES SECTION

1. BAGHDAD SECTION

IMMEDIATELY following the capture of Baghdad, on March 11th, 1917, an Inland Water Transport Office was established there by Lieut.-Colonel Hughes, D.S.O., who had commanded the forward transport during the advance. This office was situated on the river front, adjacent to G.H.Q., and was at that time principally concerned with the discharge and loading of craft on either bank of the river in the vicinity of Baghdad city, at the same time forming the headquarters of the Assistant Director I.W.T., Forward Area.

No facilities in the shape of wharves or jetties existed in Baghdad at this time, with the single exception of a small ramp at the railway terminus, this being a masonry construction which could only be used at times of moderately high water. The steam cranes and other mechanical appliances in connection with it had been destroyed by the Turks before evacuation. The first action taken, therefore, was to select suitable sites in the vicinity of Baghdad on which to establish supply bases for future operations.

The main Turkish army had retreated in two directions, viz. (1) up the right bank of the Tigris, following the Samarra Railway, and (2) towards the Euphrates. It was therefore expected that the greater portion of our troops would be operating on the right bank of the river. An excellent site was found on this bank, about six miles below Baghdad and immediately up-stream of the entrance to the

Maude Bridge, Baghdad shewing cut partly open.

Khirr Canal, which provided a straight water frontage some two miles in length, with deep water alongside the bank and unlimited stacking ground in rear to form supply, ammunition, and engineer dumps. The Advanced Base was formed here, and immediate steps were taken to mark off the water frontage and apportion the ground to various departments.

To supply the troops operating to the north-eastward of Baghdad, and in order to deal with the requirements of Baghdad itself, it also became necessary to establish a Supply Base on the left bank of the river. A suitable site was found for this at Hinaidi, situated seven miles below the Advanced Base, though only three miles from Baghdad by land. This became the port for the left bank, and subsequently the terminus of the Kut-Baghdad Railway. The development of both these ports, as I.W.T. stations, will be dealt with later.

The headquarters of the Lines of Communication was established at Karradah, opposite Advanced Base, and as the Inland Water Transport, so far as their mission on the Line of Transport was concerned, were working directly under Lines of Communication, a second office was opened in close proximity to the above, which had been chosen as being centrally situated for either Advanced Base, Hinaidi, or Baghdad itself.

In May, 1917, Lieut.-Colonel Hughes, D.S.O., was recalled to Basrah to relieve Brig.-General Grey, and was relieved in turn by Lieut.-Colonel Ward, who was appointed D.D.I.W.T., Forward Area. As this section developed, it was found that its more important work was with G.H.Q. in connection with areas outside the Lines of Communication. The Deputy Director therefore decided to give up his office at Karradah, and move back to the original office at Baghdad. In July, 1917, a Deputy Assistant Director was appointed to deal with all matters in connection with the Lines of Communication at Advanced Base.

Baghdad City.—The improvement and extension of existing facilities in and around the city of Baghdad was commenced in June, 1917, and in this the I.W.T. largely co-operated. One of the first items undertaken was the re-erection by the sappers and miners of the pontoon bridge, which had been towed up in sections from Gurmat Ali, on the present site of the " Maude " Bridge. Whilst this work was in progress a portion of the bridge unfortunately sank. Salvage operations were carried out by the I.W.T., and successfully completed by the end of the month. In September, 1917, the I.W.T. took over entire control of this and the North Bridge. Later, with a view to the protection of the two bridges, a mine defence boom was placed across the river well above the North Bridge.

Meanwhile improvements to the railway wharf, which had now been completed, greatly facilitated the rapid discharge of railway material and other stores.

By the end of 1917 a total of 18,303 tons had been landed in the Baghdad area, whilst 8697 tons of stores had been loaded here for despatch elsewhere.

Early in 1918 several Red Cross motor launches were lifted on to trucks at the railway wharf and despatched to the Euphrates in connection with military operations in that area ; a number of steam launches and small barges being similarly dealt with at a later date.

In April, 1918, during exceptionally high floods, the South Bridge was carried away, owing to a mahaila fouling the " Cut." This was eventually replaced by the present " Maude " Bridge, which is fully described under " Construction." The pontoons of the old bridge were, however, salved and subsequently converted to oil-tanks, some being mounted on railway trucks for the transport of oil in bulk, and others erected ashore.

During 1918, extensions to the Customs and Blockade Wharves were completed, and many other improvements introduced, amongst them being the stationing of a motor fire and salvage vessel in this area, which has since proved invaluable on several occasions.

From January 1st, 1918, to the conclusion of hostilities, 78,276 tons had been discharged in this section, whilst 16,229 tons of stores had been loaded for despatch else-

General View of Maude Bridge, Baghdad on day of opening ceremony.
December 11th, 1918.

Steel frame transomes for check weight lifting gear "Maude Bridge"
(Old South Bridge) Baghdad.

October 15th, 1918.

where. This is exclusive of the large quantity of civil merchandise handled by the Government fleet, which during the latter part of 1918 averaged over a thousand tons per week. The personnel maintained at this station is shown on page 159.

Advanced Base.—An I.W.T. Office was opened here on March 14th, 1917. The station rapidly developed ; a Stores branch, which then included coal and oil fuel, was established at once, and in July, 1917, an Accounts branch was also included.

The Coal and Oil Fuel Depot soon assumed large proportions and was separated from the Stores, a special officer being appointed to supervise this, directly under the I.W.T. Officer, Advanced Base. By August, 1917, a stock of two thousand tons of coal had been accumulated, which has been maintained ever since, whilst the erection of bulk storage tanks for fuel oil, kerosene, and petrol was proceeded with by the Construction Department. The capacities of these tanks are shown in Appendix E1.

A fleet of about ten Samana tugs and six shallow draught stern-wheelers, with a large number of suitable barges, was usually based on this station to cope with transport requirements in the Forward Area. The tonnage handled by this fleet, over the periods mentioned, when accurate statistics were available, was as follows :—

1917 (middle of November to end of December) 48,274 tons
1918 (whole year) .   .   .   .   .   463,651 ,,

In addition, during 1918, 37,637 tons were loaded here for despatch elsewhere.

A Steam Ferry Service was instituted at an early date between Baghdad city and Advanced Base, which was later extended to Hinaidi. The extent to which this service was utilised may be gauged by the fact that the number of passengers carried averaged over fifteen thousand per week. The central camp for the distribution of I.W.T. personnel and maintenance of discipline in the Forward Area was situated at Advanced Base. The personnel maintained at this station is shown on page 159.

Hinaidi.—This was first opened as a port on March 24th, 1917, on which date a Ferry Service was started for troops and supplies to Advanced Base. This was at first operated by mahailas, and the tonnage handled for the month of April amounted to 2187 tons, but this increased so rapidly that it became necessary to establish a regular steam ferry service shortly afterwards. The tonnage handled had more than doubled by August, and large numbers of troops were being landed and embarked here in addition.

A Medical Inspection Station was also established, at which vessels from down-river were boarded before receiving pratique.

During 1918 considerable work was done improving the foreshore by building ramps to facilitate the loading and unloading of vessels ; quarters and offices were erected, and an oil fuel and kerosene bulk storage installation completed. The latter is described under " Construction," and capacities of tanks are shown in Appendix E1. The total tonnage handled at this station, exclusive of that carried by native craft, was as follows :—

During 1917 (April to December) . . . 34,244 tons
   „   1918 . . . . . . 107,580 „

The I.W.T. staff maintained at Hinaidi is shown on page 159.

Karradah Workshops.—The Floating Workshop P.S. 34 arrived at Advanced Base on March 23rd, 1917, and commenced work there forthwith. A week later she was moved to the left bank and moored alongside the site selected for the present workshop at Karradah, which was completed and handed over to the dockyards by the Construction Department on March 10th, 1918. They are more fully described under these departmental headings.

Motor Repair Workshops is situated adjacent to G.H.Q., and is also dealt with under " Dockyards." Previous to completion, repairs to motors were nearly all effected by the

River-head Floating Workshop, P.S. 34 at Baghdad.
June 10th, 1917

Building marked with X. I.W.T. Offices, Baghdad.
October 15th, 1918

floating workshop *Ngawun*. A school for instructing locally engaged motor-boat drivers was instituted in connection with this establishment.

Native Craft Depot, Karradah.—This was opened in March, 1917, shortly after the occupation of Baghdad. The staff then consisted of one B.O., and three B.O.R.'s, and the fleet of thirty vessels, all of the latter having been commandeered in the Baghdad area. This fleet was considerably augmented by the arrival of the Mat Convoy, consisting of sixty-one mahailas, from Basrah in May, 1917, and which brought with it 534 tons of coal and 1824 tons of mats and general stores.

Native craft were principally employed in this area ferrying supplies up-stream to Sindiyah, Khan Jadidah, Chaldari, Es Salek and Kazimain, and down-stream to Ctesiphon, Bustan, and Azizieh. A regular service of small native craft was also maintained on the Diala during such times as the draft of water permitted.

A Mahaila Repair Yard was opened in June, 1917, and largely extended in August, 1918, a sailmaking loft being then included in this establishment.

This was also the main depot for the storage and repair of buoyage craft working in the Baghdad area.

At the end of 1917 the fleet of native craft had increased to :

66 mahailas,
45 Baghdad dinghies, and
65 goofahs.

The tonnage handled by native craft, over the periods mentioned, was as follows :

From March, 1917, to December 31st, 1917 . 37,555 tons
,, December 31st, 1917, to November 11th, 1918 . . . . . . 81,892 ,,

The personnel of the establishment at the conclusion of hostilities consisted of :

B.O.'s . . . 2
B.O.R.'s . . . 17
Eastern races . . 60

These are included in the return shown on page 159.

Zeur.—An I.W.T. Station was established at Azizieh during the advance. In February, 1918, this was removed some twenty-six miles up-stream to Zeur, which offered a more central and convenient site as an oiling station. A fuel oil-tank of 220 tons capacity was erected there by the Construction Department and a pumping plant installed. Zeur was also a centre of activity of the Buoyage Department, more particularly during the low-water season.

The staff maintained at Zeur is shown on page 159.

Tigris Stations above Baghdad.—Whilst the development of Baghdad and Advanced Base was proceeding, other stations were being opened up above Baghdad as the advance proceeded, but these were merely tentative organisations until the 26th May, 1917, when the first permanent station was opened at Khan Jadidah, where supplies for the troops operating in that area were discharged, and, as required, ferried to numerous small temporary posts beyond. This station was closed down, and the I.W.T. officer and his staff moved to Sadiyah on the 8th September, 1917. The principal work of the new station consisted of ferrying stores to Tuwair and Akab. Up to the end of 1917, 13,605 tons of stores, etc., had been discharged here, whilst 7253 tons had been reloaded and ferried to other posts. The vessels employed on this service were small stern-wheelers, though during the high river tugs of the *Sumana* class and quarter-wheelers of the S.40 class were occasionally used. During the Samarra advance vessels of the P.S. 50 class ascended to above Akab.

In March, 1918, a ferry across the Tigris at Samarra was established with a *Sumana* class tug and tractor barges. In April, 1918, and during the May advance, a large quantity of stores was ferried right up to Tekrit, without any previous survey of this part of the river having been made. The vessels employed, however, viz. S. 40, S. 2, and T.L. 10, had to be recalled at the end of May, owing to a falling river.

During the October and November advance, the steamers *Baghdad*, *Khalifa*, *Hamidieh*, and *Bahrinieh* were captured from the Turks at Shargat ; the two former were in fair condition, and a working party was sent up to put in hand the necessary repairs so that they could be floated down on the next high river. The two latter were so damaged that they were not considered worth salving. It was during this advance that a service of " killicks," or rafts, made of inflated skins, was instituted by the I.W.T. for the purpose of bringing sick and wounded down-river to Tekrit.

Both Sadiyah and Akab were closed down as I.W.T. stations at the end of October, 1918 ; from the end of 1917 to which date, 13,700 tons of stores had been landed at these places.

Diala Bridges.—1. The Boat Bridge at Diala mouth was taken over from the sappers and miners on the 15th September, 1917.

2. Cassels Post Bridge was taken over on the 18th December, 1917. This bridge was replaced by a bridge of peculiar and interesting construction, being made up of trestles, supported on goofahs in pairs. This bridge was, however, abolished soon after its completion in March, 1918.

3. Baqubah Bridge, forty-three miles above Diala mouth, was taken over on the 24th December, 1917. An I.W.T. officer was stationed here at the same time, for the purpose of controlling the traffic of native craft, which was then considerable.

The staff maintained on the Diala is shown below.

Personnel.—The staff maintained in the Baghdad section, excluding the Euphrates area, on the date specified consisted of :

Stations.	December 31st, 1917.			November 11th, 1918.		
	B.O.'s.	B.O.R.'s.	Eastern Races.	B'O.'s.	B.O.R.'s.	Eastern Races.
Baghdad:						
D.D.I.W.T.'s Office	3	11	18	4	13	17
I.W.T.O.'s Office	2	5	14	1	12	18
Bridges	3	33	194	3	15	101
Motor Repair Workshops	3	19	59	4	29	167
Construction Department	7	2	485	24	90	1288
Karradah Workshops	3	32	53	6	28	330
Native Craft Depot	3	11	24	2	17	60
Advanced Base	7	36	174	16	50	241
Hinaidi	3	2	36	4	5	33
Diala Stations	1	4	—	2	5	68
Tigris Stations above Baghdad	3	1	51	1	2	20
Zeur	—	—	—	1	2	24
Total	38	156	1108	68	268	2367

2. The Upper Euphrates Section

Shortly after the occupation of Baghdad, and with the purpose of securing the left flank of the force, an advance was made across the desert towards the Euphrates. This resulted in the capture of Feluja and the establishment of the Inland Water Transport at that place on April 23rd, 1917. A number of native craft of various kinds were found there, together with a steam barge of about 100 tons capacity ; this formed the nucleus of a fleet which was eventually destined to contribute materially to the success of future operations on the Euphrates.

With a view to utilising water communication via the Khirr-Saklawiyah Canals, which, leaving the Tigris just below Advanced Base, joins the Euphrates at a point some 18 miles above Feluja, a reconnaisance was made with a shallow-draught launch (T.L. 27) towing a bellum of some 12 tons capacity. They proved successful in reaching the Euphrates after encountering serious difficulty in navigating the shallow waters of the Akar-Kufa Lake, lying between the above-mentioned canals.

This route to the Euphrates was, however, never utilised, as it became necessary to rebuild the dam in the Saklawiyah Canal as a protection for the Baghdad-Samarra Railway during floods. This dam had been breached by the Turks in their retreat after evacuating Feluja. The work of rebuilding it was successfully accomplished by the Construction Department of the Inland Water Transport and was completed by the end of October.

It was found on examination that the steam barge captured at Feluja required extensive overhaul before she could be used. This left the force entirely dependent for river transport on such native craft as were available with the exception of the one towing launch. These were principally engaged at first in collecting country produce and in transporting supplies to small detachments posted above Feluja. In July, 1917, they proved of great value in the advance on Ramadie when they accompanied the force to a point some 26 miles above Feluja, supplying the road transport as required.

At this time the department of local resources requested assistance in the registration of native craft required for the collection and conveyance of produce in the Museyib, Hindiyah, and Hillah districts. For this purpose the Inland Water Transport opened an office at Hillah, and from information gathered, as a result of enquiries, it was found that large numbers of native craft of all sizes were trading on the Hindiyah and Hillah branches of the Euphrates and would be available for Government purposes if required. Some thirty of these craft were selected immediately and taken on the strength of the fleet under I.W.T. control. They were at first employed in carrying material for rebuilding the Saklawiyah bund from Mufraz, but the results attained were so satisfactory that in August it was decided to supply the force at Feluja by utilising this route in connection with the light railway from Advanced Base, thus obviating the difficulties of mechanical transport across the desert.

The utilisation of native craft for military purposes on the Euphrates was now becoming more general, and in addition to the delivery of supplies and stores from Baghdad at Feluja via Mufraz, large quantities of grain, fodder, and wood were being collected from the Museyib, Hindiyah, and Hillah districts. This traffic was at first handled entirely by the department of local resources, but as demands increased it became evident that a more effective system of control was necessary. It was, therefore, handed over to the Inland Water Transport, and representatives of this department were stationed at Museyib and Hindiyah Barrage in September. Preparations were then being made for the advance on Ramadie, more craft being commandeered for this purpose and taken on the strength of the fleet. The tonnage requirements of Feluja at the time amounted to 50 tons per day, and no difficulty was experienced in dealing with this quantity in addition to the other demands from Mufraz. As the force moved forward from

T. 63 on truck at Khirs Railway Depot. Advanced Base, Baghdad for transportation to Euphrates.

April, 1918

I.W.T. Station, Zeur.

October 21st, 1918

Feluja the 50 tons daily was diverted on to Madhij, which now became river-head, thus causing an extension of the line and consequent additional strain on the fleet. Ramadie was captured on September 28th, and the mileage to be operated had again increased.

The fleet was now augmented by two steam launches, two gun barges, and six bellums, the latter of an average capacity of 25 tons each, captured here. Both the launches and barges had been sunk by the Turks, but were successfully salved and sent to Mufraz to refit. The same salvage party also succeeded in raising a 4·2 gun here. By December 21st a broad gauge railway had been completed to Feluja, which eliminated the necessity of transport via Mufraz. The tonnage handled to the end of 1917 was as follows :—

By native craft under I.W.T. control .   . 14,116 tons
  ,, steam craft . . . .   317 ,,

The fleet of native craft at this time comprised 162 vessels of a total carrying capacity of 2028 tons. Steam craft included the towing launch (T.L. 27) previously referred to, one steam barge captured at Feluja (renamed S.B. 13) and the two launches captured at Ramadie (renamed L. 101 and L. 104). Control had gradually been extended and I.W.T. Stations were now open at Hillah, Mufraz Feluja, Hindiyah Barrage, Kufa, Museyib, Madhij, and Ramadie, the fleet being organised on definite runs between these places.

Early in 1918 preparations were being made for a further advance up the Euphrates, and in this connection, it was decided to establish a new loading base at Dhibban, some 17 miles above Feluja, and also to extend the railway to this point. All available native craft were ordered up from Museyib and below, but there was still a serious shortage of self-propelled craft for transport purposes. Several Red Cross motor launches had already been loaded on to railway trucks at Baghdad and railed across to Feluja for work between that place and Ramadie. The same method was, therefore, adopted with larger craft which were dismantled at Karradah workshops, the hulls being placed on a cradle resting on two railway trucks and the engines and boilers on two more ; they were then railed over, launched and refitted at Feluja, where a workshop had now been erected. Several 30-ton barges were also taken over in this manner. By the end of February, military requirements had increased to 175 tons per day to Ramadie, which still further increased in March to 240 tons per day, a considerable amount of which had to be diverted onwards as the troops advanced. The steady arrival of additional steam craft from Baghdad and more native craft from Museyib enabled all demands to be dealt with satisfactorily.

Whilst these operations were proceeding, a further call was made upon river transport as owing to the murder of a political officer at Nejef and unrest amongst the Arabs in that district, a brigade had to be despatched there, and native craft were called upon to provide the transport necessary to maintain it. Meanwhile, officers of the Buoyage Department, who had been surveying and buoying the river between Feluja and Ramadie, followed the advance and marked the channel as far as Khan Baghdadi, greatly facilitating the passage of craft of all kinds. Some 12 miles above Khan Baghdadi another gun barge and a motor launch of German make were captured and added to the fleet.

The farthest point to which regular river transport extended was Sahaliyah, some 16 miles beyond Hit. A number of specially selected native craft with double crews were employed ferrying supplies to this point, the difficulties of navigation rendering the use of self-propelled craft prohibitive on this section.

Tonnage.—By the end of March, when operations had temporarily ceased, the fleet on the Upper Euphrates consisted of 1 steam tug, 1 steam barge, 6 steam launches, and 12 " E Class " barges, representing a tonnage of about 360 tons, and 300 native craft representing a total carrying capacity of about 2700 tons. During the quarter ending March 31st, 7382 tons had been carried by the steam fleet and nearly 22,000 tons by native craft.

Personnel.—The staff maintained on this section at the end of March consisted of :—

B.O.'s	.	.	.	18
B.O.R.'s.	.	.	.	56
*Eastern races		.	.	180

Reorganisation.—The Inland Water Transport on the Euphrates had now expanded to such an extent and so many new stations had been opened both above Feluja and below Museyib, that it was decided to divide the section north of Shenafiyah, which had been known up to this time as the Upper Euphrates, into two sections, for the purpose of better administration. The Upper Section still retained the same name and extended from above Museyib northwards, whilst that portion lying between but including Museyib and Shenafiyah was named the Middle Euphrates. This change came into operation on the 6th April, 1918, and a Deputy Assistant Director was appointed to control each section, under the Deputy Director, Baghdad.

It will now be convenient to consider these sections separately, and it is proposed to deal first with the Upper Euphrates. Ten " Fly " Class gunboats, with their guns removed and converted to ordinary towing vessels, had been despatched from Basrah to the Upper Euphrates earlier in the year in order to enable as many native craft as possible to be released from this section and transferred to the Middle Euphrates, where a large fleet was being concentrated in readiness for the collection of the 1918 harvest, which, it was estimated, would be an exceptionally heavy one. These vessels after a lengthy and adventurous voyage were successfully navigated across Hamar and Shenafiyah Lakes, through the Hindiyah Barrage to Dhibban. With them arrived the floating repair workshop *Vulcan*, which permitted the workshop at Feluja to be closed down. In addition, more steam launches and small barges were railed across from Baghdad with a view to releasing all native craft possible for harvest work on the Middle Euphrates.

---

* Exclusive of crews of native craft.

The " E Class " tugs, though they arrived after completion of the Hit-Khan Bagdhadi operations, proved very useful units, each vessel being capable of towing three " E Class " barges containing from 60 to 70 tons of supplies during the flood season, and four similar barges when the river became normal again, and making the round trip from Dhibban to Hit and back in three days. The return tonnage was fully utilised for the conveyance of captured ordnance, stores, and lime. To provide for the fuel requirements of these vessels, bulk oil storage tanks were erected at Feluja, Dhibban, Ramadie, and Hit (see Appendix E1.)

A large number of shakturs had been captured during the above operations ; a number of these were placed at the disposal of the Department of Local Resources for work in the vicinity of Hit, whilst others were transferred to the Middle Euphrates, where they were principally used in the construction of floating bridges. As a means of transport they proved unsatisfactory.

Towards the end of April, Sahaliyah was closed down as an I.W.T. station, supplies being no longer required there, and the headquarters of the section was moved to Ramadie in order to be in closer touch with Divisional Headquarters.

By the end of June military requirements had so considerably reduced that it was possible to transfer 227 native craft to the Middle Euphrates.

In July the export of lime from Hit was largely increased owing to extensive irrigation works in progress, but as a further reduction in military requirements took place no difficulty was experienced in meeting all demands, and by the end of August 47 more native craft had been released. Abu Ryatt and Ugbah were closed down as I.W.T. stations about this time ; the remaining stations left open on this section then being Feluja, Dhibban, Madhij, Ramadie, and Hit.

Bridges.—The floating bridges at Dhibban and Ramadie were taken over, controlled, and maintained by the Inland Water Transport.

Tonnage.—From the date on which this section was divided up (April 6th, 1918) to the conclusion of hostilities, the tonnage handled was as follows :—

	Tons.	Corresponding ton mileage.
By steam craft	33,849	1,675,723
„ native craft	21,234	1,018,415
	55,083	2,694,138

In addition, 9492 troops and followers had been carried.

Personnel.—The staff of this section at the conclusion of hostilities consisted of :—

B.O.'s	24
B.O.R.'s	78
*Eastern races	684

3. THE MIDDLE EUPHRATES SECTION

Transport.—In preparation for the anticipated harvest of 1918 from this area, large numbers of native craft had been concentrated here to provide for its collection. In this connection it had been estimated that provision would have to be made to transport some 240,000 tons of produce. It therefore became necessary to augment the establishment, and an A.D.I.W.T., with an adequate staff was stationed at Hillah in May, 1918. Three new I.W.T. stations on the Hindiyah branch and six on the Hillah branch were opened almost immediately, and a stringent control of all craft operating in this area was established.

At this time the total tonnage of native craft available on this section amounted to about 3500 tons, the craft varying in size from 1 to 60 tons capacity. A large convoy of bellums despatched from Basrah, including 17 motor-driven bellums, brought the available tonnage up to 5500 tons. A motor repair workshop was established at Hillah and native craft repair yards opened at Hillah, Kufa, and Museyib. Shipment of the harvest was to have commenced in May when river conditions provided sufficient water to

* Exclusive of crews of native craft.

L

float the larger bellums loaded to their full capacity, but owing to defective road transport and the incomplete organisation of the Department of Local Resources, river transport preparations were not taken full advantage of, for, by the end of June, only 7392 tons had been shipped. Progress was then somewhat accelerated and by the beginning of August the average weekly tonnage shipped amounted to 2516 tons. Meanwhile, the fleet capacity had risen to 9150 tons, having been steadily augmented by additional craft from the Tigris. By the end of August, collecting facilities having somewhat improved, the weekly tonnage shipped had increased to 4065 tons. River restrictions necessitated by the course of irrigation development now began to be felt, considerably retarding the full use of available tonnage. Due to rotation at the Barrage the larger bellums could only be used during 14 days of each month, whilst the draught of even the smaller ones was restricted. Had shipments commenced in May a very much greater tonnage could have been handled had it been available.

In September the utility of the larger native craft sent from Basrah became doubtful. Working in shoal water and in narrow channels, casualties were of frequent occurrence, and out of a total fleet strength of 703 bellums no less than 112 were simultaneously under repair at the various dockyards. The locally owned craft of a build and size adapted to conditions were found to be more efficient. The steady decrease in tonnage, which now became perceptible, was partly due to these causes and partly due to the amount of bulk bhoosa shipped instead of grain which was not forthcoming. Shipments of even this commodity also fell off, resulting in much loss of tonnage. A resumption of grain purchases later, however, gave the highest tonnage figures yet attained in the week ending October 12th, 1918, when shipments amounted to 4771 tons. This was merely a temporary improvement, and at no time afterwards was it exceeded or even equalled. With the cessation of hostilities it was decided to curtail further attempts to purchase grain, and transport work was in consequence reduced as the various stations were cleared. Arrangements were, therefore, made to reduce the fleet and return vessels not needed to their owners, the establishment being also reduced in accordance.

Tonnage.—From the date on which the Middle Euphrates had been opened as a separate section up to the conclusion of hostilities, the tonnage handled was as follows :—

	Tons.	Corresponding tons mileage.
Native craft . .	72,979	2,065,661

Less than 50,000 tons of grain were actually collected in the Euphrates Area, and as the I.W.T. had been instructed to prepare for a possible 240,000 tons and had done so, it is evident that their personnel and craft were by no means fully employed, and the cost of collecting the grain was proportionately high.

Oil Distribution.—When order amongst the Arab tribes in this area had been once thoroughly established, every encouragement was given by the political department to the extension of cultivation, and facilities were given for renewal of the irrigation appliances which had been damaged by the enemy. In this connection a scheme of oil distribution was inaugurated, which was placed in the hands of the Inland Water Transport. Bulk storage for kerosene was installed at Hillah, Dewaniyah, and Kufa (see Appendix E1), the supply being maintained at these places by the I.W.T., and the actual retailing being done by the political.

Bridges.—Floating bridges were opened and maintained by the I.W.T. in this section at Hillah, Dewaniyah, Afaj, Rumetha, Kufa, Abbasiyah, Tuerij, and Museyib.

Personnel.—The staff maintained on this section at the conclusion of hostilities consisted of :—

B.O.'s	24
B.O.R.'s . . .	102
Eastern races . .	474

Summary.—The following table shows the tonnage carried and corresponding ton mileage on the Upper and Middle Euphrates before and after the sections were divided and between March, 1917, and November, 1918 :—

	NATIVE CRAFT.		STEAM CRAFT.	
	Tons.	Ton Miles.	Tons.	Ton Miles.
UPPER EUPHRATES :				
Before division .	35,610·75	1,604,576·5	7,995·75	67,025·5
After division .	21,234	1,018,416·25	33,848·75	1,675,723
MIDDLE EUPHRATES	69,000·75	1,879,722	Nil	Nil
Total. .	125,845·5	4,502,713·75	41,844·5	1,744,748·5

	Tons.	Tons Miles.
Total native craft	125,845·5	4,502,713·75
Total steam craft	41,844·5	1,744,748·5
	167,690	6,247,462·25
In addition carried on merchants' account	5,649·5	262,947
Grand total .	173,339	6,510,409·25

The strength and composition of the fleet on the Euphrates at the conclusion of hostilities is shown in Appendix B5.

AMARA SECTION

A MARINE Transport Office was established at Amara immediately following the British occupation of that place in June, 1915. The station developed as necessity demanded, and in October, 1915, a small workshop was established on the right bank capable of carrying out light running repairs to vessels passing through.

In December, 1915, Amara was made Advanced Base for the relieving force concentrated at Ali Gharbi for the relief of Kut, thus becoming an important shipping and fuelling station. The small workshop was inadequate to cope with the increasing amount of work required. A larger one was therefore erected on an adjoining site. It was at this shop that the *Julnar* was fitted out previous to her ill-fated endeavour to carry supplies to Kut. After the fall of Kut, large numbers of troops were recalled to Amara for rest and training during the hot weather, which thus gradually grew in importance. Towards the end of the summer, 1916, preparations were being made for a renewed offensive towards Kut, and all these troops, plus reinforcements, stores, transport, etc., had to be taken back to river-head. About the same time the Kurna-Amara Railway was commenced, and it became necessary to have a portion of the fleet based on Amara. These events coincided with the assumption of control of river transport by the Inland Water Transport, and one of the first things done was to effect a concentration of the various departments included within the Directorate, which had up to that time been scattered at various points up and down the river in the vicinity of Amara. The present site was selected and the erection of quarters, offices, workshops, stores, etc., commenced, finally resulting in the establishment of a compact,

149

self-contained, well-equipped, and thoroughly up-to-date station. The progress made may be gauged by the following figures regarding the number of ships passing through and tonnage handled :—

(a) In 1916 vessels passing through averaged 180 per month.
,, 1917   ,,   ,,   ,,   ,,   325   ,,
,, 1918   ,,   ,,   ,,   ,,   370   ,,
(b) In 1916 an average of   8,936 tons was handled
,, 1917 ,,   ,,   ,,   32,670 ,,   ,,   ,, [monthly.
,, 1918 ,,   ,,   ,, nearly 50,000 ,,   ,,   ,,   ,,

By tonnage handled is meant tonnage despatched up-stream and down-stream in Amara based vessels and barges.

Fleet.—In 1916 only a few vessels were based on Amara, such as P.S. 1, 2, 21, and a few tugs and barges, the remainder of the fleet being on the Basrah-Sheikh Sa'ad run, only calling at Amara to disembark troops and stores on the upward voyage and sick on the downward voyage. In 1917 this fleet was increased to approximately 25 towing vessels and 70 barges. The vessels included such of the P.S. 90 class as were then in the country, P.S. 1–7, P.S. 16 class, P.S. 25 class, and several Sumana tugs. In 1918 the Amara fleet was again increased by additional vessels of the P.S. 90 class, and about twenty 225-feet barges, capable of carrying 700–800 tons D.W. each. A direct service from Amara to Kut was inaugurated with these craft, resulting in an average of 1500 tons being shipped daily over considerable periods.

Coal.—The average monthly stock balance of coal maintained at Amara was :

During 1916   .   .   717 tons.
   ,,   1917   .   .   1610 ,,
   ,,   1918   .   .   2219 ,,

The average number of vessels bunkered per month was :

During 1916   .   .   .   90
   ,,   1917   .   .   .   165
   ,,   1918   .   .   .   200

Amara I.W.T. Offices and Officers' Quarters. To the left is the new Lookout and
Signal Tower.

March 27th, 1919

Birdseye view of port of Amara taken from the top of lookout tower.
March 27th, 1919

Oil Fuel.—Two steel tanks, one of 1000 tons capacity and a second one of 400 tons capacity, were erected for the storage of oil fuel between December, 1916, and June, 1917. In addition an elevated steel tank of 50 tons capacity was erected for the use of the railways. These tanks, though separated by some distance, were all connected and could be filled from the same source.

The average monthly stock balance of oil fuel carried was :

During 1916	.	.	224 tons.
„ 1917	.	.	523 „
„ 1918	.	.	1068 „

The average number of vessels oiled per month was :

During 1916	.	.	.	26
„ 1917	.	.	.	97
„ 1918	.	.	.	130

Works.—Amongst the more important works carried out by the Construction Department at Amara since September, 1916, are :—

  The Amara Bridge,
  The signal tower for the control of shipping,
  The I.W.T. Headquarters building,
  The workshops and numerous piers, jetties, etc.

The Conservancy Department have carried out a large amount of reclamation, dredging, revetting, and constructing dams and training walls across effluents of the Tigris in the vicinity of Amara. These are more fully dealt with under departmental headings.

Out-Stations.—Ali Gharbi is situated about half-way between Amara and Kut and has been in use as a fuelling station since December, 1915. It was the Advanced Shipping Base and final port of destination for all vessels up to January, 1916. It still retained considerable importance as a fuelling station after the recapture of Kut, and was also a centre of activity of the Buoyage Department. An average stock of about 200 tons of coal was maintained, and a fuel oil barge was also stationed there. The staff on the dates indicated consisted of :

	Dec., 1916.	Dec. 31st, 1917.	Nov. 11th, 1918.
B.O.'s	4	3	4
B.O.R.'s . . .	7	13	5
Eastern races . .	35	55	69

Personnel.—The I.W.T. staff at Amara on the dates indicated was as follows :

	Dec. 31st, 1916.	Dec. 31st, 1917.	Nov. 11th, 1918.
B.O.'s	11	27	27
W.O.'s	2	5	—
B.O.R.'s and B.W.I.'s .	36	114	141
Eastern races . .	205	554	840

E. Class Barge on truck at Khirs Railway Depot, Advanced Base, Baghdad, for transportation to Euphrates.

April, 1918

Section of Cylindrical Oil Tank on Railway Truck.

KUT SECTION

KUT has played a prominent part from an early date in the history of the Mesopotamian campaign, but it is only proposed to deal in this record with events subsequent to its recapture by General Maude in February, 1917, shortly after which date the Inland Water Transport became established there. Its situation rendered it a point of peculiar importance to river transport, and early steps were taken to select a site for a port in the vicinity. Kut town itself was not considered suitable either from a marine or a medical point of view, neither was there the necessary space available for the establishment of a supply depot on a large scale, as had been decided upon. Two sites were proposed in the first place, one at Shumran, 8 miles above Kut town, and the other on the present site. The first one was rejected owing to the presence of a shoal which it was anticipated would cause difficulty to navigation in the low-water season. Nor was this anticipation wrong, there having been only 3 feet of water on this shoal (Kut-Saba crossing) in August, 1918. The present site, which is situated about 4 miles below Kut town, extends for a distance of 1½ miles along the left bank, and besides providing ample water for berthing and mooring vessels, also offers every facility for the loading or discharging of vessels and barges at any state of the river. In support of the advantages of Kut as a port it may be remarked that during August, 1918, when shipping was held up owing to a block on the Kut-Saba crossing, there were 37 vessels and 83 barges in port at one time, without causing serious congestion.

Amara-Kut Ferry.—Shortly after the occupation of Baghdad, and owing to the uncertain nature of the river between Kut and that place, it was decided to construct a railway as an alternative route. Very large quantities of railway material had therefore to be brought up-river for this purpose and landed at Kut, in addition to military stores of every description. On the completion of this railway at the end of July, 1917, Kut became an important transhipping station, and a regular ferry service to Amara was instituted, the vessels principally employed on this run being the P.S. 90 class towing two 225-feet barges. The tonnage handled by this ferry service soon assumed very large proportions, an average of nearly 1500 tons per day being dealt with throughout 1918.

Workshop.—As early as December, 1915, a complete workshop had been ordered in India in anticipation of the recapture of Kut. This machinery and shedding had been stored at Amara, where a certain quantity of it had been temporarily put into use. The new workshop at Amara being completed about this time, some of the machinery from the old shop was transferred to Kut in addition to the above. This has been added to as circumstances permitted, and eventually a most efficient and complete workshop came into being at Kut. This is more fully dealt with under dockyards.

Fleet.—During the low-water season a certain portion of the fleet of suitable draught was based on Kut to tow on barges which had been brought from the Base and Amara by deeper draught vessels. As the railway could never handle more than about 800 tons per day, any balance remaining above this had to be sent up by river. Washouts on this railway were of fairly frequent occurrence during the high river which threw all the work on to the river transport, until such time as repairs could be effected.

A number of hospital ships in accordance with medical requirements were also based on Kut.

Coal.—The coal dump at Kut assumed larger proportions than that at any other station on the river, excepting at the Base, there being at one time, in September, 1918, over 7000 tons of coal in stock. The majority of the coal demanded by railways for the forward area was handled here ;

this sometimes amounted to as much as 2500 tons per month. In all, an average of 4500 tons of coal was handled monthly.

Oil.—Previous to the erection of bulk storage tanks, a 1000-ton oil barge belonging to the A.P.O.C. was utilised here, but in March, 1918, six 220-ton tanks were completed and a pumping plant installed. These had originally been intended for water tanks, but they were successfully adapted to this new purpose. About 2000 tons of oil fuel were handled monthly.

Stocks of petrol and kerosene were also maintained.

Accidents and Groundings.—Records show that a very large proportion of groundings have taken place in the Kut Area. These have all been dealt with by the Buoyage Department in a highly creditable manner. A diving unit is maintained here which has proved invaluable, notably in the cases of P.A. 5 and P.S. 90, both of which were badly holed and in danger of foundering, and both of which vessels were successfully salved.

Bridges.—The bridge from Sheikh Sa'ad was brought up to Kut in February, 1918. This bridge was in the low water, the only means of communication with Hai. In April, 1918, the S.S. *Blosse Lynch* collided with the bridge causing damage to the extent of Rs.50,000. Apart from this one incident the bridge has been " broken " and " made " during even the highest floods without accident.

Out-Stations.—*Sheikh Sa'ad.*—Up to time of the advance this was the principal I.W.T. station in the Forward Area. At that time there was a small workshop also P.S. 34 together with an establishment of 6 B.O.'s and about 500 men. It included in addition a coal and oil fuel depot. As Kut developed Sheikh Sa'ad declined in importance and was finally evacuated as an I.W.T. station in March, 1918.

Arab Village—known as River Head—was a subsidiary port to Sheikh Sa'ad during the period preceding the advance. A small I.W.T. staff was maintained there, also coal and oil fuel dumps. It was evacuated in April, 1917.

Baghaila.—An I.W.T. officer was established here during the advance, but in February, 1918, this post was moved to

Sumar, 7 miles up-river. Sumar is used as a coaling and oiling station, and is also a depot for Buoyage stores. The *Ngawum*, a floating motor-boat repair shop, is stationed here.

The Hai River is open to navigation from January to June, and light-draught steamers can then proceed as far as Qualet-Sikker. Considerable quantities of grain have been brought to Kut during the high-water season by vessels of the I.W.T. fleet.

Summary.—At the conclusion of hostilities Kut was in every way a most efficiently equipped port, possessing amongst it more prominent features.

1. Repair workshops complete with foundry, moulding sheds, carpenter's shop, and electric light plant, employing over 200 men of all trades.

2. Quarters and offices built by the Construction Department of a special type, considered most suitable for Mesopotamia. The Construction Department alone employed over 200 men here, principally of the building trades.

3. A mahaila slipway, with a slipway capable of taking the largest mahaila on the river. About 40 men, mostly Arab caulkers and carpenters, were employed in this connection.

4. A floating bridge with a crew of about 100 men, which contained sixty-four (64) native boats, and was capable of carrying vehicles up to $3\frac{1}{2}$ tons.

5. A camp with 30 huts capable of accommodating 1000 men.

6. An Accounts Department handling approximately Rs.100,000 per month.

7. A coal and oil fuel depot handling roughtly 4500 tons of coal and 2000 tons of fuel oil monthly.

8. A fully equipped stores department.

Personnel.—The staff of the section on the dates indicated consisted of :

B.O.'s .	.	15	21
B.O.R.'s	.	40	55
Eastern races		1200	850

THE NARROWS SECTION

A SYSTEM of control in the Narrows was instituted in March, 1916, and extended from the Northern Station below Qualet Saleh to South Station. The personnel then consisted of 2 British officers, 1 gunner, and 19 Indian other ranks.

In February, 1917, the control was extended to Chumaijah Shargiy or New Station (Southern Entrance), and to Michyria Canal. Shortly afterwards three new reporting stations were added between Michyria and Amara, viz. Lower, Sayazid, and Majar Kebir, with two British other ranks at each, the three stations being under the officer in charge of local buoyage duties. This was known as the " Narrows Extension."

The Inland Water Transport Station at Ezra's Tomb was included in control in December, 1917, when it was extended to, but not including, Kurna, the whole distance from Majar Kebir being known as the " Narrows Section."

System of Control.—All shipping is controlled from Central Station. There is a mast at each station each fitted with a crossyard and semaphore arm. Vessels in the Narrows are always in sight of two of these masts. Movements of downward bound vessels are controlled by the signals of the station ahead of them, upward bound vessels conform to the movements of the former. Suitable banking-in stations are marked by mooring posts painted with black and white horizontal stripes. Downward bound vessels are given the right of way except in special cases, and upward bound vessels bank in to allow them to pass.

Owing to continual looting by Marsh Arabs from vessels banked in for the night, " banking-in " boards were erected in suitable reaches at which Shebana Guards were posted, and the Sheikh of the district was held responsible for loss of property.

Control regulations do not apply to launches, motorboats, or small craft.

There are in all ten stations throughout the control system, two B.O.R.'s being in charge of each. These pass information concerning all shipping through to the Central Control. In this way information of any grounding or breakdown is received practically as soon as it occurs.

Pilotage.—A pilot service was instituted in February, 1917, ten qualified Arab pilots being employed until September, 1917, when they were relieved by non-commissioned officers and sappers who had been trained in this section. In further advancement of this scheme a British Officer Pilot Service for both upward and downward-bound vessels was instituted in June, 1918, which proved a great success, in that delays were reduced to a minimum.

Telephones.—In March, 1916, a single wire local telephone system was installed in the control. This system was gradually improved and extended, all outlying stations being kept in touch with Central Control. In December, 1917, a regular exchange was installed at Central Station, and at the same time an overhead wire was erected across the river, to replace the submarine cable, which had been a constant source of trouble. These wires were carried on lattice-work masts, and allowed a clearance of 90 feet for traffic.

In January, 1918, the trunk line from Basrah to Amara was brought into the exchange at Central Station.

All local wires are maintained by personnel of the section.

Lighting System.—As the number of vessels on the river increased it was found impossible to pass all of them through the Narrows during the daytime on account of the delays due to banking in to pass one another. It was therefore decided to light the worst bends and use the Narrows by night for the passage of upward-bound ships as they could easily clear the controlled section before daylight, and leave a practically clear run during daytime for downward-bound vessels.

The erection of the existing system was commenced in March, 1917, and actually commenced running on May 1st of the same year, all extension work being completed by May 18th. Five lighting sets were installed in the vicinity of the worst bends, viz. at South Station, Hadama Bend, Central Station, North Station, and Qualet Saleh. Mosquito Corner, Abu Tamir, and Hadama Bends were subsequently supplied with current from Central Station, as the power house and lighting set from Hadama Bend was removed to Abu Raba. From South Station the line was extended southwards to the right bank, two 112-feet lattice-work masts being employed to carry the wires across the river at this point.

At Qualet Saleh, in addition to river lighting, current was supplied for fans and lighting in the hospital and political buildings, the wiring and fitting of them being carried out by the Inland Water Transport Department. An additional lighting set was installed here in July, 1918, as one was found to be insufficient to meet requirements.

In the same month a lighting set was installed at Ezra's Tomb to supply current for fans and lighting purposes in the pilot's bungalow there.

A portable lighting set, erected on a pontoon, has been employed at out-stations, wherever it was necessary to remove any of the lighting sets for overhaul.

All lighting sets are periodically dismantled and brought to the workshops for renewals of bearings and complete overhaul.

The lighting system has proved invaluable as an aid to navigation, particularly during the low-water season, as upward-bound vessels entering the Narrows at night cleared them well before daylight, and thus avoided the delays they would otherwise have incurred, whilst awaiting downward-bound vessels, in the daytime.

In view of the considerable amount of Government property stolen from Central Station by Arab thieves a searchlight was erected on the roof of the officers' quarters with excellent results.

Central Station Workshop.—The workshop at Central Station was commenced in November, 1917, and was in use in January, 1918, being fully completed in March of that year. It was erected for the purpose of maintaining the lighting system, and for the upkeep of both motor and steam launches belonging to the section.

In addition, a considerable amount of work was undertaken at various times for river craft, thus minimising delays where otherwise these vessels would have had to be towed to either Basrah or Amara to effect repairs.

Ezra's Tomb.—The Inland Water Transport Station and oil tank at Ezra's Tomb were commenced in January, 1917, and completed in June of that year. It was the farthest point to which deep-draught tugs could ascend in the low-water season, and here their barges were transferred to tugs suitable for navigating the Narrows. It was also intended as an oiling station for such craft as had not sufficient bunker capacity to carry them through to Amara. The upkeep and maintenance of the pumping plant and tank were carried out by personnel attached to this section.

Qualet Saleh.—The Lines of Communication cross the river at Qualet Saleh, the floating bridge at this point has been used as required both for military purposes and local traffic.

The following figures show the record amount of traffic which has passed over the bridge in any one month :—

All ranks	. . . .	6291
Gun wagons .	. . .	210
Guns .	. . . .	52
Horses, bullocks, camels	.	5958
Bullock wagons	. . .	403
Motor-cars .	. . .	76

In December, 1917.

Remarks.—All groundings, breakdowns, and buoyage duties in the Control, are attended to by a trained working party under the direction of an officer of the section.

Owing to the marshland and the river flooding its banks

between Ezra's Tomb and Kurna, it was found essential, for the safety of navigation, to mark the banks with bamboo poles. For this purpose two sappers and seven Lascars were employed to carry out the marking during the period from January to June of each year.

Accidents and Delays.—Among the most serious accidents and delays which have occurred in this section the following may be quoted :—

Accidents :—

20.3.1917. B. 4. Put over the bank below North Station by P.S. 53 downward bound. Finally dug out and refloated on the 25th March, 1917.

10.5.1917. A. 223. In tow of S.T. 16, loaded with 200 tons of coal and pontoons for the MacMunn Bridge at Amara. Sunk clear of the channel with her back broken in Jhamsha Reach. Fifty tons of coal were salved, and the pontoons towed to Amara. On September 14th, 1917, salvage operations were commenced, with the result that the barge and the remainder of the coal were salved. She was temporarily repaired and towed to Basrah on the 20th October, 1917.

9.11.1917. L. 92. Upward bound, capsized in Hair Pin Bend, and sunk in 52 feet of water. She was lifted on to the bank with the assistance of the *Pahlwan* and diving unit. Pumped out and towed to Basrah on the 29th November, 1917. No traffic delayed.

16.1.1918. B. 3. In tow of P.S. 60, downward bound. Put over the bank above Ezra's Tomb. Finally dug out and refloated on the 17th January, 1918.

14.2.1918. S.B. 4. Upward bound. Struck a submerged object below Lower Station, springing a bad leak. Cargo was discharged and she proceeded down. Temporarily repaired on the 16th February, 1918.

1.7.1918. A. 48. In tow of P.S. 28. Upward bound. Ran aground in Nahair Corner, causing her back to be broken. Cargo was discharged and she was towed down. Temporarily repaired on the 4th July, 1918.

M

3.11.1918. D. 292. In tow of P.S. 15, upward bound. Sunk clear of channel in Jhamsha Reach, badly holed through alleged striking of part of the *Marmaris*. Cargo salved and she was temporarily repaired and towed to Amara on the 12th November, 1918.

31.3.1919. P.S. 12. Upward bound above Micherya. Sunk by the head badly holed in forward hold. Alleged to have struck unknown object. She was temporarily repaired and proceeded down on the 2nd April, 1919.

Delays :—

16.8.1916. P.S. 2. Downward bound. Grounded badly in Lower Abu Muzaiyah, delaying all traffic for six days. Refloated and channel cleared on 22nd August, 1916.

30.1.1917. H.M.S. *Gnat*. Downward bound. Grounded badly below North Station, delaying all traffic for one day. Refloated and channel clear 31st January, 1917.

30.8.1917. P.S. 20. Downward bound. Grounded badly in Jhamsha Reach causing a silt to form across the river with a maximum depth of two feet. Personnel and loaded barges were transferred to downward-bound vessels and vice versa. Channel clear to all traffic on 3rd September, 1917.

2.1.1918. B. 108. In tow of P.S. 3. Upward bound. Was run badly aground below Central Station. She was refloated after lightening cargo on the 4th January, 1918.

3.2.1918. S.T. 19. Downward bound. Grounded badly in Majar Crossing, delaying all traffic for two days. Refloated and channel clear on 5th February, 1918.

23.2.1919. P.S. 54. Upward bound. Ran over the bank in Hair Pin Bend. Refloated and proceeded up undamaged on the 25th February, 1919.

In all cases the salvage parties were from the personnel of this section.

Shipping Records.—The greatest number of vessels passing through the Narrows in any one month was :

Vessels .	.	362 (July, 1918).
Mahailas .	.	270 ,, ,,

By night :—

    Vessels . . 171 (March, 1918).

Establishment.—For year ending 31st December, 1916 :—

British officers	4
British other ranks . . .	12
Indian other ranks . . .	44

For year ending 31st December, 1917 :—

British officers	9
British other ranks . . .	49
Indian other ranks . . .	314

At the end of hostilities :—

British officers	20
British other ranks . . .	52
Indian other ranks . . .	235

LOWER EUPHRATES SECTION

THE section was opened on January 1st, 1918, previous to which date there had been an Inland Water Transport officer at Nasariyah only since the occupation of that town by the British in 1915.

It extends from, but excluding, Kurna to Shenafiyah on the Euphrates, a total distance of about 270 miles.

This section was organised in anticipation of developments which did not subsequently take place.

Nasariyah is the headquarters of the Deputy Assistant Director of Inland Water Transport of this section. The original offices and quarters were situated in the town, but as expansion took place they were found to be quite inadequate for the efficient running of the station and section. Accordingly new offices and quarters were built at Khandaq Wharf on the opposite bank, and above the town, and were completed in August, 1918.

Fuel oil, kerosene, petrol, and stores depots were also opened to supply the whole section, whilst a railway siding was put in for convenience in handling cargo and stores for shipment up-river.

The workshops were erected in the town shortly after the occupation in 1915, and have been maintained there ever since.

Darraji was opened as an Inland Water Transport station in January, 1918, and used as a transhipping station for cargo from steamers into native craft during the low-water period, January to March, to maintain communication with Samawa and Shenafiyah. It was abolished as a transhipping station in April and converted into a subsidiary station under a non-commissioned officer, and abolished entirely as an I.W.T. post on April 1st, 1919.

Samawa was opened as an Inland Water Transport post in January, 1918, and became the principal station on the section after Nasariyah. Permanent quarters were erected for the staff in March, and fuel oil and kerosene storage tanks installed for the supply of shipping and the supply and transport depot.

Shenafiyah was opened as an Inland Water Transport station in January and administered by an officer until the withdrawal of the garrison in June, when the post was reduced to a non-commissioned officer for the maintenance working in Shenafiyah Lake.

Hamar Lake.—A dredged cut channel with a mean depth of 8 feet was completed through the lake on 29th January, 1919, making through navigation possible from the Tigris to Shenafiyah Lake.

Shenafiyah Lake.—A temporary shallow navigable channel was made through this lake at the end of 1918, but the abandonment of the work combined with the abnormal rise of the river in February, 1919, resulted in the destruction of the containing bunds, and caused the silting up of all the channels.

In April, 1918, a flotilla consisting of 10 " Fly " class steamers, 2 stern-wheelers, 6 motor bellums, 4 barges, and 131 native craft, were with great difficulty passed across the lake for work in connection with military operations on the Upper Euphrates.

Remarks.—Between Nasiriyah and Shenafiyah the river, as a navigable fairway, during the low-water period is controlled entirely by the opening and closing of the Hindiyah Barrage. When the Barrage has been closed for some days, only the shallowest draught vessels can navigate the river, the least depth of water on some of the bars being as low as 2 feet between Darraji and Samawa, near which place five bad bars exist.

Personnel.—The strength of the personnel employed of this section was on the dates specified :

	British officers.	British other ranks.	Eastern races.
Dec. 31st, 1917 . .	4	17	162
Nov. 11th, 1918 . .	24	74	676

Fleet.—The strength of the fleet based on this section was on the dates specified :

	Steam vessels.	Motor boats.	Barges.
Dec. 31st, 1917 . .	3	9	3
Nov. 11th, 1918 . .	10	22	14

Tonnage.—The tonnage handled by this department during the period under review is as follows :—

			Total tonnage.
In the quarter ending	March 31st, 1918	.	2,600 tons.
,,	,, June 30th, 1918	.	4,581 ,,
,,	,, Sept. 30th, 1918	.	5,760 ,,
,,	,, Dec, 31st, 1918	.	6,992 ,,
	Total for the year 1918.		19,933 ,,

PART III

THE FLEET

A SHORT description of some of the more important units comprising the River Fleet will be of interest here. For more complete details reference should be made to the *Inland Water Transport Fleet Register*, which is issued as a separate publication. The actual strength of the fleet in commission at various times is shown in Appendices B1, B2, B3, and B4. The following distinctive initial letters have been adopted to designate the various classes of vessels according to their respective types :—

Class.	Type.
S.S.	Sea-going vessels.
P.S.	Paddle steamers.
S.	Stern-wheelers.
S.B.	Steam barges.
M.L.	Motor lighters.
S.T.	Sea and harbour tugs.
P.T.	Paddle-tugs.
T.	Up-River tugs (screw).
M.T.	Motor-tugs.
F.	Converted gunboats.
FLY	Gunboats.
T.L.	Towing launches.
L.	Steam Launches.
P.A.	Ambulance paddlers.
H.P.	Hospital paddlers.
H.S.	Hospital stern-wheelers.
H.M.	Hospital screw motor vessels.
H.	Hospital screw steamers and steam launches.
M.	Motor-boats.
M.B.	Motor bellums.
H.G.	Hydro-Glisseurs.

Representative vessels selected from various classes are described below :

Barges.—Classes of barges are indicated according to their length by the following initial letters :—

A indicates length from 170 feet upwards.
B   ,,   ,,   ,,   140 ,,   (inclusive) to 170 feet.
C   ,,   ,,   ,,   100 ,,   ,,   ,, 140 ,,
D   ,,   ,,   ,,   75 ,,   ,,   ,, 100 ,,
E   ,,   ,,   ,,   50 ,,   ,,   ,, 75 ,,

Native Craft.—Classes of mahailas are indicated according to their tonnage by the following initial letters :—

A Class—50 tons and upwards.
B Class—35 ,,   to 49 tons.
C Class—25 ,,   ,, 34 ,,
D Class—12 ,,   ,, 24 ,,
E Class—under 12 tons.

Tonnage being estimated as capacity of cargo hold in cubic feet divided by forty, i.e. " freight tons."

The assembly of a River Fleet of such magnitude in Mesopotamia, collected as it had been from all parts of the world, capable of supplying such craft obviously presented extraordinary difficulties, and a few details concerning these and the methods by which they were eventually overcome will be of interest. In the earlier part of the campaign all vessels were obtained from India, Burma, the Malay States, and the Nile ; but as the needs of the Expeditionary Force increased and the resources of India became somewhat exhausted, it was necessary to place large orders for vessels in the United Kingdom. The problem of getting such fragile and unseaworthy craft to the scene of operations was attended with considerable risk and though at first many were lost, with their crews, *en route*, it will be seen by the statistics given below that these were reduced to a minimum as experience was gained.

It will be convenient to consider this subject under two headings, viz :

(1) Vessels obtained from India and places east of Suez.

(2) Vessels obtained from the United Kingdom and places west of Suez.

(1) TOWAGE OF CRAFT FROM INDIA

Towage operations from India and Burma during the whole period of the War were under the direction of the Royal Indian Marine, by whom, as many suitable towing vessels as possible were impressed for the work each year. In many cases, owing to a shortage of suitable towing craft, cargo vessels had to be impressed for these duties.

During the seasons 1914-15, 1915-16, 1916-17, the supervision of the preparation of the craft for despatch was entirely carried out by the Royal Indian Marine ; but in 1917, Inland Water Transport officers were stationed at Karachi and Bombay to supervise the construction and re-erection of craft sent out from the United Kingdom and Canada in plates and angles, after which date the preparation and fitting out of craft for despatch onwards was entirely carried out by Inland Water Transport officers.

Below will be found a brief summary of craft despatched (towed or convoyed) from India and Burma during the periods indicated :—

By R.I.M. officers :
1914-15.—13 despatched to Mesopotamia :
    12 arrived, 1 lost. 7·7 per cent loss.
1915-16.—184 despatched to Mesopotamia :
    132 arrived, 52 lost. 28·1 per cent loss.
1916-17.—269 despatched to Mesopotamia :
    236 arrived, 33 lost. 12·3 per cent loss.

By I.W.T. officers :
1917-18.—180 despatched to Mesopotamia :
    179 arrived, 1 lost. 0·5 per cent loss.
1918-19.—63 despatched to Mesopotamia :
    63 arrived.

It will be seen from the above figures that during the seasons 1917-18 and 1918-19 the percentage of losses was reduced to a minimum, which may be ascribed to the following reasons :—

(1) Special towing equipment being devised, plans of which were sent to all ports of despatch.

(2) Additional experience gained by officers commanding towing steamers as to the handling of their craft.

(3) Most of the craft being newly constructed.

Nearly all the craft and barges which had been obtained from Calcutta and Rangoon had to undergo extensive repairs at Bombay before proceeding to Mesopotamia. These craft being only lightly constructed for river work had worked so badly on the sea voyage that they required in some cases to be re-riveted as much as 50 per cent.

No records are available of any notable occurrences of the 1914–15 and 1915–16 seasons, but a few incidents regarding those of 1917–18 and 1918–19 are given below.

(1) Barge R. 30.—This barge was reported as lost in January, 1917, but was subsequently reported ashore on the Maldive Islands in January, 1918. A towing steamer was sent there to endeavour to bring the barge on to Bombay. She was then docked and repaired and despatched onward to Mesopotamia, but unfortunately foundered 117 miles from Bombay during heavy weather.

(2) Barge No. 7.—This barge outward-bound from the United Kingdom broke adrift from her towing steamer and was picked up by the S.S. *Lady McCallum*, after having been five days adrift in the Persian Gulf with six Europeans on board, and towed to Basrah. As the *Lady McCallum* was at the time towing two large A. Class barges, this may be considered a marvellous piece of work, the total length of the tow being over one-third of a mile.

(3) The *Ban-Whatt-Hin* was despatched from Bushire to search for a hopper barge which had broken adrift from her towing steamer in the western portion of the Persian Gulf. After several days' search she found the barge and towed it safely to Basrah.

(4) Both the S.S. *Kistna* and the S.S. *Zira*, in December, 1918, when towing two A. Class barges from Rangoon to Colombo had trouble with their tows owing to heavy weather. The tows both broke adrift, and when picked up again two days later it was found that all the barges had made a lot of water and were badly down by the head, so they were towed stern first for the remainder of the voyage.

(5) The *Ramapoora*, when towing two A. Class barges, was caught in a "shamal" in the Persian Gulf, and only managed with difficulty to reach Bushire before one of the barges sank owing to having sprung a leak. This barge was afterwards salved and taken to Basrah.

During the 1917-18 season over 29,000 tons (dead weight) of cargo and stores was shipped to Basrah, either on towing steamers or on craft towed ; also approximately 2000 troops, besides a large number of cattle, were transported to Basrah on towing steamers.

In addition to the vessels which either proceeded under their own power or were towed there, the following craft, including motor-tugs, motor-boats, steam launches, barges, anchor boats, hospital and Red Cross launches, were shipped to Mesopotamia on the decks of transports during the seasons mentioned :—

1916–17	1917–18	1918–19
168	252	237

A tribute to the manner in which the towing programme of 1917–18 was carried out is contained in the following despatch from the Commander-in-Chief in India :—

"I am directed to convey the high appreciation of His Excellency, the Commander-in-Chief, of the results of the towage of river craft—season 1917-18—and am to say that the results reflect great credit upon those responsible for the fitting-out preparation for despatch and safe towage of these craft to Mesopotamia.

"I am to ask that you will kindly convey to all Officers concerned, viz. Inland Water Transport and Royal Indian Marine

Officers at Bombay, Karachi, Calcutta, and Rangoon, His Excellency's appreciation of the good work performed by them."

(2) Towage of Craft from the United Kingdom and Places West of Suez

The majority of the vessels intended for Mesopotamia were built on the Clyde, and very shortly following the assumption of control of affairs in that country by the War Office, a depot was established at Glasgow for the purpose of recruiting and training suitable personnel, to man the ships, to supply drafts for Mesopotamia, and to carry out the storing, fitting for the sea voyage and despatch of all vessels as they were completed. This depot was known as the Mesopotamian Home Section, and was under the command of Lieut.-Colonel M. B. Sayer, C.B.E., R.E.

A sub-depot, controlled from Glasgow, was shortly afterwards established at Fowey in Cornwall. Here the Great Western Railway wharf was requisitioned, a small repair shop erected and oil storage tanks built, in order to ensure that vessels were fuelled to their utmost capacity and to make good any defects that might have been discovered after leaving Glasgow, before their final departure from the United Kingdom.

An additional sub-depot, also controlled from Glasgow, was subsequently opened at Barry Dock, this depot being principally concerned with the shipment of vessels in sections and in plates and angles for re-erection either in Mesopotamia or India, and with the shipment of engineering and constructional materials and stores, an average of three thousand tons per month of which were shipped there for a period extending over eighteen months.

The voyage of lightly designed shallow-draft river craft to Mesopotamia was attended by grave danger, as apart from enemy action, success was almost entirely dependent on their passage being negotiated whilst weather conditions remained favourable. To facilitate matters, a relay system was therefore introduced—two powerful deep-sea tugs

H.M. The King Inspecting I.W.T. ratings at Richborough.

being employed on each relay, either for towing or for escorting duties. The relays were arranged as follows :—

Port.		Approximate distances.
Fowey—Gibraltar	. . . . .	1200 miles.
Gibraltar—Malta	. . . . .	1000 ,,
Malta—Port Said	. . . . .	1100 ,,
Suez—Aden	. . . . . .	900 ,,
Aden—Muscat	. . . . .	1250 ,,
Muscat—Basrah	. . . . .	·770 ,,
	Total distance .	6220 ,,

The tugs employed were all well-armed and based on one or other of the ports mentioned, where their services were utilised, when not employed on their regular duties, for carrying out such salvage work as might be required from time to time by the naval authorities. Many daring feats, such as rescuing the crews of torpedoed vessels, etc., were performed by these vessels in the execution of these duties.

Before leaving the United Kingdom all vessels were fitted with longitudinal fore and aft beams on both lower and main decks, extending nearly the whole length of the ship, to stiffen them and to prevent them working in a sea-way, the forepeaks being also "tommed" and stiffened with timber as much as possible. A further precaution adopted was to fit tanks containing fish-oil at each bow and quarter, so that in the event of bad weather occurring the taps could be turned on and the oil allowed to percolate overboard. This procedure was stated on several occasions to have saved vessels from foundering. A method was also adopted of heaving vessels to beam-on by means of two large sea-anchors fitted with oil-bags made fast by their cables to the sponson. In this position, though against all the accepted principles of heaving-to bow-on, these shallow-draft vessels lay comfortably and shipped no heavy water ; in fact, it was found by experience to be the only effective way to handle such craft. Any attempt to keep them bow-on usually resulted in the forward structure being broken up.

Some of the vessels despatched created world's records
for this class of craft, by proceeding under their own power
from the United Kingdom to Basrah, a distance of approximately 6500 miles. The practice hitherto had been to un-
ship their paddle-wheels, board them in, and then to tow
them to their destination. Of a total of sixty-three vessels
despatched to Mesopotamia, either under their own power
or in tow of the relay tugs, only the following casualties
occurred :

P.S. 57 stranded in the Red Sea, and finally abandoned.

P.T. 1 foundered off the Isle of Man (seven lives lost).

P.T. 62 sunk by an enemy submarine in the Mediterranean.

S.P. 17 foundered in the Mediterranean in bad weather.

S.P. 21 foundered in the Arabian Sea.

The numbers given are United Kingdom numbers.

In addition, two of the relay tugs, H.S. 3 and H.S. 4,
were sunk by an enemy submarine off the coast of Spain,
together with the refrigerating barge which each vessel
was towing. (Reference will be made to these incidents
later.)

Considerable difficulty was experienced with the 110-feet
paddle tugs, owing to their limited bunker capacity, which
was only sufficient to last them for six days' steaming. The
method generally adopted was for one of the relay tugs to
tow them for the first five hundred miles, their own engine
meanwhile working at " slow," whilst they proceeded under
their own power entirely for the remainder of the distance.

About five hundred officers and one thousand men in all
were recruited and trained at the Glasgow depot, and the
great courage and resource shown on several occasions, in
extricating their vessels from positions of grave peril, on
the part of many of the above, has been frequently recognised.

A few of the more exciting incidents which occurred in
connection with the voyages of some of these vessels to
Mesopotamia will, perhaps, prove of interest here :

P.A.I.—Ambulance Steamer running Steam Trials on the Clyde, previous to proceeding to Mesopotamia.

(1) P.T. 62 (U.K. No.) was in action with an enemy submarine, one day's sail from Port Said. This vessel was only armed with one 6-pounder gun, with which, after an action lasting 1¼ hours, she succeeded in sinking the submarine, this fact being eventually officially recognised by the Admiralty.

(2) P.T. 12 left Greenock on Dec. 3rd, 1916, during fine weather. At about 8.30 p.m. the same day the boiler and engine-room suddenly burst into flame, filling the engine-room and all parts of the superstructure with clouds of dense black smoke and flame. The crew took to the boats, but hung on to the vessel at a safe distance until the boat's painters were burnt through. They were eventually picked up by H.M. patrol vessel *Ashlyn*, and landed at Ardrossan. Two days later the S.S. *Fodhla* sighted a "curious looking steamer," which turned out to be the remains of P.T. 12, still afloat. They dropped alongside, and after playing a hose upon her for threequarters of an hour they succeeded in extinguishing the fire and towing the burnt-out hull to Ayr.

(3) P.T. 1 left Glasgow on May 9th, 1917. The next morning, when off the Isle of Man, the weather became bad, a moderate gale springing up from the south-east. The vessel commenced to labour heavily and to fill up forward. The pumps were started, but the water gained on them, and at 9.30 p.m. the boats were ordered away. The starboard boat, with the chief officer and eight men on board, got safely away ; but before the port boat could get clear, a heavy sea washed her under the sponson, throwing the occupants into the water. Five of these were picked up by the other boat, which came to their assistance immediately, the remaining seven being drowned.

(4) P.S. 57 struck a reef in the Red Sea on Feb. 22nd, 1917, and rapidly began to fill up. She was beached as soon as possible off Akaki (one hundred miles south-east of Part Sudan). Salvage operations were commenced immediately, being carried out by H.M. ships *Minto* and *Northbrook*, and large quantities of stores and equipment were saved.

Efforts to refloat her were, however, unsuccessful, and on Feb. 28th it was found that she had broken her back. She was therefore abandoned. No lives were lost on this occasion.

(5) H.S. 3 and R.B. 10. This tug, towing a refrigerating barge, left Plymouth on Sept. 5th, 1917. On the 11th inst. she put into Lisbon to replenish her bunkers from the barge, it being impossible to carry out this operation at sea owing to heavy weather. On the 12th inst., after getting clear of the Tagus, they were fired on by an enemy submarine. The crews of both vessels took to their boats, which were immediately ordered alongside the submarine. An officer and three men from the submarine went on board the tug and barge and after removing all arms and instruments placed bombs on board and sank them. The officer in charge and three non-commissioned officers were detained aboard the submarine, the rest of the crew being ordered to pull for the shore the next day. The former were later found to have reached the Prisoners of War Camp at Brandenburg in Germany.

(6) H.S. 4 and R.B. 6. These two vessels were sunk by an enemy submarine in the Bay of Biscay. The crews were allowed to proceed in their boats, being eventually picked up by a French schooner and landed at Pampolle in France.

(7) S.T. 21 and R.B. 1 left Aden on May 21st, 1917. On the 25th inst. the weather became bad and the barge broke adrift from the tug. On the 26th inst. the tug was lost sight of. On the 27th the crew of the barge rigged a jury mast and improvised a sail. The weather showed no signs of moderating and no land was in sight. At daybreak on the 28th land was sighted dead to leeward, distant about two miles ; but owing to an excellent display of seamanship and judgment on the part of the N.C.O. in charge of the barge, she was prevented from stranding until June 8th, when she dragged both anchors and grounded. She was immediately boarded by hostile Arabs, who looted everything and maltreated the crew. The latter, however, eventually managed

to escape, with the assistance of some friendly Arabs, and after enduring many hardships and privations reached Muscat fifteen days later. The tug was never heard of again, and it is presumed she foundered during the cyclone reported on May 26th.

A summary of the self-propelled vessels and barges despatched from the United Kingdom and Canada to Mesopotamia is given below :—

N

BARGES DESPATCHED OR SHIPPED TO MESOPOTAMIA FROM UNITED KINGDOM OR CANADA

Type of Craft	Class Letter	Total Craft	Craft Diverted	No. Lost in Transit	Towed	Shipped on Transports and Re-erected at Basrah or in India		Complete Shipped Hulls	Port Work at Karachi
General transport	B.	253	3 Egypt, 30 France, 6 Home	13 ex S.S. *Karonga* / 9	7	100	58(a)	13	14(b)
Oil barges	O.B.	23	—	—	—	—	—	23	—
Refrigeration barges	R.B.	16	—	3	7	6(c)	—	—	—
Filtration barges	F.B.	6	—	—	4	2(d)	—	—	—
Water tank	W.E.	14	—	1	—	—	—	13(e)	—
Tractor barges	T.D.	2	—	—	—	2(f)	—	—	—
Ice barges	I.E.	11	—	1	—	5	2(g)	3	—
Hospital barges	H.B.	4	—	—	—	4	—	—	—
Totals		329	39	27	18	119	60	52	14

(a) Includes 40 Canadian barges.
(b)   ,,   8   ,,   ,,
(c)   ,,   6 Converted from "B" type.
(d)   ,,   2   ,,   ,,   ,,

(e) Includes 1 Converted from "B" type.
(f)   ,,   2   ,,   ,,   ,,
(g)   ,,   2 Canadian barges.

SELF-PROPELLED CRAFT DESPATCHED OR SHIPPED TO MESOPOTAMIA FROM THE UNITED KINGDOM

No.	Type of Craft	Class Letter.	Total Craft.	Craft Diverted.	No. of Craft Lost.	Towed out.	Own Steam.	Shipped per Transport.	Returned to England.	Disposed of.	Remarks.
1.	Dredgers	—	4	—	—	1	—	3	—	—	Includes *Quorra*.
2.	Paddle steamers	P.S.	12	—	1 (a)	—	11	9	1	—	(a) P.S. 57.
3.	Paddle tugs	P.T.	27	1 (b)	2	15	—	9	—	—	(b) P.T. 11 (hull only).
4.	Hospital paddlers	H.P.	9	2 Egypt	1	—	6	—	2	—	
5.	Hospital motor vessels	H.M.	4	—	—	4	—	—	—	—	
6.	Ambulance vessels	P.A.	7	—	—	—	7	—	5	—	
7.	Stern-wheelers	S.	25	6 Egypt	—	—	—	18	—	—	
8.	Hospital stern-wheelers	H.S.W.	7	—	—	—	—	7	—	1 (c)	(c) S. 50.
9.	Up-river tugs	T.	59	11 Egypt 12 Admlty.	2 (d)	—	—	34	15	—	(d) T.78, T.85
10.	Sea and harbour tugs	S.T.	2	—	1 (e)	—	1	—	—	—	(e) S.T. 21
11.	Motor-tugs (ex M. launches)	M.T.	7	—	—	—	—	7	—	—	
12.	Steam launches	L.	1	—	—	—	—	1	—	—	
13.	Motor launches	M.	160	40	6	—	—	114	—	—	
	Motor fire-floats	—	4	—	—	—	—	4	—	—	
	Motor buoyage	B.L.	17	—	—	—	—	17	—	—	
	Totals		345	72	13	20	25	214	23	1	

THE GUNBOAT FLOTILLA

THE present gunboat flotilla, consisting of the four shallow-draught monitors *Firefly*, *Greenfly*, *Grayfly*, and *Sedgefly*, was handed over to this department by the Royal Navy on March 2nd, 1918.

Their duties as Defence vessels are to patrol the rivers of Mesopotamia, usually two of them being stationed on the Tigris and two on the Euphrates.

All four vessels are of practically the same dimensions and capacity, their length being 126 feet, breadth, 18 feet, depth, 6 feet, with a maximum draft of 3 feet and speed of 10 knots.

They carried an armament of one 4-inch B.L. Mark VIII gun, one 12-pounder 12 cwt. Mark VI gun, one three-pounder Vickers' (anti-aircraft) gun, four ·303 Maxims, besides the usual complement of rifles and pistols.

The 4-inch guns were removed in August, 1918, for the purpose of arming vessels on the Caspian. (See par. 38).

They are also fitted with searchlights and wireless installations, the latter having a radius of between 200 and 250 miles.

Each vessel has a complement of :

> 2 navigating officers,
> 1 engine-room officer,
> 8 gunner ratings,
> 1 engine-room mechanic,
> 17 deck and engine-room ratings (Indians).

The native crews take a keen interest in their work, and with European supervision all four vessels are maintained in a high state of efficiency.

During the short period these vessels have been under the

H.M.S. Mantis on Slipway, I.W.T. Dockyard, Basra. February 21st, 1918.

("Fly Class Gunboats.")

Dimensions: length, 126'; breadth. 20' 10"; depth, 4' 6". Service draft, 2' 11½". Engines, S/S., T., S/C.; 3 cylinders; N.H.P. 17'14. Speed 9'5 knots. Boilers. Yarrow W.T. Fuel capacity, 13 tons oil. Consumption, 3'5 tons per 24 hours. Armament, 1—4" gun, 1—12 pounder, 1—3 pounder, A.A., 5 machine guns.

Four vessels of this class taken over from the Royal Navy and operated by I.W.T. for defence purposes.

In the photograph they are flying the R.N. paying-off pennant.

See special article "The Gunboat Flotilla' on page 180.

Twelve vessels of this class now used for towing purposes. All from the Royal Navy.

Inland Water Transport, they have been engaged in two or three minor actions against hostile Arabs, particularly in the vicinity of Hamar Lake, where on May 29th, 1918, the town of Badr was practically destroyed by gunfire from the *Firefly* and *Greenfly*, and on February 26th, 1919, owing to further trouble the town was captured by infantry under cover of the guns of these vessels.

On March 29th, 1918, the *Sedgefly* hoisted the Union Jack over Hai Town, and repeated this operation at Qal-'at-Sikkar, some thirty-four miles beyond Hai, on June 14th, 1918. For a vessel of this size to navigate a river like the Hai to this distance is in itself no easy task.

The *Firefly* is the historic vessel captured by the Turks on the retreat from Ctesiphon, and eventually recaptured by the Royal Navy on the advance to Baghdad.

TROOPS

THE personnel of the troops serving in the Inland Water Transport in Mesopotamia has included, besides the British officers and British other ranks who joined the Unit direct, or were transferred from other units on account of their technical qualifications, contingents from the undermentioned :

(1) The British West Indies Regiment.
(2) The Nigerian Marine.
(3) The West African contingent.
(4) The Coloured Section, R.E.
(5) The Mauritius Labour Battalion.
(6) The Egyptian Labour Corps.
(7) A large number of skilled and unskilled Indian and Chinese followers. These amounted at their maximum to nearly 40,000 men.
*

The grand total of the whole of the above amounted at its maximum to nearly 50,000 men.

It will be seen from these figures, and also owing to the varying composition of respective detachments, that their housing, welfare, and discipline was a question of some importance.

Camps.—The main depots where men were accommodated away from the actual place of their work were :

(1) The Inland Water Transport Barracks, Ashar, for British other ranks.
(2) Tanooma Camp, for British officers and all Eastern Races arriving in the country or awaiting repatriation. This came under the department of Personnel, and is dealt with under this heading.

* These were administered by A.D.I.W.T. Personnel.

B.O.R. Staff at Headquarters, Basrah

I.W.T. Barracks, Ashar, including Keshla Camp.—In September, 1916, the Inland Water Transport took over a part of the old Turkish barracks at Ashar. It is situated 1½ miles to the northward of Headquarters, and covers an area of about six acres. The main building is constructed of mud bricks. It comprises an officers' mess, quartermaster's stores, sergeants' mess, and several offices ; also a recreation room for British other ranks.

In addition to the Commandant, there are usually four officers in residence. One officer for the maintenance of discipline and for Orderly Officer's duties, a Quartermaster, a Medical Officer, and the Discipline Officer for Keshla Camp.

The Camp has a dispensary, heatstroke station, bathrooms, and huts and tents for the accommodation of the men. There is also a small stage and cinema for their recreation.

All British other ranks newly arrived in the country are sent to this Camp to await allocation, and all men who are discharged from hospital pass through on their way to their original or new appointments. Men on leave are detailed to the Camp for kit inspection and the preparation of documents.

A number of motor dockyard British other ranks are quartered here ; also some of the personnel of the Inland Water Transport dockyard, to which the Camp is adjacent.

The Camp can accommodate between six hundred and seven hundred B.O.R.'s.

The whole area is lighted by electricity, and fans have been installed.

The supply of water is obtained from the main pumping station, and when necessary it is heated by a steam pipe from the rapid destructor at the dockyard.

After the cessation of hostilities Low Lane became the Base Concentration Camp, to which all British other ranks were sent in anticipation of and preparation for demobilisation.

Keshla Camp is under the same Commandant. It has an area of about ten acres, and is adjacent and to the south of the barracks. This Camp was originally arranged for the Egyptian Labour Corps. It is now set apart wholly for the accommodation of Oriental labour, and has accommodation for eight hundred Indians and the same number of Chinamen, all of whom have regular employment close to their quarters. The Chinese accommodation has recently been taken over by the Dockyard Department.

There are still a few of the original native brick buildings remaining, which are used for offices and accommodation for the six British other ranks who are there to assist the Officer Commanding in maintaining discipline.

Gardilan Camp.—Owing to complaints from the medical authorities regarding overcrowding in the dockyard area, this Camp was started in June, 1918. It accommodated in tents twelve hundred ratings of the Construction Department, who crossed the river daily to their work. This Camp was later handed over to the Personnel Department, and is dealt with under this head. The Camp staff consisted of one B.O. as Camp Commandant and three B.O.R.'s.

Khora Creek has accommodation for twelve hundred ratings, and contains specially constructed huts for the use of Indian clerks.

The Camp Commandants are under the control of the Officer Commanding Inland Water Transport Troops at Headquarters, who is himself responsible to A.D.I.W.T., Headquarters. It is his special duty to visit all camps at frequent intervals, to compare and improve, as far as possible, the conditions obtaining in the various camps. All court-martial work is supervised by him.

To provide recreation, an Athletic Association was formed, under which football (Rugby and Association), hockey, tennis, cricket, boxing, and athletic sports were encouraged. The Inland Water Transport teams were always well to the fore, and as a final achievement both the Rugby and Association teams proceeded to Baghdad in February, 1919, as Base champions, and succeeded in winning the championships of the Mesopotamian Expeditionary Force for these two events.

The remaining personnel at the Base was accommodated in the vicinity of their work, namely at :

Margil	5000 personnel	
Muftieh	1200 ,,	
Main Dockyard . . .	4000 ,,	} Later
Motor Dockyard . . .	600 ,,	} combined.
Headquarters	400 ,,	

Camp Commandants responsible for discipline, etc., to the administrative C.O. were appointed in each case. These camps are being dealt with under their respective departmental headings.

A few remarks regarding the Coloured Troops attached to the Inland Water Transport are appended :

British West Indies Regiment.—The first draft of the British West Indies Regiment, consisting of thirty-eight non-commissioned officers and men, under Captain Devenish, arrived in Mesopotamia on the 4th July, 1916.

On the 31st July, 1916, Lieut. Morgan arrived with sixty-one non-commissioned officers and men.

In December, 1916, Captain L. A. Jeffreys, with three officers and 328 non-commissioned officers and men arrived. A further draft of forty-two men (mostly recruited in British Honduras) arrived in August, 1918.

These troops were mainly employed doing guard duty at the various Inland Water Transport camps. About one hundred were employed as motor-boat drivers, and a number as carpenters, blacksmiths, and clerks.

This contingent has been awarded three Meritorious Service Medals, and has had seven Mentions in Despatches.

Nigerian Marine.—Sixty-seven Marine Ratings arrived in Mesopotamia in February, 1917, on board the convoy steamer *Ivy*. They had all previously served throughout the Cameroons Expedition, and were now detailed for various duties with the river fleet. They returned to Nigeria in the *Ivy* in the summer of 1918. Two Distinguished

Service Medals had been awarded them during the operations in West Africa.

West African Contingent.—The first draft of 168 officers and men of the West African contingent arrived in Mesopotamia in August, 1917. The second draft of 508 arrived in October, 1917. The third draft, consisting of twenty-six men, arrived in December, 1917.

Captain Nosworthy, R.E., was in command of the whole contingent.

They were mostly employed as labourers and stevedores. They were repatriated in July, 1918. One Meritorious Service Medal was awarded to this contingent.

Coloured Labour Section, R.E.—Two hundred and twenty-four of the Coloured Labour Section, Royal Engineers, were taken on the Mesopotamian strength on the 31st December, 1916. They were brought from England by Captain D. J. Marriott, R.E., and were employed in Mesopotamia as crane drivers, clerks, motor-boat drivers, and a number of them formed crews of ships. They were repatriated at the beginning of April, 1918.

European Personnel.—The following summary shows the strength of B.O.'s and B.O.R.'s on the dates indicated :—

	Dec., 1916.	Dec., 1917.	1918. (Armistice.)
Officers. . . .	292	703	804
Warrant Officers, Class I	11	8	5
,, ,, Class II	18	43	94
Sergeants . . .	66	120	177
Corporals . . .	84	133	167
2nd Corporals . .	38	60	158
Lance-Corporals . .	65	171	425
Sappers . . .	1192	1793	1669
Total .	1756	3031	3499

CASUALTIES

LIST OF OFFICERS OF THE I.W.T. BURIED IN MESOPOTAMIA AND ELSEWHERE

Name.	Rank.	Unit.	Date died.	Where buried.
Crichton, J. R.	Major	1/5th/Hants	6.2.17	Hakimiyah. Row D, No. 11
King, D. A.	Lieut.	R.E., I.W.T.	22.7.17	Baghailah. Row A, No. 2
Lindsay, A. C.	Lieut.	R.E., I.W.T.	10.2.18	Makina New. Row H, No. 5
Meharg, R. J.	Lieut.	I.W.T.	4.3.17	Sheikh Sa'ad. Row 5, No. 331
Tibbs, B. E.	Lieut.	I.W.T.	9.1.18	Drowned. Body not recovered
Guerrier, E. G.	Lieut.	I.W.T.	30.11.18	Baghailah. Row 1, No. 1a
Grote, A. L.	Capt.	R.E., I.W.T.	9.7.18	Makina New. Row K, No. 17
Fennemore, G. C.	2/Lieut.	R.E.	3.11.18	Base Isolation, Tanooma. Row H, No. 24
Perrin, T. F.	Capt.	R.E., I.W.T.	24.7.17	Hakimiyah. Row J, No. 27
Stewart, A. C.	2/Lieut.	I.W.T.	19.4.18	Drowned. Body not recovered
Tully, T. M.	2/Lieut.	I.W.T.	9.10.18	Makina New. Row O, No. 2
Pattison, T.	Lieut.	I.W.T.	22.12.18	Advanced Base, Baghdad. Row C, No.154
Dadds, I. L. L.	Lieut.	R.E., I.W.T.	17.7.17	Hakimiyah. Row 1, No. 11
Price, S. A.	2/Lieut.	R.E., I.W.T.	11.7.17	Hakimiyah. Row E, No. 39
Morgan, J.	Lieut.	I.W.T.	6.10.18	British Cemetery, Muscat
Learoyd, D. G.	Lieut.	R.E., I.W.T.	13.12.17	Makina New. Row F, No. 17
Smith, R. J.	Lieut.	I.W.T.	31.7.18	Makina New. Row L, No. 15
Armstrong, J.	Lieut.	R.I.M. att.I.W.T.	1917	Killed by Turks. Grave unknown
Christie, L. W.	Lieut.	R.I.M. att.I.W.T.	7.5.17	Hakimiyah. Row E, No. 3
Collins, F. J.	Lieut.	R.I.M. att.I.W.T.	25.3.17	Hakimiyah. Row E, No. 14
Lamond, G. A. W.	Lt.-Col.	R.E., I.W.T.	25.2.18	General Cemetery, Kanatta.
Sczulezeswki, O.	Lieut.	R.N.V.R.	26.10.17	Military Cemetery, Amara

Name.	Rank.	Unit.	Date died.	Where buried.
McLean, J.	Lieut.	I.W.T.	16.7.18	Kerman Khah Cemetery, Der-i-Khazineh, Persia
Wallace, A. R.	Lieut.	I.W.T.	18.1.19	Fallujah. Row H, No. 1
Nairin, F. W.	Eng.-Lieut.	R.I.M.	9.11.16	Hakimiyah. Row A, No. 23
Keil, A. P. M.	Eng.-Lieut.	R.I.M.	11.10.16	Amara Cemetery. Plot 7, Row C, No. 5
Corlett, D.	Lieut.	R.I.M.	9.10.16 ;	Makina Masus Old Cemetery. Row H1, No. 22
Anderson, R.	Lieut.	I.W.T.	29.5.18	Missing, believed drowned
Sydney, H.	T/Lieut.	I.W.T.	26.5.17	Drowned at sea
Davies, T. L.	2/Lieut.	I.W.T.	26.5.17	Drowned at sea
Overton, C.	2/Lieut.	I.W.T.	26.5.17	Drowned at sea
White, A. G.	Lieut.	I.W.T.	15.7.17	Died at sea
Shephard, W. H. J.	2/Lieut.	I.W.T.	23.9.17	Makina Cemetery.
Smith, L. O.	Lieut.	I.W.T.	30.6.19	Makina Cemetery

NON-COMMISSIONED OFFICERS AND PRIVATES OF THE I.W.T. BURIED IN MESOPOTAMIA AND ELSEWHERE

I.W.T., R.E,

Name.	Rank.	Number.	Date of death.	Where buried.
Harrison, J. E.	A/Cpl.	157525	11.11.16 }	Base Isolation Cemetery. Grave E. 13
Young, J.	C.S.M.	109953	26.12.16 }	
Swinborne, B. B.	A/Sgt.	149626	2.3.17	T.C. 74 Sq. 220, near Baghailah
Attwood,	Spr.	208260	1.4.17	Hakimiyah Cemetery. Grave E.13
McCormack, J.	Spr.	227127	30.4.17	Hakimiyah Cemetery. Grave E.6

I.W.T., R.E. (*continued*)

Name.	Rank.	Number.	Date of death.	Where buried.
Mitchell, J.	Spr.	205430	14.5.17	Base Isolation Cemetery. Grave E.9
Gooda, T. G.	Spr.	208137	21.5.17	Hakimiyah Cemetery. Grave B.30
McDonald, A.	Spr.	214060	14.6.17	Hakimiyah Cemetery. Grave F.1
Kelley, J. H.	Spr.	206005	28.6.17	Tanooma Cemetery. Grave A.11
Smith, H. E.	Spr.	271351	10.7.17	Hakimiyah Cemetery. Grave E.17
Rowe, W. S.	Spr.	150705	11.7.17	Hakimiyah Cemetery. Grave E.26
Girling, E. J.	Spr.	200342	11.7.17	Hakimiyah Cemetery. Grave E.25
Poree, P. J. A.	Spr.	202264	12.7.17	Hakimiyah Cemetery. Grave H.3
Lockett, H. M.	Spr.	197052	12.7.17	Hakimiyah Cemetery. Grave H.9
Mathias, J.	Spr.	200280	12.7.17	Hakimiyah Cemetery. Grave E.30
Price, W. J.	Spr.	200552	15.7.17	Hakimiyah Cemetery. Grave G.25
George, P.	Spr.	201026	15.7.17	Hakimiyah Cemetery. Grave G.26
Rampling, H. J.	Spr.	208318	17.7.17	Hakimiyah Cemetery. Grave I.8
Richards, E. F.	Spr.	243500	17.7.17	Hakimiyah Cemetery. Grave L.26
Smith, H. H.	Spr.	200714	18.7.17	Hakimiyah Cemetery. Grave L.28
Tolson, T.	Spr.	200716	17.7.17	Near Ctesiphon. T.C. 85a
Archer, A.	Spr.	200681	19.7.17	Hakimiyah Cemetery. Grave H.27
Philip, J	Spr.	271214	20.7.17	Hakimiyah Cemetery. Grave J.2
Holley, R.	Spr.	228515	16.7.17	Hakimiyah Cemetery. Grave I.22
Johnston, J. C.	Cpl.	196711	23.7.17	Kut (Camp) Cemetery. Grave No. 7
Brown, C.	Spr.	243510	23.7.17	Drowned
MacLeod, J.	Spr.	205160	26.7.17	Kurna Cemetery. Grave No. 44
Young, C.	Spr.	200924	26.7.17	Hakimiyah Cemetery. Grave K.23
Bragg, W. J.	Spr.	195458	21.7.17	Hakimiyah Cemetery. Grave J.11

I.W.T., R.E. (continued)

Name.	Rank.	Number.	Date of death.	Where buried.
Manley, E.	Spr.	200997	13.8.17	Hakimiyah Cemetery. Grave K.4
Faulkner, E. G.	Spr.	510626	14.8.17	Makina Masus New Ext. Cemetery. Block 1, A.1
Crosbie, W.	Spr.	208435	21.8.17	Makina Masus New Ext. Cemetery. Block 1, A.12
Foden, D. B.	Cpl.	178623	4.9.17	Drowned
Cantwell, M.	Spr.	174861	8.9.17	Makina Masus New Ext. Cemetery. Block 1, C.16
Mathews, J.	2/Cpl.	204701	13.9.17	Kurna Cemetery. Grave No. 45
Thomas, H. P.	Spr.	200442	27.9.17	Makina Masus New Ext. Cemetery. Block 1, D.4
Jackson, A. J.	Cpl.	235113	22.7.17	North British Cemetery, Baghdad. Block 1, L.11
Fielding, J.	L/Cpl.	131967	16.12.17	Base Isolation Cemetery. Grave G.12
Bradbrook, J.	A/2/Cpl.	196938	11.3.18	Makina Masus New Ext. Cemetery. Block 1, H.16
Charles, J.	Spr.	287499	30.3.18	Drowned. Body not recovered
Clinton, T.	Spr.	215546	8.4.18	Drowned. Body not recovered
Wilson, G.	A/L/Cpl.	205955	5.5.18	Christian Cemetery, Koweit. Persian Gulf
Miller, J. I.	Spr.	WR.323441	18.5.18	Base Isolation Cemetery. Grave A1.19
Mercer, S. A.	A/Cpl.	168453	22.5.18	Makina Masus New Ext. Cemetery. Block 1, I.21
Knight, H. E.	L/Cpl.	280844	7.6.18–	Makina Masus New Ext. Cemetery. Block 1, J.7
Cannon, A. J.	Spr.	204672	9.6.18	Drowned. Body not recovered
Lynch, J.	L/Cpl.	200967	20.6.18	Makina Masus New Ext. Cemetery. Block 1, J.15
Miller, H. J.	Spr.	205424	28.6.18	Makina Masus New Ext. Cemetery. Block 1, K.1
Finch, P.	A/L/Cpl.	271174	29.6.18	Died whilst on leave in India.
Shepherd, W.	Spr.	264989	1.7.18	Kurna Cemetery. Grave No. 40
Ellison, W.	Spr.	195644	2.7.18	Makina Masus New Ext. Cemetery. Block 1, K.9
Blundel, F.	Spr.	200824	6.7.18	Tanooma Cemetery. Grave D.4
Hastings, W. J.	Spr.	320088	7.7.18	Makina Masus New Ext. Cemetery. Block 1, K.16

I.W.T., R.E. (continued)

Name.	Rank.	Number.	Date of death.	Where buried.
Guest, P. O.	A/L/Cpl.	195782	21.7.18	Drowned. Body not recovered.
Wilkinson, S.	Spr.	271698	12.8.18	South Cemetery, Baghdad. Grave B.14
Hampton, A. J.	Spr.	554236	18.8.18	Makina Masus New Ext. Cemetery. Block 1, M.1
Green, H.	Spr.	150178	20.8.18	North British Cemetery, Baghdad. Block 1, J.14
Barbour, A.	Spr.	281432	24.8.18	Kut Camp Cemetery. Grave C.7
Blackmore, W. H.	C.S.M.(A/R.S.M.)	88602	31.8.18	Base Isolation Cemetery. Grave H.10
Wilson, G.	A/L/Cpl.	215218	3.9.18	Makina Masus New Ext. Cemetery. Block 1, M.4
Huston, S.	Spr.	WR.553750	25.9.18	Base Isolation Cemetery. Grave H.15
Reeves, L. J.	Cpl.	WR.303545	30.9.18	Makina Masus New Ext. Cemetery. Block 1, M.21
Evans, H	Spr.	WR.552779	30.9.18	Makina Masus New Ext. Cemetery. Block 1, M.22
Whiting, R. F.	Spr.	WR.200296	4.10.18	Amara New Cemetery. Block 1, C.7
Knott, E.	Spr.	WR.505680	8.10.18	Makina Masus New Ext. Cemetery. Block 1, N.14
Smith, G.	Spr.	259143	12.10.18	Base Isolation Cemetery. Grave H.19
Didsbury, A.	Spr.	281024	14.10.18	Makina Masus New Ext. Cemetery. Block 1, O.22
Sadler, J	Spr.	271146	15.10.18	Makina Masus New Ext. Cemetery. Block 1, P.7
Elias, H. J.	A/C.S.M.	228840	8.10.18	Makina Masus New Ext. Cemetery. Block 1, N.20
Mitchell, R.	Spr.	200201	18.10.18	Makina Masus New Ext. Cemetery. Block 1, P.19
Anderson, W.	Spr.	320462	20.10.18	Makina Masus New Ext. Cemetery. Block 1, Q.3
Hewitt, A. E.	A/C.S.M.	196706	23.10.18	Kut Camp Cemetery. Grave C.20
King, W.	Sgt.	149624	23.10.18	Makina Masus New Ext. Cemetery. Block 1, Q.16
Taylor, W.	Spr.	346761	10.11.18	Base Isolation Cemetery. Grave H.25
Dollon, M.	Spr.	505691	16.11.18	Base Isolation Cemetery. Grave H.27
Foley, D.	Spr.	WR.330067	20.11.18	Amara Cemetery. Plot 8, D.6
Higgins, W.	A/L/Cpl.	271409	13.11.18	Bangalore
McDonald, J.	Spr.	WR.553620	18.3.19	Makina Masus New Ext. Cemetery. Block 2, T.17
Santley, J.	A/Sgt.	WR.552038	19.2.19	Makina Masus New Ext. Cemetery. Block 2, T.7

I.W.T., R.E. (continued)

Name.	Rank.	Number.	Date of death.	Where buried.
Bowen, W.	A/Sgt.	WR.553318	21.5.19	Makina Masus New Ext. Cemetery. Block 2, A.15
Whittaker, F.	Spr.	WR.553052	30.5.19	Makina Masus New Ext. Cemetery. Block 2, A.21
King, C. W.	A/R.S.M.	WR.552121	3.6.19	Amara New Cemetery. Grave E.10, Block 1
Winkley, W.	Spr.	WR.553127	12.6.19	Makina Masus New Ext. Cemetery. Block 2, B.7
Smith, R.	A/Sgt.	WR.340165	1.7.19	Makina Masus New Ext. Cemetery. Block 2, C.6
Flook, F. W.	A/2/Cpl.	WR.553420	1.7.19	Makina Masus New Ext. Cemetery. Block 2, C.7
Feehan, J.	2/Cpl.	WR.552403	4.7.19	Makina Masus New Ext. Cemetery. Block 2, C.13
Carruthers, J.	A/L/Cpl.	WR.553031	10.7.19	Makina Masus New Ext. Cemetery. Block 2, D.1
Anderson, N. E.	A/L/Cpl.	WR.553303	10.8.19	Makina Masus New Ext. Cemetery. Block 2, E.1
Pearce, W. H.	L/Cpl.	WR.553715	11.8.19	Amara Left Bank Cemetery. Plot 13, Row C.31
Phillips, T. H.	A/Cpl.	WR.305967	11.8.19	Makina Masus New Ext. Cemetery. Block 2, E.2
White, L.	Cpl.	204853	12.7.17	Hakimiyah Cemetery. Row H, No. 14
Rogers, J.	Spr.	195707	12.7.17	Hakimiyah Cemetery. Row H, No. 13
Smith, W.	Spr.	200976	13.7.17	Hakimiyah Cemetery. Row F, No. 21
Hickling, W.	C.S.M.	205742	14.7.17	Adv. Base Cemetery, Baghdad. Row A, No. 47
Rose, S.	Spr.	271291	15.7.17	Adv. Base Cemetery, Baghdad. Row B, No. 52
Boyle, J.	Spr.	205589	13.11.17	Makina New Ext. Cemetery. Block 1, Row F, No. 8
Carey, E.	A/C.S.M.	178461	7.12.17	Base Isolation Cemetery. Block 1, Row G, No.10
Giles, G. F.	A/L/Cpl.	505727	11.1.18	Makina New Ext. Cemetery. Block 1, Row G, No. 6
Henwood, W. J.	Sgt.	505731	27.6.18	Fallujah Cemetery. Row G, No. 4
Lavis, L. L.	Spr.	WR.553134 (formerly 205288)	20.9.18	Base Isolation Cemetery. Row H, No. 13.
Colcomb	A/L/Cpl.	WR.553571 (formerly 259128)	4.11.18	Makina New Ext. Cemetery. Block 1, Row R, No. 11

M.V.G. ATTACHED I.W.T.

Name.	Rank.	Number.	Date of death.
Jobard, R.	L/Cpl.	7956	22.10.16

B.W.I. ATTACHED I.W.T.

Seacombe	Pte.	1780	12.11.16
Rouse, A.	Pte.	1059	29.1.17
Duncan, C.	Pte.	5208	23.2.17
Diamond, J.	Pte.	1614	13.4.17
Gabourel, S.	Pte.	1838	16.8.17
Masson, J.	Sgt.	1715	14.9.17
Collie, W.	Pte.	5073	17.12.17
Gabourel, E. W.	Pte.	5119	29.6.18.
Gabb, F. B.	Pte.	5117	5.9.18
Burgess, A. C. H.	Pte.	5048	9.10.18
Usher, G. E. P.	Sgt.	1813	10.10.18
Baker, J.	Pte.	5023	22.10.18
Lowell	Pte.	5211	22.3.19

14TH HUSSARS. ATTACHED I.W.T.

Stanley, R.	Pte.	5410	2.1.17

BANGALORE V.R.'s. ATTACHED I.W.T.

Brown, C.	Cpl.	3965	17.3.17

E.I.R.V.'s. ATTACHED I.W.T.

Newton, J.	A/C.S.M.	J.38	13.5.17

D.C.L.I. ATTACHED I.W.T.

Brownsell, R.	Pte.	4508	12.7.17

COLOURED SECTION, I.W.T.

McCarth, F.	L/Cpl.	199694	22.7.17
Brown, C.	Pnr.	199689	2.12.17
Silver, J.	Pnr.	199719	9.1.18

W.A.C. ATTACHED I.W.T.

O'Kay, Jacob	Pte.	306	31.8.17
Amavi, M.	2/Cpl.	137	19.9.17

o

W.A.C. Attached I.W.T. (continued)

Name.	Rank.	Number.	Date of death
Jengetta	Pte.	29	20.9.17
Ekot, T.	Pte.	364	13.10.17
Currenta	Pte.	964	21.10.17
Bestman, T.	Pte.	409	30.10.17
Braimah	Pte.	65	1.11.17
Tambahomia	Pte.	866	3.11.17
Calabar	Pte.	301	4.11.17
Yandibama	Pte.	492	16.11.17
Fine Boy	Pte.	43	20.11.17
Cong	Pte.	75	18.11.17
Jenkins, E.	L/Cpl.	51	19.11.17
Alichali Konakry	Pte.	801	22.11.17
Bassi Kamara	Pte.	436	23.11.17
Fodel Aorca	Pte.	693	28.11.17
Sori Kanu I.	Pte.	712	25.11.17
Sampson	Pte.	591	25.11.17
Blackie	Pte.	652	8.12.17
Sam	Pte.	N44	10.12.17
Lamina Bandara	Pte.	726	13.12.17
Ajo	2/Cpl.	N125	16.12.17
Kammanda	Pte.	928	12.12.17
Daneman	Pte.	31	19.12.17
Aleokuta Alli	Pte.	N267	29.12.17
Nathaniel Patrick	Pte.	N186	25.12.17
Samseh	Pte.	374	20.12.17
Sori Kamara II.	Pte.	28	30.12.17
Benjimin	Pte.	366	3.1.18
Momo	Pte.	13	14.1.18
Simbo John	Pte.	237	4.1.18
Tommy	Pte.	145	13.1.18
Doinji	Pte.	36	11.2.18
Joe Amara	Pte.	50	19.2.18
Bio	Pte.	245	22.2.18
Kwanah	Pte.	7	26.3.18
Momodu Katah	Pte.	788	6.4.18
Alpha Kamara	Pte.	661	17.4.18
Coffe Ben	Pte.	317	30.4.18
Tohunie	Pte.	281	1.7.18
Jabbo Daniel	Pte.	148	18.7.18
Komes, W. N.	Pte.	N194	28.7.18
Try Best	Pte.	N64	28.7.18
Sunday Tia.	Pte.	N157	30.7.18
Kamarra, K.	Pte.	852	30.7.18

R.I.M. ATTACHED I.W.T.

Name.	Rank.	Number.	Date of death.
Thackney, J. J.	Gnr.		18.8.17
Patulo, A. J.	Gnr.		20.10.17
Johnson, F.	Gnr.		16.2.18

NIGERIAN MARINE. ATTACHED I.W.T.

Anthony	Cpl.	33	13.9.17

R.F.A. ATTACHED I.W.T.

Humphreys, H.	Gnr.	14204	7.5.18

LIST OF HONOURS GRANTED TO OFFICERS OF THE INLAND WATER TRANSPORT, ROYAL ENGINEERS, FOR SERVICES WITH THE I.W.T. IN MESOPOTAMIA.

Companion of the Order of the Bath.
Major-General W. H. Grey, C.M.G., R.E.

Companion of the Star of India.
Brigadier-General R. H. W. Hughes, C.M.G., D.S.O., R.E.

Companion of the Order St. Michael and St. George.
Brigadier-General R. H. W. Hughes, C.S.I., D.S.O., R.E.
Colonel H. Robertson, R.E.

Companion of the Order of the Indian Empire.
Colonel J. C. Ward, D.S.O., M.B.E., R.E.

Commanders of the Order of the British Empire.
Lieut.-Colonel R. S. F. Macrae, C.I.E.
Colonel H. E. Ratsey, D.S.O., R.E.
Colonel E. D. Truman, O.B.E., R.E.

Companions of the Distinguished Service Order.
Lieut.-Colonel R. D. T. Alexander, O.B.E., London Rgt.
Major J. H. Brown, O.B.E.
Lieut.-Colonel C. R. Campbell, R.E.
Lieut.-Colonel G. F. C. Corfield, R.E.
Lieut.-Colonel H. Fairweather, R.E.
Major E. R. Frankland.
Lieut.-Colonel H. W. Johns, R.E.
Lieut. W. R. King, O.B.E., R.N.V.R.
Major H. MacCallum.
Colonel H. E. Ratsey, O.B.E., R.E.
Colonel J. C. Ward, C.I.E., M.B.E., R.E.

Officers of the Order of the British Empire.

Lieut.-Colonel R. D. T. Alexander, D.S.O., London Rgt.
Major R. Angus, R.E.
Major A. H. Baker, R.E.
Lieut.-Colonel J. H. Boyd, R.E.
Lieut.-Colonel P. H. Browne.
Lieut.-Colonel W. G. Burn, R.E.
Major A. H. F. de Woolfson, R.E.
Lieut.-Colonel R. H. Garstin, R.E.
Lieut.-Colonel L. J. Hall, R.E.
Major B. L. Harvey, I.A.R.O.
Major A. L. Hill, M.C., I.A.R.O.
Major R. McG. Innes.
Captain H. C. Jones.
Major E. W. B. Kidby.
Lieut. W. R. King, D.S.O., R.N.V.R.
Captain E. O. Knowles.
Major A. Macdonald, R.E.
Lieut.-Colonel R. S. F. Macrae, C.I.E., C.B.E.
Major D. J. Marriott, R.E.
Lieut.-Colonel J. N. Metcalfe, D.S.C., R.E.
Lieut.-Colonel T. M. S. Milne Henderson, R.E.
Lieut.-Colonel H. M. K. Moilliet, R.E.
Major A. L. Rowlings.
Major H. J. Starkey, R.E.
Major T. A. O. Thompson.
Colonel E. D. Truman, C.B.E., R.E.
J. W. Medland, Esq.

Members of the Order of the British Empire.

Lieut. M. Cambell.
Captain C. Coutts.
Lieut. G. A. Duncan.
Lieut. G. E. Griffiths.
Second-Lieut. G. J. Mercer.
Captain T. V. Monks.
Captain P. R. Morgan.
Captain R. Renfrew.
Lieut. T. Smith.
Captain E. Smithson.
G. Blaney, Esq.

Military Cross.

Captain J. Armstrong.
Captain D. T. Fulton.
Captain H. S. Shepherd.

Meritorious Service Medal.

Major J. H. Haiste, R.E.

FOREIGN DECORATIONS.

Officier Legion d'Honneur.

Brigadier-General R. H. W. Hughes, C.S.I., C.M.G., D.S.O., R.E.

Croix de Guerre.

Lieut.-Colonel R. H. Garstin, O.B.E., R.E.

Order of St. Maurice and St. Lazarus.

Major-General W. H. Grey, C.B., C.M.G., R.E.

LIST OF HONOURS GRANTED TO W.O.'s, N.C.O.'s, AND MEN OF THE I.W.T., R.E., FOR SERVICE WITH THE I.W.T. IN MESOPOTAMIA.

Distinguished Conduct Medal.

No.	Name.	Date.
W.R.553403	Sapper A/Cpl. J. Harte . . .	25.5.18

Meritorious Service Medal.

WR.552744	Sergeant H. Banks	12.2.19
WR.552142	T/R.S.M. A. E. Benge . . .	29.8.17
WR.553305	Sergeant H. Burgess . . .	29.8.17
WR.552197	T/R.S.M. W. H. Cherry . . .	29.8.17
WR.552027	C.S.M. T. Corps	29.12.18
WR.553029	C.S.M. G. H. Cottom . . .	29.12.18
WR.501634	T/C.S.M. (A/R.S.M.) J. O. Deane .	29.12.18
WR.303564	T/R.S.M. T. Dowson . . .	12.2.19
WR.552150	T/R.S.M. A. Fagan	29.8.17
WR.552369	C.S.M. J. Hammond . . .	29.12.18
WR.552128	T/R.S.M. L. W. Long . . .	29.12.18
WR.301917	Sgt. (A/C.S.M.) F. H. E. McDonald (B.W.I.R.)	29.12.18
WR.201720	C.Q.M.S. G. McDonald (B.W.I.R.) .	25.2.18
WR.309104	C.S.M. (A/R.S.M.) P. V. Manning .	12.2.19
WR.552116	C.S.M. D. A. Mead	29.12.18
WR.553308	T/R.S.M. A. Muir , . . .	3.8.18

No.	Name.	Date.
WR.303531	C.S.M. (A/R.S.M.) W. T. Musslewhite	12.2.19
WR.301275	Private Oken Ifian (W.A.C.) . .	29.12.18
WR.552319	Sergeant J. F. Piatt . . .	29.12.18
WR.554149	Sapper J. Scotland	29.12.18
WR.552048	C.S.M. H. Shires	29.12.18
WR.552145	C.S.M. J. G. Shore	24.8.17
WR.309277	C.S.M. J. J. Toy	29.12.18
WR.553229	T/R.S.M. R. Watts	29.12.18
WR.303506	T/C.S.M. (A/R.S.M.) R. Whitefield .	1917
WR.155301	Sgt. (A/C.S.M.) S. E. Woods (B.W.I.R.)	4.2.18

Indian Distinguished Service Medal.

1st Class Engine Driver Asah Ali.
2nd Class Master Aziz Meah.
1st Class Engine Driver Bassa Meah.
Serang Emos Shaikh Ali.
Head Clerk Framroze Manekji Katrak.
Hony. Subadar Gyan Chandra Roy.
Gunner Kanchoo Bala Malmajee.
2nd Class Master Lall Meah.
1st Class Engine Driver Victor Carvalho.

STAFF OF INLAND WATER TRANSPORT AT THE CONCLUSION OF HOSTILITIES

Director :

Brigadier-General R. H. W. Hughes, C.S.I., C.M.G., D.S.O., R.E.

Deputy Directors :

Colonel J. C. Ward, D.S.O., M.B.E., R.E.	. On leave.
Colonel H. E. Ratsey, D.S.O., R.E.	. Chief Engnr.
Colonel G. B. Barton, R.E.	. Baghdad.

Assistant Directors :

Lieut.-Colonel H. Robertson, C.M.G., R.E.	. Dockyards.
Lieut.-Colonel R. D. T. Alexander, D.S.O.	. Construction.
Lieut.-Colonel C. R. Campbell, D.S.O., R.E.	. Personnel.
Lieut.-Colonel R. S. F. Macrae, C.I.E., O.B.E..	Native Craft.
Lieut.-Colonel R. H. Garstin, O.B.E., R.E.	. Norperforce.
Lieut.-Colonel J. H. Boyd, O.B.E., R.E..	. C. and R.
Lieut.-Colonel H. W. Johns, D.S.O., R.E.	. Marine Engr.
Lieut.-Colonel G. F. C. Corfield, D.S.O., R.E.	. Vessels.
Lieut.-Colonel E. D. Truman, O.B.E., R.E.	. Headquarters
Lieut.-Colonel J. N. Metcalfe, D.S.C., R.E.	. Transport.
Lieut.-Colonel H. Fairweather, D.S.O., R.E.	. B. and P.
Lieut.-Colonel A. G. Kinch, D.S.O., R.E.	. Amara.
Lieut.-Colonel H. M. K. Moilliet, R.E.	. Baghdad.

Deputy Assistant Directors :

Major R. Angus, O.B.E., R.E.	. Re-erection.
Major A. H. Baker, O.B.E., R.E.	. Dockyards.
Major B. L. Harvey, I.A.R.O.	. Construction.
Captain G. W. Thompson	. Baghdad.
Major D. P. Lamb	. M. Dockyard.
Major W. G. Burn, R.E.	. Stores.
Major A. L. Rowllings, O.B.E.	. B. and P.
Major A. D. Lewis, R.E.	. C. and R.
Major J. H. Haiste, R.E.	. C. and R.

Captain A. Macdonald, O.B.E., R.E.	. . Native Craft.
Captain A. L. Hill, M.C.	. . . Native Craft.
Captain B. F. Peverell .	. . . Native Craft.
Major E. M. Bayfield, R.E. .	. . . L. Euphrates.
Major E. R. Frankland, D.S.O.	. . . Coal and Oil.
Major L. J. Hall, R.E. .	. . . Caspian Sea.
Major A. D. Butler	. . . . T. and L.
Major W. A. Milne.	. . . . M. Euphrates.
Major H. L. Emmerson, R.E.	. . . On leave.
Major J. H. Brown, D.S.O. .	. . . Norperforce.
Major N. P. Hocking	. . . . Vessels.
Major D. J. Marriott, R.E.	. . . Headquarters
Major T. A. Choate, R.E.	. . . Construction.
Major W. V. Butcher, R.E.	. . . Construction.
Captain W. Marshall	. . . . Marine Engr.
Captain W. J. James	. . . . M. Euphrates.
Major T. M. S. Milne-Henderson, R.E.	. . Kut.
Major H. MacCallum, D.S.O.	. . . Narrows.

NOTE.—Reference should be made to the "List of Officers," Inland Water Transport, Mesopotamian Expeditionary Force, which is issued as a separate publication, for complete particulars of all other Officers attached to this Directorate.

AFTERWORD

In view of the length of time during which this record has been under preparation it will hardly be complete without some reference to the post-bellum activities of the Inland Water Transport.

Over nine months has elapsed since the Armistice was signed. Peace with Germany is now an accomplished fact, and though the Treaty with Turkey has not yet been presented there is little fear of that country being able to again renew hostilities in Mesopotamia. The Expeditionary Force has been reduced to an Army of Occupation, consisting approximately of two infantry divisions, a cavalry brigade, and the necessary administrative services, included amongst which the Inland Water Transport remains a factor of considerable importance.

1. Personnel.—Many of the Directorates, such as irrigation, works, port, railways, telegraphs, etc., have become quasi-civil, and for them the question of carrying on is comparatively easy as they are able to engage their personnel on civil contracts. The I.W.T., however, is not apparently to be maintained under civil conditions, and as it is an essential organisation for military purposes it still requires to be kept going by military personnel. Of the 799 officers serving in the department at the time of Armistice, only 120 expressed any desire to remain with the Army of Occupation, the remainder being anxious to return to their civil employment. To carry on the service, it has therefore been necessary to compulsorily retain a certain number of these men until such time as replacements can be sent from England, a matter regarding which some difficulty would appear to exist.

Wherever possible, British N.C.O.'s and men have been

relieved by Indians, and though efficiency has undoubtedly suffered there is no doubt that under peace conditions a great deal can be done by Asiatics in positions in which it was formerly essential to employ Europeans. The actual strength of the I.W.T. has now been reduced to :

Officers	325
B.N.C.O.'s and men . . .	766
Eastern races	22,770
Civilians	597
Total . . .	24,458
Attached or local labour . .	2,378
Grand total . .	26,836

2. Transport.—The amount of tonnage now being handled amounts to 900 tons per day delivered from Basrah to Kut, and 500 tons per day from Basrah to Baghdad, corresponding to 3,577,000 ton miles per week over and above the maintenance of subsidiary services.

The Basrah-Amara railway line has been taken up, thus throwing an additional burden on river transport, and the above services would appear to be required until such time as the Euphrates Valley railway from Basrah to Baghdad is in working order. This is expected to be an accomplished fact about June, 1920.

3. The Fleet.—The fleet has been reduced as far as compatible with estimated requirements. Previous to the outbreak of the monsoon in April, the following vessels were equipped and despatched overseas for further service in North Russia :—

5 ambulance paddlers (P.A.),
2 90-Class paddlers (P.S.),
2 hospital paddlers (H.P.),
1 captured paddler, *Basrah*, (P.S.),
3 refrigeration barges (R.B.).

These vessels were officered and manned throughout by I.W.T. personnel. With the exception of one of the

90-Class paddlers, which broke her back, but was able to crawl into Malta without loss of life, all these vessels have safely arrived in the United Kingdom.

In addition to the above, fifteen *Sumana* tugs were dismantled and despatched to the U.K. on the decks of cargo steamers.

The following vessels were also sent to India for sale or return to their original owners :—

    5 paddle steamers (P.S.),
  16 transport barges,
   1 dredger, *Campbell*,
   1 terminal pontoon,
   1 stern-wheeler (S.).

All of these arrived safely at their destinations in India or Burma.

At the present moment there are waiting in Basrah for the next fine weather season to enable them to be sent to India, most of them already prepared for sea :—

   7 90-Class paddlers (P.S.),
   9 other paddlers (P.S.),
   4 tugs (S.T.),
   3 steam barges (S.B.),
   3 motor lighters (M.L.),
   1 sea-going vessel, *Kalika*, (S.S.),
  50 transport barges.

With the exception of 10 London County Council steamers which have been hired out to local merchants for service between Basrah and Baghdad since March, the remainder of the general transport fleet is still fully employed for military purposes.

4. Mail and Civil Cargo Services.—Since the taking up of the Amara Railway a daily fast mail service has been maintained between Basrah and Kut by the creek steamers (T. Class). These run to time-table, doing the upward journey in 52 hours and the downward one in 34 hours.

To replace the railway the I.W.T. also run a bi-weekly

freight and passenger service from Basrah to Amara for the civil community. This is well patronised and much appreciated by the inhabitants of Amara.

5. Construction.—With the completion of the bulk-oil storage scheme, the Construction Department of the I.W.T. has been reduced to the minimum staff required for the maintenance of technical works and buildings and the construction of such wharves and jetties as may be required up-river.

6. Bridges.—All of the floating bridges have now been handed over to the Irrigation or Works Directorates with the exception of the large mechanically worked bridges on the Tigris, which are still maintained by the I.W.T.

7. Conservancy and Reclamation.—The Conservancy and Reclamation Department closed down on completion of the Hamar Lake dredging scheme, but it has been found necessary to form a small Dredging Department in its place, as further work from the dredgers has been required which is now being carried out. This for the present includes two reclamation schemes at Baghdad, one at Amara in conjunction with conservancy work, and one at Basrah.

8. Narrows Control.—In the Narrows the lighting system has been done away with, though " Control " is still maintained, but as most of the vessels remaining on the river have searchlights no undue delay is caused, and upward night running is carried out as before.

The Irrigation department have built a permanent regulator across the Majar Kebir Canal and a semi-permanent one in the Chahala, with the result that there has been an adequate supply of water passing through the Narrows throughout the low-river season, and no delays to vessels due to insufficient depth of water has occurred.

9. Buoyage and Pilotage.—The Buoyage Department is still at full strength. The original railway policy included the taking up of the Kut-Baghdad line, and as this would have thrown the entire maintenance of the force upon the river above Kut, it was considered necessary to preserve an adequate buoyage staff.

10. Gunboats.—The four Defence vessels are still carrying out their duties, and continue to exercise at least a moral effect on such portions of the Arab population as are inclined to be unruly. Two of the converted vessels of this class on the Upper Euphrates have been added to this fleet, having been armed with Maxims and 18-pounder field guns.

11. Control of Traffic on the Rivers and Registration of Civil Owned Vessels.—A Proclamation has been drawn up in collaboration with the Judicial Adviser to the Civil Administration, comprising complete and exhaustive rules and regulations for the better control of civil shipping on the rivers, to register and survey all such vessels, to license the masters and engineers in charge of them, and to inflict penalties for infringement of these regulations. This Proclamation embodies and legalises all previous regulations that have been made on this subject from time to time. The Director of I.W.T. is appointed the Chief Navigation Authority under the Proclamation with the powers of a first class magistrate.

CONCLUSIONS

1. Organisation and Administration.—A brief consideration of the lessons to be learnt from the working of the Inland Water Transport in Mesopotamia will be of some value in assisting to eliminate such errors as have been made in the past and should materially contribute to prepare for future eventualities. In this connection it must be emphasised that all large rivers possess their natural peculiarities or characteristics, and vessels which have proved in practice the most suitable for Mesopotamia may possibly be quite unsatisfactory in some other part of the world. For instance, conditions in Mesopotamia totally differed from those prevailing in France or Egypt. In the former case Inland Water Transport work was of primary importance, the rivers being the only highroads for supplies until the campaign was far advanced and forming the principal means of communication throughout, whilst in

the latter case, though it immensely relieved congestion on
the railways and roads, and contributed extensively to the
general transportation effort, the work was mainly carried
out on canals or canalised rivers, which presented neither
the same difficulties, nor did it present the same relative
importance to the success of operations generally. In such
circumstances comparison regarding the actual work accomplished or staff involved will serve no useful purpose, but a
common factor which is of value and applies equally to all
parts of the world is the I.W.T. organisation. This has
worked smoothly and efficiently from start to finish, responsibility having been adequately distributed, without the
Director in any way losing complete control of even his
most distant operations.

The I.W.T. in Mesopotamia was an entirely self-contained
Directorate. Generally speaking it is not economical, nor
does it tend to efficiency, for each Directorate to have its
own subsidiary departments, but the principle was fully
justified in this particular instance owing to the size of this
Directorate and the scope of its work. It may safely be
said that had the I.W.T. to depend upon other departments
of the Army for the construction of their huts and offices,
their workshops and store buildings, their bridges and
wharves, their oil tanks and pumping installations, the
reclamation of their areas, the building of their ships and
barges, the conservancy of the rivers, including an adequate
supply of the varied stores and equipment necessary, they
would not have been able to carry on as they have done.

It has frequently been said that the I.W.T. was doing
work which rightly belonged to other departments, and
this has sometimes been registered against the department.
The answer to such charges, however, was always simple,
i.e. it was being done because other departments were
unable to cope with the work, and therein lies one of the
secrets of Inland Water Transport success in Mesopotamia.
In addition to this, there was behind the department a
powerful and efficient department at the War Office who
never failed to respond to demands for officers, men, or

material. Without this support we could not possibly have accomplished what we did in Mesopotamia, and owing to this help we were able, besides doing our own work, to render extensive and valuable assistance in both men and material to other departments not so favourably situated. The extent of this assistance to others on the part of the Inland Water Transport is perhaps not fully appreciated.

A Directorate General of Transportation was never actually established in Mesopotamia, although it was intended to do so. I am of opinion that greater economy in working would have resulted had it been done. Loss of tonnage, frequently at vital moments, resulted through "Transportation" being made subservient to "Embarkation" requirements, whereas under a technical administration both might possibly have been combined with no loss to either. In other words, with a freer hand to load and despatch, the same amount of work might have been done with fewer vessels. As it was, our aim was to meet the needs of the Army irrespective of cost, and we had to make allowances for demands which in a commercial enterprise might be considered uneconomical.

2. **Personnel.**—The administration of an organisation such as the I.W.T. in Mesopotamia demands officers with unusual experience. It is necessary for them to possess sufficient education for ordinary official business, they must have a thorough grounding in seafaring knowledge, which can only be learnt at sea, they should also be accustomed to discipline and the handling of men, and have general knowledge of ship construction, dockyard organisation, rivers and their conservancy, surveying, stevedoring, construction of wharves and bridges, and a knowledge of the world. The naval officer, though possessing many of the above attributes, is not considered altogether suitable, as his training is not sufficiently elastic, whilst naval discipline, and routine loom perhaps too large on his horizon. The ordinary merchant service officer is also not altogether suitable, as generally speaking he has too little administrative experience. The best recruiting ground for the ideal

type of officer for this purpose is, in my opinion, the Marine Services of the Colonial, India, and Foreign Offices. Their marine officers being generally taken from the Royal Naval Reserve have both Naval and Merchant Service experience to start on, with the advantage of subsequent work of varied characters connected with rivers and river craft. They should also be acquainted with Government methods of office procedure, store-keeping, etc., and dealing with raw untrained natives. As the supply of these officers in the world is limited the question might be worth considering of forming a reserve from them for War service, or of maintaining a nucleus or skeleton organisation at the War Office to be completed in time of War for service in any part of the world.

The above remarks apply, of course, in general, as it is recognised that in both the Navy and Merchant Service there are many equally suitable men, if they can be found when wanted. A nucleus organisation, as outlined above, might enrol and arrange for the training of a reserve from these sources.

3. Type of Vessels.—The types of vessels used on the Mesopotamian rivers are too numerous to be described in detail here, consisting as they do, of the original craft in use in the country, a large number of vessels raked up here and there from India and Burma, and new vessels of various types from the United Kingdom.

As much criticism has been given at various times on the suitability or otherwise of the craft employed it might be as well, however, to record the considered verdict as to which type has proved the most satisfactory.

The conditions to be taken into account on the Tigris were, primarily, draught ; secondly, strength and power for towing ; thirdly, accommodation for troops ; fourthly, fuel or cargo carrying capacity. The above qualifications were all again governed by size. The original vessels in use in the country were paddle steamers and small screw tugs, and it was on these lines that the minds of the authorities responsible for ordering the first new vessels would

P

appear to have worked. For some reason or other there was a prejudice against stern-wheelers, possibly because so many were lost in the early days on the voyage from Burma to Mesopotamia ; possibly again because the really up-to-date twin-wheel stern-wheel steamer of high power, light draught, and great strength was then unknown in the East.

The vessels picked up in India were mostly paddle steamers, whose draught in the early days was much against them and caused endless trouble in the low river, otherwise they proved useful all round craft.

The first vessel ordered by India Office from the United Kingdom, known as the " 50-Class paddlers," were certainly an improvement on the lynch steamers that had been running in the country before the War. Although their actual draught turned out some six inches in excess of their specifications they proved most useful vessels. Their defects are (1) the machinery is too complicated, requiring skilled European engineers to run them ; (2) their horse-power (1000) is far too high, as it can never be fully utilised on the river and is a waste of about 30 per cent ; (3) their steering gear is badly designed ; (4) their windlass and ground tackle is too light, and their size and sponsons render them very liable to damage in navigating the Narrows.

The other vessels originally ordered from England were small screw tugs similar to those in use on the Tigris before the War. These also have proved most useful vessels, their only defect being that in shoal water during the low river they suck the bottom and require more water to work in than paddle vessels do.

It has already been mentioned that the requirements for the ideal troop and cargo carrying Tigris steamer were all governed by size. Above Amara the river is broad and draught is the governing factor, but between Amara and Kurna, particularly in the Narrows, length and breadth become of equal if not of greater importance. The 50-Class vessels are excellent for the above Amara service (the larger 90-Class vessels from India were only really suitable in the low river between Amara and Kut), but below Amara their repair bills were excessive, due to damage to their sponsons in passing through the Narrows.

The difficulty of getting a suitable vessel to meet all conditions was at once recognised by the Commission which came out in July, 1916, and the result of their representations to the War Office was the arrival, in due course, of the S. 40 and H.S. 13 Classes of quarter wheelers. These vessels were modifications of the quarter wheelers of "Richard Lander" type in use on the River Niger, and were designed by Colonel Ratsey. They are of strong build, light draught, have high-power simple machinery, carry a large supply of oil fuel, a fair amount of cargo, and accommodate a considerable number of troops.

The S.40 Class, which may properly be called "tugs," have fixed floats on their paddles, which though it detracts about 10 per cent from their speed, considerably reduces their repair bills as there are no bushes to renew.

The upper deck of this class of vessel is "Tumbled Home" 1 foot 9 inches each side, thus obviating damage to upper works by contact with barges.

The H.S. 13 Class have feathering paddle floats, these ships being 25 feet longer, and the upper deck the same width as the main deck. Originally built as hospital vessels, three of these have since been converted to ordinary transport vessels.

Both types have independent paddles which gives them practically the same manœuvring powers as side paddle steamers without the disadvantage of their vulnerability to damage owing to the extra beam and overhanging sponsons of the latter, and they are undoubtedly the most efficient and suitable vessels on the River Tigris. They fulfil draught, strength, and power conditions admirably. Having no sponsons and less beam than paddle steamers they sustain little or no damage when navigating the Narrows. The carrying capacity in troops, fuel, and cargo compares very well with any other vessels, and having no complicated machinery they can if necessary be run by native engineers.

As regards barges, the same mistake as with steamers

was made in following too blindly the early Mesopotamian models. Apart from the square swim ends of the first barges sent out, which were totally unsuitable for work in the Narrows, the barges were of too little depth for safe towing alongside paddle steamers, and advantage could not be taken during the high-water season to load these barges to their correct draught. The effect of such a barge alongside a paddler on striking the bank was for the outer side to tilt up with the result that the inner side often slipped under the paddle sponsors causing serious damage to the floats. The later barges ordered by the I.W.T. Commission were of deeper build and to a great extent obviated this danger. These were the C. 400 Class barges of 125 feet by 25 feet by 6 feet 9 inches dimensions.

The most efficient transport unit of all the various types and conditions on the river has been found to be one of the "Richard Lander" type of H.S. 13 (S. 14, 15, 16) or the S. 40 Class of steamers with two of the C. 400 Class of barges. And as this unit is one which would undoubtedly prove suitable for practically any river in the world, it might be standardised for future use. (For further particulars see chapter on "The Fleet.")

Motor-boats.—Many types of motor-boats were in use in Mesopotamia of all makes and sizes. Of these there can be no doubt that for rough handling, hard work, general reliability and usefulness the Kelvin engine comes easily first. This engine is simple in its construction, of good if somewhat roughly finished material, and is capable of being run by the most inexperienced motor drivers. Where more expensive and higher class engines have given constant trouble through silt in the water choking or wearing out their pumps, or through the inexperience of their drivers, the Kelvin ran with practically unfailing regularity. It is recommended as a standard type for operations such as the Mesopotamian Expedition.

4. Bandalling.—Bandalling has been used to a greater extent and with greater success as the limitations of that form of training are better understood. For instance, bandalling is now found to be quite useless in making the

P.A. 7.

Dimensions: length. 218'; breadth. 52' 6"; depth. 6' 3". Service draft, 3' 6". Engines, D.C. S/C., (1/P); 4 cylinders; Yarrow W. t'. boilers, N.H.P. 103'2. Speed, 10 knots. Towing 7'5 knots. Fuel capacity, 82 tons oil. Consum tion, 21 per 24 hours. Patients fitted for 200.
Seven vessels of this class all built in Great Britain.

S. 47

Length: 150'; extreme breadth, 34' 10"; depth, 6'. Loaded draft, 4' 3". Engines, H.C., S/C. (1/P); 4 cylinders; N H.P. 63'5. Spee·i, 10 4 knots. Fuel capacity, 46 tons oil. Consumption, 7 tons per 24 hours Cargo capacity. 100 tons. Troop capacity, 150.
Eleven vessels of this class constructed originally in Great Britain, some being re-erected in India or Mesopotamia.

water take a course that for some unapparent reason it does not want to, but, on the other hand, it is of the very greatest assistance in improving the natural (or possibly apparently unnatural) course it wishes to take.

Again it is found that bandals are useless when the current falls below a certain velocity, not only because the amount of silt in suspension is so small, but also because no scour will then set up.

The methods and effects of bandalling last year were much criticised in Mesopotamia. One charge was that unnatural instead of natural channels had been preserved, whilst another made was that extra depth in the channels had been secured at the expense of width.

The answer to the first is that bandals will not always make the river take the course required no matter how early operations are started nor how well the bandals are placed, and it is better to accept and improve the apparently unnatural course the river has taken than close the river to navigation altogether in the vain endeavour to conserve an ideal channel.

To the second charge—in the low river there is only a certain volume of water in the river and you cannot have it both ways. For obvious reasons depth is preferable to width. At the worst a narrow reach in the river can be controlled so that traffic does not meet in it, or a ship can bank in and drop her barges to let another pass. *Whereas without the depth there is no traffic at all.*

Finally, I consider that bandalling on the Tigris is of the very greatest assistance in improving and maintaining the channels, and in very many cases in actually forming them, and it has fully justified the expense and energy that have been expended upon it. But to the Buoyage service I give the palm for the principal success of the river transport in Mesopotamia. The system of marking the crossings and reaches has been excellent, and the devotion displayed by the Buoyage officers in patrolling the river, regulating traffic, piloting vessels over new or particularly bad crossings, and generally superintending operations, and this during the hottest months of the year, has been beyond all praise.

It will be interesting to watch what happens in the Tigris when bandalling is abandoned, as it threatens to be when the I.W.T. is finally demobilised. The Karun River which last year was kept open by this means, is this year unnavigable by vessels drawing more than 2 feet 6 inches, no bandalling having been carried out there this season. In concluding this afterword I wish to take the opportunity of placing on record my sincere thanks to all, both officers and men of the I.W.T. for the splendid way in which they have assisted me and worked together for the common cause. Without the great loyalty and " esprit de corps " which they have shown it would have been impossible to keep together such a large department as the I.W.T. in Mesopotamia. We had practically no regular soldiers in our organisation and no mutual traditions to maintain, yet in spite of this lack of the elements of cohesion, friction and bickering were conspicuous by their absence, and no department ever worked better together than ours has done. It is with the greatest regret that I have seen the breaking up for ever of our comradeship in this country. Of the three Deputy Directors all are now gone. Colonel Ratsey, back to his duties on the Niger, Colonel Ward to the Directorship of the port of Basrah, and Colonel Barton to London to his own affairs. Colonel Robertson and Colonel Truman now reign in their stead. Lieut.-Colonel Alexander has gone back to the Indian Railways, and Lieut.-Colonel Boyd to Northern Nigeria. The Royal Indian Marine have recalled nearly all their splendid young officers, and the Colonial Office have only left to us two of theirs. I cannot mention all the old friends who have left us, but what they have done is not forgotten, and those left are endeavouring to maintain the traditions that we and they have created. I again extend my heart-felt thanks to all and wish them the best of luck in the future.

R. H. W. HUGHES,

Brigadier-General,

27th *August,* 1919.   D.I.W.T.

P.S. 2 (" Kentung ").

Dimensions: length. 179'; breadth 60'; depth. 7' 6". Loaded draft. 5' 3". Engines.
D.C.. S/C. (C P); 2 Cylinders N.H P 49 6 Speed light. 8 knots. Towing, 5'5 knots
Fuel capacity, 60 tons oil. Consumption, 10 tons oil per 24 hours. Cargo capacity. 65
tons. Troop capacity, 300.

Eleven vessels of he same general features, but dimensions varying slightly; all
obtained from the Irrawadi Flotilla Company.

P.S. 16 (" Bhagabatti").

Dimensions: length, 192'; breadth, 48'; depth. 8'. Loaded draft, 4' 9". Engines.
D.C , S/C. (C/P); 2 cylinders; N.H.P. 81'4. Babcock W.T. boiler. Speed, 10 knots.
Towing, 5'5 knots. Fuel capacity, 65 tons coal. Consumption, 17 tons per 24 hours.
Cargo capacity, 66 tons. Troop capacity, 200.

Three vessels of this class, all from East India Railway Company

RIVER TIGRIS.

Mosul	Hammam Ali	Qaiyarah	Shargat	Lesser Zab	Fat-hah	Tikrit	Samarrah	Sinijah	Sindiyah	Sadiyah	Kasirin	Khan Jadidah	Nassawa	Kadhimain	Baghdad	Advanced Base	Hinaidi	Diyala	Station
																			Mosul
15																			Hammam Ali
50	35																		Qaiyarah
75	60	25																	Shargat
97	82	47	22																Lesser Zab
115	100	65	40	18															Fat-hah
152	137	102	77	55	37														Tikrit
186	171	136	111	89	71	34													Samarrah
218	203	168	143	121	103	66	32												Sinijah
242	227	192	167	145	127	90	56	24											Sindiyah
247	232	197	172	150	132	95	61	29	5										Sadiyah
257	242	207	182	160	142	105	71	39	15	10									Kasirin
263	248	213	188	166	148	111	77	45	21	16	6								Khan Jadidah
277	262	227	202	180	162	125	91	59	35	30	20	14							Nassawa
289	274	239	214	192	174	137	103	71	47	42	32	26	12						Kadhimain
294	279	244	219	197	179	142	108	76	52	47	37	31	17	5					Baghdad
299	284	249	224	202	184	147	113	81	57	52	42	36	22	10	5				Advanced Base
306	291	256	231	209	191	154	120	88	64	59	49	43	29	17	12	7			Hinaidi
314	299	264	239	217	199	162	128	96	72	67	57	51	37	25	20	15	8		Diyala
324	309	274	249	227	209	172	138	106	82	77	67	61	47	35	30	25	18	10	B
329	314	279	254	232	214	177	143	111	87	82	72	66	52	40	35	30	23	15	
338	323	288	263	241	223	186	152	120	96	91	81	75	61	49	44	39	32	24	
352	337	302	277	255	237	200	166	134	110	105	95	89	75	63	58	53	46	38	
379	364	329	304	282	264	227	193	161	137	132	122	116	102	90	85	80	73	65	
405	390	355	330	308	290	253	219	187	163	158	148	142	128	116	111	106	99	91	
453	438	403	378	356	338	301	267	235	211	200	196	190	176	164	159	154	147	139	
461	446	411	386	364	346	309	275	243	219	208	204	198	184	172	167	162	155	147	
507	492	457	432	410	392	355	321	289	265	254	250	244	230	218	213	208	201	193	
549	534	499	474	452	434	397	363	331	307	296	292	286	272	260	255	250	243	235	
581	566	531	506	484	466	429	395	363	339	328	324	318	304	292	287	282	275	267	
595	580	545	520	498	480	443	409	477	353	342	338	332	318	306	301	296	289	281	
618	603	568	543	521	503	466	432	400	376	365	361	355	341	329	324	319	312	304	
633	618	583	558	536	518	481	447	415	391	380	376	370	356	344	339	334	327	319	
660	645	610	585	563	545	508	474	442	418	407	403	397	383	371	366	361	354	346	
689	674	639	614	592	574	537	503	471	447	436	432	426	412	400	395	390	383	375	
717	702	667	642	620	602	565	531	499	475	464	460	454	440	428	423	418	411	403	
746	731	696	671	649	631	594	560	528	504	493	489	483	469	457	452	447	440	432	
770	755	720	695	673	655	618	584	552	528	517	513	507	493	481	476	471	464	456	
792	777	742	717	695	677	640	606	574	550	539	535	529	515	503	498	493	486	478	
812	797	762	737	715	697	660	626	594	570	559	555	549	535	523	518	513	506	498	
823	808	773	748	726	708	671	637	605	581	570	566	560	546	534	529	524	517	509	
854	839	804	779	757	739	702	668	636	612	601	597	591	577	565	560	555	548	540	

RIVER KARUN.

```
Basrah
20  Muhammerah
34  14  Salmanch
54  34  20  Ali-ibu Al Husain
74  54  40  20  Idrisiyah
94  74  60  40  20  Farsiat
100  86  72  52  32  12  Milainan
124 104  90  70  60  30  18  Bait Haidar
130 110  96  76  66  36  24  6  Ahwaz
```

RIVER DIYALAH.

```
Diyalah Bridge
9    Police Post
22   13   Cassell's Post
35   26   13   Coningham's Post
52   43   30   17   Baqubah
60   51   38   25   8    Qarnabit
77   58   55   42   25   17   Abu Giyeh
83   74   61   48   31   23   6    Sarfet
90   81   68   55   38   30   13   7    Akrat
103  94   81   68   51   43   26   20   13   Mansuriyah
130  121  108  95   78   70   53   47   40   27   Khanikin
```

```
esiphon
9    Bustan
3    14   Lajj
)    41   27   Zeur
6    67   53   26   Aziziyah
4    115  101  74   48   Sumar
2    123  109  82   56   8    Baghailah
8    169  155  128  102  54   46   Kut
)    211  197  170  144  96   88   42   Sheikh Sa'ad
2    243  299  202  176  128  120  74   32   Ali Gharbi
5    257  243  216  190  142  133  88   46   14   Filaifilah
4    280  266  239  213  165  157  111  69   37   23   Ali Ash Sharqi
4    295  281  254  228  180  172  126  84   52   38   15   Kumait
1    322  308  281  255  207  199  153  111  79   65   42   27   Amara
4    351  337  310  284  236  228  182  140  108  94   71   56   29   Qal'at Salih
5    379  365  338  312  264  256  210  168  136  122  99   84   57   28   Ezra's Tomb
7    408  394  367  341  293  285  239  197  165  151  128  113  86   57   29   Qurnah
     432  418  391  365  317  309  263  221  189  175  152  137  110  81   53   24   Nahr Umar
4    454  440  413  387  339  331  285  243  211  197  174  159  132  103  75   46   22   Basrah
5    474  460  433  407  359  351  305  263  231  217  194  179  152  123  95   66   42   20   Muhammerah
2    485  471  444  418  370  362  316  274  242  228  205  190  163  134  106  77   53   31   11   Abadan
5    516  502  475  449  401  393  347  305  273  259  236  221  194  165  137  108  84   62   42   31   Fao
```

DISTANCE

RIVER EUPHRATES.

Hit															
10	Aqubah														
20	10	Abu Rayat													
39	29	19	Ramadie												
61	51	41	22	Madhij Post											
84	74	64	45	23	Fallujah										
131	121	111	92	70	47	Mufraz Post									
162	152	142	123	101	78	31	Musaiyib								
168	158	148	129	107	84	37	6	Hindiyah Barrage							
182	172	162	143	121	98	51	20	14	Tuwairij						
208	198	188	169	147	124	77	46	40	26	Kifl					
226	216	206	187	165	142	95	64	58	44	18	Kufah				
238	228	218	199	177	154	107	76	70	56	30	12	Abu Sukhair			
268	258	248	229	207	184	137	106	100	86	60	42	30	Shenafiyah		
333	323	313	294	272	249	202	171	165	151	125	107	95	65	Samawah	
365	355	345	326	304	281	234	203	197	183	157	139	127	97	32	Kh
380	370	360	341	319	296	249	218	212	198	172	154	142	112	47	1
425	415	405	386	364	341	294	263	257	243	217	199	187	157	92	6
446	436	426	407	385	362	315	284	278	264	238	220	208	178	113	8
454	444	434	415	393	370	323	292	286	272	246	228	216	186	121	
459	449	439	420	398	375	328	297	291	277	251	233	221	191	126	
462	452	442	423	401	378	331	300	294	280	254	236	224	194	129	
467·5	457·5	447·5	428·5	406·5	383·5	336·5	305·5	299·5	285·5	259·5	241·5	229·5	199·5	134·5	1
471·5	461·5	451·5	432·5	410·5	387·5	340·5	309·5	303·5	289·5	263·5	245·5	233·5	203·5	138·5	1
473	463	453	434	412	389	342	311	305	291	265	247	235	205	140	1
482	472	462	443	421	398	351	320	314	300	274	256	244	214	149	1
499	489	479	460	438	415	368	337	331	317	291	273	261	231	166	1
512·5	502·5	492·5	473·5	451·5	428·5	381·5	350·5	344·5	330·5	304·5	286·5	274·5	244·5	179·5	1
513	503	493	474	452	429	382	351	345	331	305	287	275	245	180	1

BASRAH, APRIL. 1920.

TABLES.

DISTANCE TABLE OF HILLAH BRANCH FROM HINDIYAH BARRAGE TO SAMAWAH

Hindiyah Barrage															
9	Bustan Hantush														
21·5	12·5	Jumjumah													
26	17	4·5	Hillah												
35	26	13·5	9	Husain											
40	31	18·5	14	5	Jarbuiyah										
46	37	24·5	20	11	6	Allaq									
52	43	30·5	26	17	12	6	Qasr Kharqan								
64	55	42·5	38	29	24	18	12	Shattal Dagharah							
85	76	63·5	59	50	45	39	33	21	Khan Jadwal						
97	88	75·5	71	62	57	51	45	33	12	Diwaniyah					
118	109	96·5	92	83	78	72	66	54	33	21	Imam Hamza				
134	125	112·5	108	99	94	88	82	70	49	37	16	Abu Kawar			
141	132	119·5	115	106	101	95	89	77	56	44	23	7	Rumaithah		
151	142	129·5	125	116	111	105	99	87	66	54	33	17	10	Hamrah	
160	151	138·5	134	125	120	114	108	96	75	63	42	26	19	9	Samawah

raji										
Nasiriyah										
21	Suq-ash-Shuyukh									
29	8	Beni Said								
34	13	5	Mezlik							
37	16	8	3	Ismailie Camp						
·5 42·5	21·5	13·5	8·5	5·5	Three Ball Beacon					
·5 46·5	25·5	17·5	12·5	9·5	4	Beni Hutait				
48	27	19	14	11	5·5	1·5	Telegraph Corner			
57	36	28	23	20	14·5	10·5	9	Chibaish		
74	53	45	40	37	31·5	27·5	26	17	Medina Jetty	
5 87·5	66·5	58·5	53·5	50·5	45	41	39·5	30·5	13·5	Qurnah Railway Bridge
88	67	59	54	51	45·5	41·5	40	31	14	·5 Qurnah Boat Bridge

P.S. 89 (" Busreh ").

Dimensions: length 219'; breadth, 60'; depth, 9' 8". Loaded draft, 4' 9". Engines, D.Q. S C. (I/P) or (C/P); 4 cylinders; Yarrow W.T. Boilers; N.H.P. 252. Speed, light. 12 knots. Towing. 7·5 knots. Fuel capacity, 80 tons coal. Consumption. 20 tons per 24 hours. Has since been converted to oil fuel. Cargo capacity, 100 tons. Troop capacity, 500.
Captured from Turks.

P.S. 25 (" Marjoria ").

Dimensions: length, 176'; breadth, 49'; depth, 8'. Loaded draft, 5' 3". Engines, D.C., S/C. (I/P); 4 cylinders N.H.P. 76. Scotch boiler. Speed 7·5 knots. Towing, 5 knots. Fuel capacity, 55 tons oil. Consumption, 11 tons per 24 hours. Cargo Capacity, 45 tons. Troop capacity, 120.
Two vessels of this class from Assam Bengal Railway.

APPENDIX B1

RIVER FLEET IN COMMISSION WHEN TRANSFERRED FROM THE ROYAL INDIAN MARINE TO THE INLAND WATER TRANSPORT, R.E.

1.—GENERAL.

Designation Letters.	Type of Vessel.	Total.
S.S.	Sea-going steamers	4
S.T.	Sea and harbour tugs	4
P.S.	Paddle Steamers	39
S.	Stern-wheelers	7
T.	Up-River tugs	14
T.L.	Towing launches	12
L.	Steam launches	37
M.	Motor launches	95
—	River barges	84
—	Port barges	11
Y.	Small flat-bottomed lighters	39
M.I.	Motor lighters	17

2.—MEDICAL.

Designation Letters.	Type of Vessel.	Total.
H.S.	Hospital stern-wheelers	3
H.P.	Hospital paddler	1

SUMMARY

Self-propelled vessels	134
Hospital vessels	4
Barges	134
Motor-boats	95
Total	367

APPENDIX B2

RIVER FLEET IN COMMISSION AT TIME OF OCCUPATION OF BAGHDAD

1.—GENERAL.

Designation Letters.	Type of Vessel.	Total.
S.S.	Sea-going steamers	3
S.T.	Sea and harbour tugs	26
P.S.	Paddle steamers	60
S.	Stern-wheelers	13
T.	Up-River tugs	34
T.L.	Towing launches	23
L.	Steam launches	57
M.	Motor launches	187
S.B.	Steam barges	5
M.L.	Motor lighters	17
A. to E.	River barges	194
O. (A. to E.)	Oil barges	16
Port	Port barges	59
Y.	Small open lighters	40

2.—MEDICAL.

Designation Letters.	Type of Vessel.	Total.
H.P.	Hospital paddlers	1
H.S.	Hospital stern-wheelers	3
H.	Hospital screw-steamers	3
H.B.	Hospital barges	3

SUMMARY

Self-propelled vessels	242
Motor-boats	187
Barges	315
Total	744

P.S. 50.

Dimensions: length 225'; breadth, 52'; depth, 6' 3". Loaded draft, 4' 6"   Engines,
D.C., S/C. (I/P); 4 cylinders; Yarrow W.T. boilers; N.H.P. 103'2.   Speed, light 10 knots.
Towing 7'5 knots.   Fuel capacity, 82 tons oil.   Consumption, 21 tons per 24 hours.   Cargo
capacity, 80 tons.   Troop capacity, 500.
Eleven vessels of this class all built in United Kingdom.

P.S. 37 ('' Susang '').

Dimensions; length 162' 2'; breadth, 40'; depth, 7' 6". Loaded draft, 5' 3". Engines
D.C., S/C. (C/P); 3 cylinders N.H.P. 51'2.   Speed, 9'5 knots   Towing, 5 knots.   Fuel
capacity, 38 tons oil.   Consumption. 11'2 tons per 24 hours.   Cargo capacity. 80 tons.
Troop capacity. 30.
Four vessels of this class from Indian General Steam Navigation Company.

APPENDIX B3

INLAND WATER TRANSPORT CRAFT IN COMMISSION : 31ST DECEMBER, 1917

1.—GENERAL.

Designation Letters.	Type of Vessel.	Total
S.S.	Sea-going steamers	5
S.T.	Sea and harbour tugs	27
P.S.	Paddle steamers	3
S.	Stern-wheelers	19
T.	Up-River tugs	48
P.T.	Paddle tugs	15
M.T.	Motor-tugs	6
T.L.	Towing launches	26
L.	Steam launches	78
M.	Motor launches	259
H.G.	Hydro-Glissieurs	8
S.B.	Steam barges	13
M.L.	Motor lighters	14
A. to E.	River barges	391
O.	Oil barges	34
Port	Port barges	98
Y.	Small open lighters	39

2.—MEDICAL.

Designation Letters.	Type of Vessel.	Total
H.	Screw vessels	5
H.P.	Paddlers	5
P.R.	Paddlers (Ambulance)	4
H.S.	Stern-wheelers	4
H.M.	Motor-ships	2
H.B.	Barges	1
M.	Motor-boats (Red Cross Society)	64*
M.	E.M.O.'s boats	33*

3.—SPECIAL PURPOSE VESSELS.

Designation Letters or Name.	Type of Vessel.	Total
Phalwan	Floating crane	1
S.V. 1	Grab dredger and salvage	1
Nemotha	Suction dredger	1
S. 5	Small bucket dredger	1
R.B.	Refrigerator barges	6
W.B.	Water barges	6
I.B.	Ice barges	4
Hopper	Hopper	1
T.	Tractor barges	4
Fire	Motor fire-boats	3

SUMMARY.

Self-propelled vessels	. 358
Barges	. 585
Motor-boats	. 356
Total.	1299

* The total number of motor launches, general and medical, is 356.

APPENDIX B4

RIVER CRAFT IN COMMISSION AT PERIOD OF ARMISTICE: 11TH NOVEMBER, 1918

1.—General.

Designation Letters.	Type of Vessel.	Total
S.S.	Sea-going steamers	2
S.T.	Sea and harbour tugs	27
P.S.	Paddle steamers	68
S.	Stern-wheelers	26
T.	Up-River tugs	52
P.T.	Paddle tugs	21
M.T.	Motor-tugs	6
T.L.	Towing launches	22
L.	Steam launches	86
M.	Motor-boats	414
S.B.	Steam barges	13
M.L.	Motor lighters	12
A. to E.	River barges	422
O. (A. to E.)	Oil barges	75
Port	Port barges	169
Y.	Small flat-bottomed barges	33
M.B.	Motor bellums	34
H.G.	Hydro-Glisseurs	9

2.—Medical.

Designation Letters.	Type of Vessel.	Total
H.	Hospital screw steamers	5
H.P.	Hospital paddlers	6
P.A.	Ambulance paddlers	7
H.S. & S.A.	Hospital stern-wheelers	7
H.M.	Hospital motor-ships	2
H.B.	Hospital barges	3

3.—Special Purpose Vessels.

Designation Letters.	Type of Vessel.	Total
F.	"Fly" steamers	16
R.B.	Refrigeration barges	13
W.(A. to E.)	Water barges	11
L.(A. to E.)	Ice barges	9
F.(A. to E.)	Filtration barges	4
C.S.	Cold storage barges	1
	Tractor barges, hoppers, punts, diving boats	34
	Salvage vessels, dredgers, floating cranes, floating workshops, fire-floats	25

SUMMARY.

Self-propelled vessels	446
Barges	774
Motor-boats	414
Total	1634

M.L.I. ("MOTOR LIGHTER").
Dimensions: length, 105' 6"; extreme breadth, 22' 6"; depth, 8'. Loaded draft, 6'.
Engines of various types, B.H.P. about 60. Speed, 7 knots. Cargo capacity from 100 to
120 tons. Fuel capacity, 1100 gallons paraffin. Consumption, 96 gallons per 24 hours.
Twenty-five such vessels all taken over from the Royal Navy.

H.P. 7.
Dimensions: length, 218'; breadth, 52' 6"; depth, 6' 3". Service draft, 3' 6". Engines,
C., S/C. (I/P.); 4 cylinders; Yarrow W.T. boiler, N.H.P. 39·6. Speed, 8 knots. Fuel
capacity, 55 tons oil. Consumption, 7 tons per 24 hours.
Patients fitted for 98 British and 96 Indian.
Four of this class all built in Great Britain.

H.S. 13.

Dimensions: length, 174' 6"; extreme breadth, 35' 2"; depth, 6' 9". Service draft, 3' 7½". Engines, 2 sets H.C., S/C.; 4 cylinders; N.H.P. 63'5. Speed, light 9'5 knots. Towing, 5 knots. Boiler, Yarrow W.T. Fuel capacity. 30 tons oil. Consumption, 9 tons per 24 hours.

Four vessels of this class originally hospital ships, 3 of which have been converted for Military Transport purposes. All built in United Kingdom. Nos. 14, 16 re-erected at Bombay and No. 15 at Maghil.

Extra fuel oil tanks of 30 tons capacity fitted to S. 14, S. 15 and S. 16.

H.S. 16.

Dimensions: length, 174' 6"; extreme breadth, 35' 2"; depth, 6' 9". Service draft, 3' 7½". Engines, 2 sets H.C., S/C.; 4 cylinders; N.H.P. 63'5. Speed, light, 9'5 knots. Towing, 5 knots. Boiler, Yarrow W.T. Fuel capacity, 30 tons oil. Consumption, 9 tons per 24 hours.

Four vessels of this class originally hospital ships, 3 of which have been converted for Military Transport purposes. All built in United Kingdom, Nos. 14, 16 re-erected at Bombay and No. 15 at Maghil.

Extra fuel oil tanks of 30 tons capacity fitted to S. 14, S. 15, and S. 16.

APPENDIX B5

SUMMARY OF FLEET ON THE EUPHRATES AT THE CONCLUSION OF HOSTILITIES

1.—GENERAL.

Designation Letters.	Type of Vessel.	Total.
Fly	Defence vessels	2
F.	Converted gunboats	12
S.	Stern-wheel steamers	5
S.B.	Steam barges	1
T.	Up-River tugs	8
T.L.	Steam towing launches	7
L.	Steam launches	12
M.	Motor-boats	44
D. & E.	River transport barges	67
O.E.	Oil barges	5
Z.	Oil pumping plant	1
Z.	Workshop barge	1
Y.	Small flat-bottomed lighters	3

2.—MEDICAL.

Designation Letters.	Type of Vessel.	Total.
H.S.	Hospital stern-wheel steamer	1
S.A.	Stern-wheel Ambulance steamer	1
M.	Motor-boats	10

SUMMARY

Self-propelled vessels	49
Motor-boats	54
Barges	74
Flat-bottomed lighters	3
Total	180

APPENDIX B6

LIST OF FLEET AUXILIARIES

STEAM BARGES.				MOTOR LIGHTERS.			
			Tons.				Tons.
S.B. 1	.	.	132	M.L. 1	.	.	170
†2 (bulk oil)		.	132	2	.	.	170
†3	.	.	132	3	.	.	170
4	.	.	132	4	.	.	170
†5	.	.	132	5	.	.	170
6 (bulk oil)		.	237	6	.	.	170
7	.	.	237	7	.	.	170
8	.	.	122	8	.	.	170
9	.	.	132	9	.	.	170
10	.	.	170	10	.	.	170
11	.	.	170	11	.	.	170
12	.	.	123	12	.	.	170
13	.	approx.	100	13	.	.	170
				14	.	.	170
				15	.	.	170
S.S. *Saaid* (bulk oil)		.	327	16	.	.	170
				17	.	.	170
				18	.	.	170
				19	.	.	170
				20	.	.	170
†Oil burning.				21	.	.	—
				22	.	.	—
				23	.	.	—
				24	.	.	—
				25	.	.	—

H.I. ("KARMALA").

Dimensions: length, 100' 9"; extreme breadth, 25'; depth, 7' 6". Service draft. 3' 3".
Engines, T/S., T., S/C.; 6 cylinders; N H.P. 51. Speed, 10 knots. Fuel capacity, 18 tons
coal. Consumption, 7·2 tons per 24 hours.
Two vessels of this class obtained from the Port Commissioners, Calcutta.

H.M. 1.

Dimensions: length, 160'; extreme breadth. 31' 2"; depth, 6'; Service draft (maximum).
4' 1". Engines. T/S., Thorneycroft Engine, B.H.P. 300 Speed 8·5 knots. Fuel capacity.
19 tons paraffin. Consumption 2·75 tons per 24 hours.
Four such vessels built in the United Kingdom. Two similar vessels built in India—
one of slightly different dimensions built in India for Red Cross Society.

T. 80.

Dimensions: length, 81' 6"; extreme breadth, 17' 2"; depth 5'. Service draft, 3' 8". Engines, T/S C., S/C., 4 cylinders; N.H.P. 27. Speed, light, 10'5. Towing 5 knots. Fuel capacity, 9 tons oil. Consumption 3'85 tons per 24 hours.

There are 34 vessels of this class all built in the United Kingdom and shipped per transport to Mesopotamia,

S.T.1. ("LAMMADAW").

Dimensions: length 110'; extreme breadth 21' 6"; depth, 8'; Draft, 6', Engines. T/S., S/C.; 4 Cylinders; N.H P. 33'2, Speed, light, 10 knots. Towing, 6 knots. Fuel capacity, 60 tons coal. Consumption, 6 tons per 24 hours.

Four vessels of this class of slightly varying dimensions. All obtained from Irrawadi Flotilla Company.

LIST OF OIL-CARRYING, SELF-PROPELLED VESSELS AND BARGES

Barges.		Max. Load.	Max. Draught.	Remarks.
O.C.	2	150	3′ 0″	Fuel oil.
	4	155	3′ 1″	,,
	5	155	3′ 1″	,,
	6	155	3′ 1″	,,
O.B.	11	619	6′ 3″	,,
	12	419	5′ 0″	,,
	14	336	5′ 3″	,,
	15	533½	7′ 6″	,,
	16	770	8′ 0″	,,
	17	555	6′ 2″	,,
	18	555	6′ 2″	,,
O.A.	19	700	6′ 0″	,,
O.B.	20	590	6′ 0″	,,
	21	580	6′ 0″	,,
	22	550	6′ 0″	,,
	23	550	6′ 0″	,,
	24	550	6′ 0″	,,
	25	580	6′ 0″	,,
	26	580	6′ 0″	,,
	27	550	6′ 0″	,,
	28	550	6′ 0″	,,
	29	550	6′ 0″	,,
O.A.	30	700	8′ 0″	,,
O.E.	60	16·3	Lower	Fuel oil.
	61	15·7	Euphrates	,,
O.E.	62	40	4′ 6″	Tinned oil.
	63	40	4′ 6″	,,
	64	40	4′ 6″	,,
	65	40	4′ 6″	,,
	66	40	4′ 6″	,,
	67	40	4′ 6″	,,

Barges.		Max. Load.	Max. Draught.	Remarks.
O.E.	68	40	4' 6"	Tinned oil.
	69	40	4' 6"	,,
	70	40	4' 6"	,,
	71	40	4' 6"	,,
	72	40	4' 6"	,,
	73	40	4' 6"	,,
	74	40	4' 6"	,,
	75	40	4' 6"	,,
	76	40	4' 6"	,,
	77	40	4' 6"	,,
	78	40	4' 6"	,,
	79	40	4' 6"	,,
	80	40	4' 6"	,,
	81	40	4' 6"	,,
	82	40	4' 6"	,,
	83	40	4' 6"	,,
	84	40	4' 6"	,,
	85	40	4' 6"	,,
	86	11·14	—	Bulk kerosene.
	87	28	—	,,
O.C.	8	155	3' 1"	Petrol (bulk cased).
	40	234	4' 6"	,, ,,
	42	234	4' 6"	,, ,,
	43	234	4' 6"	,, ,,
	45	234	4' 6"	,, ,,
	46	234	4' 6"	,,
	47	234	4' 6"	,,
O.D.	48	72	3' 0"	,,
O.C.	49	234	4' 6"	,,
	50	234	4' 6"	,,
	51	234	4' 6"	,,
	52	234	4' 6"	,,
	53	234	4' 6"	,,
	54	234	4' 6"	,,
	55	234	4' 6"	,,
	57	234	4' 6"	,,
	58	234	4' 6"	,,
	59	234	4' 6"	,,
W.E.	4	29	3' 0"	Kerosene.
	5	29	3' 0"	,,
	6	29	3' 0"	,,
	7	29	3' 0"	,,

Barges.	Max. Load.	Max. Draught.	Remarks.
W.E. 10	48	3' 0"	Kerosene.
11	48	3' 0"	,,
O.C. 1	150	3' 0"	,,
3	155	3' 1"	,,
7	155	3' 1"	,,
O.B. 13	419	5' 0"	,,
O.C. 31	228	6' 3"	Kerosene.
32	228	6' 3"	,,
33	285	6' 3"	,,

These barges carry 4000 tins of kerosene in addition to above in bulk.

O.C. 44	Out of commission.	
O.B. 9 ⎫ 10 ⎬	Temporarily used as water barges at Bushire.	

Self-propelled oil-carrying vessels.

Saaid	310	Fuel oil.
S.B. 2	70	,,
6	248	,,
M.T. 97	15½	Kerosene.
98	15½	,,

APPENDIX C1

INLAND WATER TRANSPORT, R.E. MESOPOTAMIAN EXPEDITIONARY FORCE.

APPROVED ESTABLISHMENT, AFTER REORGANISATION, AND SUBSEQUENT TO OCCUPATION OF BAGHDAD.

	BRITISH				INDIAN		Total.
	Officers.	Warrant Officers.	Sergeants.	Rank and File.	Civilian Clerks.	Other Ratings.	
Director	1						1
Deputy Directors	2						2
Assistant Directors	7						7
Lieutenant-Colonels	(a) 4						4
Deputy Assistant Directors	17						17
Controller	(c) 1						1
Deputy Controllers	(d) 1						1
Assistant Controllers	(e) 3						3
Majors	(b) 14						14
Captains	(b)247						247
Subalterns	558						558
Warrant Officers, Class I		5					5
" " Class II		210					210
Sergeants			343				343
Corporals				489			489
2nd Corporals				497			497
Sappers				1486			1486
British West Indies Regt., N.C.O.'s				50			50
" " " Other Ranks				350			350
R.E. Pioneers				220			220
Civilian Clerks					460		460
Native Ratings						29,025	29,025
					460	29,025	29,025
Total	855	215	343	3092	460	29,025	33,990

Q

APPENDIX C2

INLAND WATER TRANSPORT, ROYAL ENGINEERS. MESOPOTAMIAN EXPEDITIONARY FORCE.

REVISED ESTABLISHMENT, 1918

(See paragraph 31 of "Summary of Events" in Part I.)

	British (including British West Indies Regt.)															Eastern Races			Grand Total.	Animals.
	Director.	Depy. Directors.	Asst. Directors.	Depty. Asst. Directors.	Majors and Captains.	Subalterns.	Total Officers.	W.O.'s, Class I.	W.O.'s, Class II.	Staff Sergeants and Sergeants.	Corporals.	2nd Corporals.	Lance-Corporals.	Sappers.	Total: B.O.R.'s.	Skilled.	Unskilled and Followers.	Total: Eastern Races.		
Headquarters	1	2	1	1	4	5	14	3	2	15	23	4	—	57	104	—	88	88	206	5
Construction	—	—	1	3	20	35	59	3	9	34	66	64	89	122	387	2028	3652	5680	6126	1
Transport and Administration	—	—	6	13	45	78	143	14	22	83	65	69	96	244	593	250	3203	3453	4189	6
Vessels	—	—	1	2	26	43	72	36	56	29	76	23	22	82	324	} 615	*15013	10751	11147	1
Marine Engineering	—	—	1	1	38	195	236	15	21	37	34	56	51	139	353			4877	5466	1
Accounts	—	—	1	1	2	11	15	—	5	9	5	10	8	33	71	—	32	32	118	1
Dockyards and Shipbuilding	—	—	1	5	36	71	113	21	30	74	98	95	125	190	633	7553	2472	10025	10771	1
Native Craft	—	—	1	4	9	20	34	2	7	16	19	16	31	97	188	321	234	555	777	1
I.W.T. Stores	—	—	—	2	1	8	11	3	2	10	16	11	18	63	113	11	151	162	286	1
Buoyage and Pilotage	—	—	1	2	16	34	53	2	4	5	10	7	12	53	95	23	883	906	1054	—
Conservancy and Reclamation	—	—	1	2	8	19	30	5	11	30	43	15	61	27	69	114	1774	1888	1987	1
Camps	—	—	—	—	7	12	19	—	—	—	—	—	—	242	407	—	415	415	841	—
Total	1	2	15	36	214	530	799	106	170	352	464	377	519	1349	3337	10915	27917	38832	42968	19

* Ships' ratings are included in this figure.

Appendix C3.

INLAND WATER TRANSPORT: MESOPOTAMIA EXPEDITIONARY FORCE

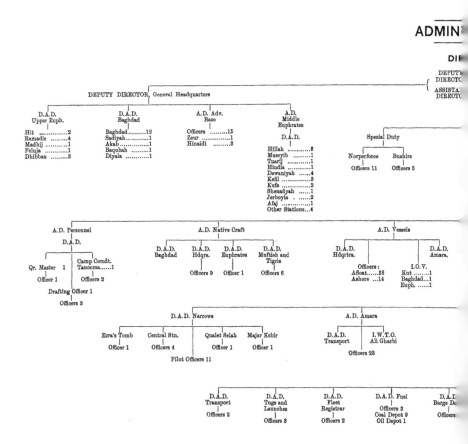

eral Duty)
eadquarters)

DEPUTY DIRECTOR, Chief Engineer

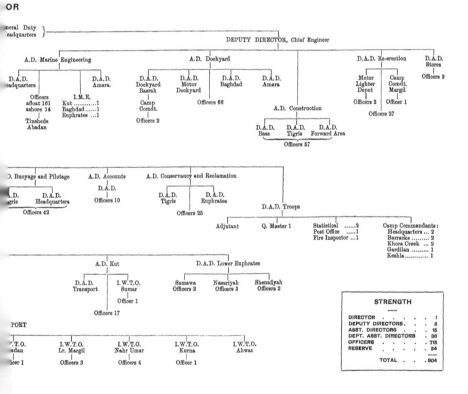

| A.D. Marine Engineering | A.D. Dockyard | D.A.D. Re-erection | D.A.D. Stores |

A.D. Marine Engineering
- D.A.D. Headquarters — Officers afloat 161, ashore 14, Tinsheds Abadan
- I.M.E. Kut ....1, Baghdad ......1, Euphrates ...1
- D.A.D. Amara.

A.D. Dockyard
- D.A.D. Dockyard Basrah — Camp Comdt. Officers 2
- D.A.D. Motor Dockyard
- D.A.D. Baghdad — Officers 66
- D.A.D. Amara — A.D. Construction
  - D.A.D. Base, D.A.D. Tigris, D.A.D. Forward Area — Officers 57

D.A.D. Re-erection
- Motor Lighter Depot — Officers 2
- Camp Comdt. Margil — Officer 1
- Officers 27

D.A.D. Stores — Officers 9

| D. Buoyage and Pilotage | A.D. Accounts | A.D. Conservancy and Reclamation |

D. Buoyage and Pilotage
- .D. gris | D.A.D. Headquarters — Officers 42

A.D. Accounts
- D.A.D. Officers 10

A.D. Conservancy and Reclamation
- D.A.D. Tigris | D.A.D. Euphrates — Officers 25
- D.A.D. Troops
  - Adjutant | Q. Master 1 | Statistical .....2, Post Office .....1, Fire Inspector ...1 | Camp Commandants: Headquarters ... 2, Barracks .... 2, Khora Creek ... 2, Gardilan .... 1, Keshla............. 1

A.D. Kut | D.A.D. Lower Euphrates
- D.A.D. Transport | I.W.T.O. Sumar — Officer 1, Officers 17
- Samawa Officers 2, Nasariyah Officers 3, Shenafiyah Officers 2

PORT

.T.O. adan icer 1 | I.W.T.O. Lr. Margil Officers 3 | I.W.T.O. Nahr Umar Officers 4 | I.W.T.O. Kurna Officer 1 | I.W.T.O. Ahwaz

STRENGTH	
DIRECTOR	1
DEPUTY DIRECTORS	3
ASST. DIRECTORS	15
DEPT. ASST. DIRECTORS	36
OFFICERS	715
RESERVE	34
TOTAL	804

APPENDIX D1.

1. Machine Fitting Shops, etc.
2. Spare Gear Store.
3. Dockyard General Stores
4. Dockyard Office.
5. Ice Plant.
6. Foremen's Quarters.
7. Large Slipways (Three)
8. Small Slipways (Five)
9. Native Huts (Mechanics)
10. Motor Dockyard Office.
11. -do- Carpenters Store.
12. -do- Machine Shop.
12.A. Steam Hauling Gear for all Slips.
12.B. Sheds over Slipways.
12.C. Wharves
12.D. Repairing Berth Jetties

13. Time Office.
14. Post Office.
15. Carpenters' Shop.
16. Power House.
17. Latrines.
18. Hospital & Quarters.
19. Sikh Temple.
20. Timber Shed.
21. Police Quarters.
22. Chinese Huts.
23. Motor Dockyard Officers' Mess.
24. Servants' Quarters.
25. Chinese Store.
26. Chinese Mess Room.
26.A. Fire Pumps & General Service
26.B. Clerks Quarters

27. Keshla Camp.
28. I.W.T. Barracks, Low Lane.
29. Construction Store & Workshop.
30. Ration Store.
31. Dispensary.
32. Chinese Cook House.
33. Refuse Destructor.
34. Canteen.
35. Castle Mess (Burnt down).
36. Dockyard Officers' Mess.
37. Officers' Quarters.
38. Chinese & Indian Wash-houses
39. Motor Boat Slipway. } Dismantled
40. do. do. do. } in 1918.

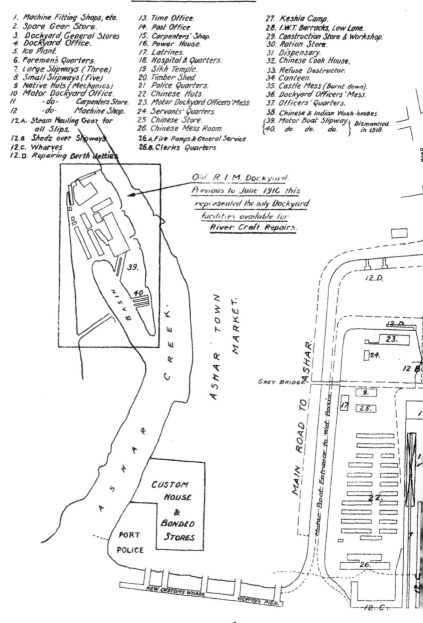

Old R.I.M. Dockyard.
Previous to June 1916 this
represented the only Dockyard
facilities available for
River Craft Repairs.

Wm Brendon & Son, Lith? Plymouth.

I. W. T. DOCKYARD. BASRAH.
And Surroundings.

Ft. 100 50 0   100   200   300   400   500   600 Ft.

SHAR BARRACKS.

DANIEL ROAD

27.

28.

26. 8

31.

32. 32.

GARDEN STREET

33.

17

29. 22   22   30.   17.   9.

RECREATION

GROUND.

WET BASIN.

17.

2. D.   12. D.   12. D.   34.

11.   19.   9.

12.   9.   18.   12. D.

14. 13.

21.

21.   15.   16.   12 D

20.   17.

3.   2.

PORTOON BRIDGE.

35   OFFICERS QUARTERS   36

4.   1.

6. 6. 4.

6.

5.

26. A

OLD RIVER BOUNDARY

12. C.

12. C.   SHIPS ENTRANCE TO WET BASIN.

37

KHANDAK CREEK.

B .

APPENDIX D2

LIST OF MACHINERY IN BASRAH DOCKYARD

Dockmaster's Department :—

4 Motor-tugs : M. 269, M. 270, M. 281, M. 282
1 Twin-screw tug, " S.T. 1."
1 Tug fitted with fire-pump, " T.L. 2."
1 Oil barge. Capacity, 2560 galls.
1 Ten-ton fixed crane.
2 Five-ton travelling cranes.
1 Three-ton travelling crane.
1 Two-ton travelling crane.

Electrical Workshops :—

1 6-in. lathe and gear complete.
1 3½-in. bench lathe with gears and chucks complete.

.Power House :—

1 Petter oil engine, 33 k.w. 50 b.h.p.
1 Dynamo (Greenwood and Batley), 33 k.w. 220 v. 150 amp.
   compound.
1 Gardner oil engine, 35 b.h.p. 4-cylinder.
1 Lancashire dynamo, 25 k.w. 220 v. 114 amp. shunt wound.
1 Bellis and Morcom steam engine, 2-cylinder.
1 Dynamo (Westinghouse Co.), 75 k.w. 220 v. 341 amp.
   interpolar.
1 Dynamo (Jessop & Co.), 220 v. compound.

Electric Motors :—

1 (No. 1) 145 amp. 220 v. 50 h.p., starter D.P., ironclad
   switch and fuses, 150 amp.
1 (No. 2) 145 amp. 220 v. 50 h.p., starter D.P., ironclad
   switch and fuses, 150 amp. Everett ammeter 0–150.
1 (No. 3) 72 amp. 220 v. G.E.C. " Reyrolle " starter D.P.,
   ironclad switch and fuses, 75 amp. Crompton ammeter
   0–120.

1 (No. 4) 75 amp. 220 v., one starter D.P., ironclad switch and fuses, 75 amp. Crompton ammeter 0–120.

1 (Foundry) 20 amp. 220 v., one starter D.P., ironclad switch and fuses, 20 amp. Everett ammeter 0–20 Verity's speed regulator.

2 (Thermo-tank blower motors), 20 amp., 220 amp. 220 v., one starter.

Carpenter's Shop :—

1 Circular saw bench for 48-in. saw.
1 Spare bevel fence for above.
1 Circular saw bench to take 40-in. saw.
1 Planing machine to take 24-in. wide.
1 Universal wood-working machine.
1 Saw-sharpening bench complete.
1 Saw-sharpening machine.
1 Four-speed wood-turning lathe with tools complete.
1 Four-speed wood-turning lathe with tools complete.

Foundry :—

1 Cupola, capacity 30 cwt. per hour, with staging and platform complete.
1 Cupola.
2 Oil-fired brass furnaces. Capacity 600 lb. each per day.

Machine and Fitting Shops:—

Lathes.	Speeds.	Centres. Inches.	Gap. Width. Inches.	Depth. Inches.	Length of bed. Feet.	Inches.
1 S.C.	4	18	27	34	26	3
1 ,,	5	17⅝	18½	24	22	0
1 ,,	4	12½	19	23¾	16	1
1 ,,	4	7½	10¾	14	6	0
1 ,,	4	7½	10½	14	6	0
1 ,,	4	8½	13	17	8	0
1 ,,	5	8½	None		12	0
1 ,,	4	6½	8	11½	6	0
1 ,,	4	8½	13½	17½	8	3
1 ,,	3	9	13	18	8	3
1 ,,	4	8	11	15½	10	2
1 ,,	4	9	13½	17½	8	0
1 ,,	4	9¾	12½	16	11	6
1 ,,	4	12½	18	23	16	3
1 ,,	4	10¼	17	20	12	6
1 ,,	3	6	12½	12¼	4	6

Machine and Fitting Shops (*continued*):—

Lathes.	Speeds.	Centres. Inches.	Width. Inches.	Gap. Depth. Inches.	Length of bed. Feet.	Inches.
1 S.C.	3	9	13½	18	8	3
1 „	4	10	14	19	12	0
1 „	3	8½	14	17	10	0
1 „	4	10	15	20½	14	6
1 „	3	6	7½	9½	6	6
1 „	3	6	7½	9	6	6
1 „	4	7½	11	13½	6	0
1 „	3	5¾	10	12	5	0
1 „	3	6½	11	12½	6	0
2 „	4	7½	11	14	6	0
1 „	5	8	None		8	0
1 „	4	6½	10	13	7	0
1 „	4	9½	14	18	12	0
1 „	3	10½	None		10	0
1 „	3	5	9	9	5	0
1 „	3	8½	12½	16	8	3
4 „	4	7½	11	14	6	0

1 4½-in. hollow spindle capstan lathe.
2 2¾-in. hollow spindle hexagonal turret lathes.

BORING MILLS :

No.	Speeds.	in.	in.	in.	ft.	in.
1 S.C.	3	24	13	34	8	2
1 „	5	37	71	37	10	0

SHAPING MACHINES :

No.	Speeds.	Stroke. in.	Length of bed. ft.	in.
1	3	10	3	6
1	4	12	4	3

PLANING MACHINES :

No.	Width. ft.	in.	Height. ft.	in.	Travel. ft.	in.
1	3	9	3	0	5	8
1	1	9	2	0	7	2
1	1	10	2	4	4	8

SLOTTING MACHINES :

No.	Speeds.	Stroke. in.	Takes. ft.	in.	Depth. in.
1	4	12	3	8	18
1	4	14	6	0	27

Machine and Fitting Shops (*continued*) :—

DRILLING MACHINES :

No.	Speeds.		Centre of spindle to column.
1	4	Double gear	2 ft.
1	4	,,	12 in.
1	4	,,	15 in.
1	4	,,	10 in.
1	4	,,	10 in.
1	4	,,	4 ft.

Radial drilling machine with upright pillar and swinging head.

1	4	Double gear.	4 ft.

Radial drilling machine with geared arm to drill at any angle.

No.	Speeds.			Centre of spindle to column.
1	4	Single gear.		13 in.
1	4	,, Sensitive drill.		10 in.
1	4	,,	,,	10 in.
1	4	,,	,,	10 in.

MILLING MACHINES :

No.

2 4-speed universal milling and cutting machines.

SCREWING MACHINES :

No.	Speeds.		
1	3	Takes up to	2½-in. pipes.
1	3	,,	1½-in. pipes.
1	3	,,	1-in. bolts.
1	Single-speed.	,,	4-in. pipes.
1	Single hand-power.		4½-in. pipes.

1 Steel bandsaw.
1 Universal grinder, length of bed 2 ft.
1 Portable crane, mounted on wheels, to lift one ton.
1 Portable testing pump, with gauge complete.
  Diameter of barrel 2 in., stroke 2 in.

Boiler and Machinery for Workshop Driving :—

No

1 Robey under-type engine with semi-loco. boiler. W.P. 100 lb. per sq. in. with feed pump.
1 Loco. type boiler. W.P. 140 lb. per sq. in.
3 Gardner feed pumps, 4 in. by 3 in. by 4 in.
1 Cochran vertical water-tube boiler with external uptake.

Boiler and Machinery for Workshop Driving (*continued*) :

No.
1 Feed pump (Dawson's vertical), 4 in. by 2¾ in. by 6 in. (No. 2676.)
1 Pressure-jet liquid fuel (Kermodes') outfit.
1 Yarrow water-tube boiler. W.P. 175 lb. per sq. in.
2 Feed pumps (Weir's), 4 in. by 8 in.
1 Worthington, 4½ in. by 2¾ in. by 4 in.

Boilermaker's Shop :—

No.
1 Punching and shearing machine, ¼-in. plate.
1 Punching and shearing machine, ½-in. plate.
1 Punching and shearing machine, 1-in. plate.
1 Bending roll machine.
1 Drilling machine.

Blacksmith's Shop :—

1 Bolt and rivet making machine with dies complete, to make from ½ in. to 1 in. bolts and rivets at a rate of fifty per hour.
1 Steam hammer, 30 cwt ; stroke 2 ft.
1 Small steam hammer ; stroke 18 in.
1 Patent pneumatic hammer ; stroke 6 in.
1 Travelling crane ; span 25 ft. 6 in., travel 154 ft., lifting capacity 2 tons.
1 Blower, 8 in. outlet.

Acetylene Welding Store :—

2 Generators complete.

Slipways :—

2 750-ton, 1 250-ton, 2 40-ton, 2 20-ton.
Haulage machinery, complete with Cochran boiler, oil-fuel and water-tanks, and all accessories.

Refrigeration House :—

1 4-cylinder paraffin engine, 30 b.h.p.
1 " Lightfoot " ammonia compressor.
1 Condenser.
2 Gwynne's No. 2 centrifugal pumps.

Pumping Station :—

1 Worthington duplex pump, 14 in. by 7 in. by 10 in.
1 Worthington duplex pump, 9 in. by 5¼ in. by 10 in.
1 Worthington duplex pump, 6 in. by 4 in. by 6 in.
1 Worthington duplex pump, 3 in. by 2 in. by 3 in.
1 Worthington duplex pump, 4 in. by 2¾ in. by 4 in.
3 Horizontal disinfectors.
1 " Burlington " tubular boiler. W.P. 75 lb.
1 Marine tubular boiler. W.P. 100 lb.
1 Weir's vertical evaporator.
1 Petrol engine, compressor and receiver.

MOTOR REPAIR DOCKYARD (BASRAH)

1.	No.	1.	21-in. Le Blond lathe, hollow spindle, heavy. Duty. 10½-in. centres, 7-ft. bed.
2.	No.	2.	9-in. lathe, 7½-in. centres, 4-ft. 6-in. bed.
3.	No.	3.	10½-in. lathe, 7½-in. centres, 8-ft. bed. (Dempster Moore.)
4.	No.	4.	8-in. lathe, 7½-in. centres, 4-ft. 6-in. bed.
5.	No.	5.	5½-in. lathe, 5½-in. centres, 4-ft. bed.
6.			D. & W. capstan lathe, 8-in. centres.
7.	No.	13.	18-in. Le Blond hollow spindle lathe.
8.			Radial sensitive drill.
9.			Drill by Turner, Hoar & Co.
10.			Drill by London Brothers.
11.			Plane (Dempster Moore).
12.			Drill ("Grinder") by Turner Horrace.
13.			Power metal saw.
14.			Grindstone.
15.			Power metal saw.
16.			Treadle lathe.
17.			Grinder.
18.			Blower (centrifugal fan).
19.			Blower (centrifugal fan).
20.			{Motor No. 39103. A.C. 30 b.h.p. {220 volts, 116 ampères, 580 r.p.m.
21.			Drill revolving bed.
22.			Shaping machine, 8-in. stroke (Dempster's).
23.			Milling machine (James Archdale's).
24.			Drill grinder.
25.			Pipe-screwing machine.
26.			Drill by Alfred Herbert.

27.   Robey engine, No. 35382. 35 h.p., complete with
               tanks, etc.
28.   29–31. Blacksmith forges.
30.   Power hammer, 60 lb. (Goliath).
32.   Copper-smith forge.

MOTOR REPAIR DOCKYARD, BAGHDAD

LIST OF MACHINERY

3½″ Drummond Lathe. S.C. Hollow spindle, ⅜″ change wheels
incomplete, full set of tools for slide-rest, nine sets of hand tools ;
also small milling cutter, spindles, and saw-blade with three saws,
wood-turning rest, overhead shafting and treadling gear, fly-
wheel, one small drill chuck, 1–4 jaw independent, 1–3 jaw scroll
chuck face plates, etc. Complete with counter-shafting.

8″ " Baghdad " Lathe. (Not S.C.) 10′ B.C. 10′ between
centres, 16″ gap in fair condition, 3-speed gear-box traverse lead
screw broken, fitter with reverse on saddle. Complete with
counter-shafting.

8″ Fay and Egan Lathe. S.C. 4′ B.C. Hollow spindle 1¼″.
New machine, complete with face plate, gear-box, S.C. changes,
and necessary change wheels. Complete with counter-shafting.

Denbigh Milling Machine. 3½″ H. × 6″ V. × 9″ H. self-acting
traverse for wheel and spindle cutters. Complete with counter-
shafting.

7″ Blonde Lathe. S.C. 2′ 6″ B.C. Hollow spindle 1¼″. New
machine, complete with face plate, 4-jaw independent chuck,
gear-box, S.C. changes. Complete with counter-shafting.

" Baghdad " Lathe. 3′ B.C., 6½″ H.G., 7″ gap, 1–3 jaw chuck,
one face plate, one set change-gear wheels, in fair condition.
Complete with counter-shafting and pulleys. Hollow spindle 1″.

Boynton and Plummer Shaping Machine. V.8″ × 14″ × 9″-
stroke in fair condition, 14″ self-acting feed. (Horizontal.)
Complete with counter-shafting.

Turner, Hoares & Co. Pillar Drilling Machine. Vertical
adjustment on post 16″, 10″ clearance, 8″ sensitive feed, 4 cone-
speeds (reduction gear in to P. cones out of section). Complete
with counter-shafting.

Jones and Shipman Sensitive Drilling Machine. Pillar
adjustment 22″, 7″ clearance, 5″ sensitive feed. Complete with
counter-shafting.

Wet Grinder by Blount. 16″ wheel centrifugal pump, friction
driven. Complete with counter-shafting.

Fan Blower (Air). *Complete with counter-shafting.*

Aster-Sieman's Electric Generating Plant. 55 k.w. 70 volts, 79 amps., 1100 revs., with switchboard, etc., for charging accumulators.

Ruston and Proctor Horizontal 10-h.p. Oil Engine. New and in good order ; drives all shop machinery.

Large Slip-way Hauling Winch.

Hornsby & Sons' One Single-cycle Oil Engine. 6-h.p. Second-hand, in good working order ; for driving slip-way winch. Complete with two circulating water-tanks and fittings.

Hand Winch on Hydro-Glisseur Slip-way.

7″ Screw-cutting Lathe, with gap-bed swinging 13″. 3′ B.C. With carrier plate, face plate, four dog chuck and self-centring chuck, and complete set of gear-wheels up to 120 ; also fitted with surface saddle traverse, by separate back-shaft drive: Complete with counter-shafting.

Wood-sawing and Planing Machine, rising, following and tilting table. Complete with counter-shafting and pulleys.

Universal Grinder. Complete with counter-shaftings.

I.W.T. REPAIR WORKSHOPS, NASIRIYAH

LIST OF MACHINERY

1 Windmill with water pump connections.
1 Hand-screwing Machine and Die.
1 Boiler Test Pump.
1 Hand-drilling Machine, and drills.
5 Hand Pumps, with four lengths of hose.
2 Lathes, with tools and fittings complete.
2 Drilling Machines, with tools and fittings complete.
1 Planing Machine, with tools and fittings complete.
1 Slotting Machine, with tools and fittings complete. '
1 Shearing and Punching Machine, complete.
1 Circular Saw, complete with saws.
2 Emery Wheels, complete.
1 Machine Hacksaw, complete.
1 Oil Engine (Hornsby type), for driving power. Shafting and belting for all machines, complete.

I.W.T. REPAIR WORKSHOPS, KARRADAH

LIST OF MACHINERY

1 Turning Lathe. $6\frac{1}{2}''$ centres.
1   ,,   ,, $7''$,,
1   ,,   ,, $24''$,,
1   ,,   ,, $7\frac{1}{2}''$,,
1   ,,   ,, $5\frac{1}{2}''$,,
1   ,,   ,, $8''$,,
1   ,,   ,, $9''$,,
1   ,,   ,, 8 ,,
2   ,,   ,, 10 ,,
1   ,,   ,, 12 ,,
1   ,,   ,, $12\frac{1}{2}''$,,
2   ,,   ,, $8''$,,
1 Milling Machine.
1 Slotting Machine.
1 Shaping Machine.
1 Planing Machine.
1 Small Vertical Drilling Machine.
1 Large Vertical Drilling Machine.
1 Radial Drilling Machine.
1 Screwing Machine (Whitworth).
1 Hand-screwing Machine (gas thread).
1 Small Shearing and Punching Machine.
1 Small Power Saw.
1 Small Emery Wheel.
1 Twist Drill Grinding Machine.
1 Wood-planing Machine.
1 Wood-turning Lathe.
1 Band Saw.
1 Circular Saw.
1 Grindstone.
1 Steam Hammer.
1 Portable Boiler and Engine.
1 Small Auxiliary Boiler.
1 Blackstone Engine.
1 Dynamo, driven from main shafting.
1 Belt-driven Hammer.
2 Blower Fans.

I.W.T. REPAIR WORKSHOPS, AMARA

LIST OF MACHINERY

LATHES :

No. 1.—London Bros., Glasgow. 6½″ centres, 3′ bed, 3-speed back gear.

No. 2.—Britannia Co., Colchester. 8″ centres, 6′ bed, 3-speed back gear.

No. 3.—Somerscales, Ltd., Keighley. 9″ centres, 4′ bed, 3-speed back gear.

No. 4.—Thompson & Co., Calcutta. 8½″ centres, 6′ bed, 4-speed back gear.

No. 5.—Machine Tool Co., Nottingham. 11¼″ centres, 12′ bed, 4-speed back gear.

No. 6.—Dean, Smith & Grace, Keighley. 12½″ centres, 10′ bed, 4-speed back gear.

No. 7.—Maker unknown. 9½″ centres, 7′ bed, 4-speed back gear.

No. 8.—J. A. Fay & Egan. 7″ centres, 4′ bed, 3-speed back gear.

No. 9.—J. A. Fay & Egan. 7″ centres, 4′ bed, 3-speed back gear.

No. 10.—Cunliff & Croom, Ltd., Manchester. 18″ centre, facing 4-speed back gear.

No. 11.—Drummond Bros., England. 5″ centres, 2′ 6″ bed, 3-speed back gear.

No. 12.—No name. Wood-turning. 6″ centres, 6′ bed.

PLANING MACHINES :

No. 1A.—Maker's name unknown. Table 2′ 6″ × 6′.
Wood Panel Segar. 18″ blade.

SHAPING MACHINE :

Make unknown. 12″ stroke, 4′ bed, 4-speed.

SLOTTING MACHINE :

No. 1C.—Muir & Co., Manchester.

MILLING MACHINE :

No. 1D.—J. Dickinson & Co. 16″ × 4′ table, 3-speed, 10″ arm to table.

DRILLING MACHINES :

No. 1E.—Radial. 4' arm, 2'×3" table, 4-speed back gear.
No. 2E.—2' 6" table, 2' pillar to drill, 4-speed back gear.
No. 3E.—4-speed back gear, self-feeding 18" table, 2' 6"
pillar to drill.
No. 4E.—Sensitive, by Washbourne Shops, U.S.A.
No. 5E.—Midgley & Sutcliffe, Bradford. 16" table, 16"
pillar to drill.

PUNCHING AND SHEERING MACHINES :

No. 1F.—By Lee & Hunt, Nottingham.

SAWS (POWER) :

No. 1G.—Power. 12" blade " Fortuna."
No. 2G.—Circular Saw. By T. Robinson & Son, Ltd.,
Rochdale. 5'×2' 6" table, 42" saw.
No. 3G.—Band Saw. 2' arm. J. Sagar & Co., Ltd.

ROLLING AND BENDING MACHINES :

No. 1H.—Made in Workshops. 3" rollers by 3' 6" long.

EMERY WHEELS :

No. 1.—" The Denbigh." 12"×2" stone.
No. 2I.—Alfred Herbert & Co. Double stones, 7"×1¼"×
6"×¾". 4.
No. 3I.—C. G. Townsend, U.S.A.
No. 4I.—Mackbeth Bros. Saw sharpening.

SCREWING MACHINE (POWER) :

No. 1J.—Chas. Winu & Co. ½"–3" Gas and Whitworth.
Screwing Machine, 1¼" bolts, 2" pipes.

POWER HAMMERS :

No. 1H.—" Hercules." Samuel Platt & Co., Wednesbury.
160 lb.
Not packed. Beaudry & Co., Boston " Champion."

BLOWERS AND FANS (BELT-DRIVEN) :

No. 1L.—18" Blackman Fan.
No. 2.—Blower. 12".
No. 3L.—Howden's Forced Draught Fan. Ex. P.S. 37¾.
Blower. " Champion " Cupola and Forge No. 8. 35".

I.W.T. REPAIR WORKSHOPS, KUT

LIST OF MACHINERY

Lathe. 16″ centres, 24″ gap, 18′ between centres, screw cutting.
Lathe. 5½″ centres, no gap, 3′ between centres, screw cutting.
Lathe. 9″ centres, 4′ between centres, screw cutting.
Lathe. 8″ centres, 4′ between centres, screw cutting.
Lathe. 8″ centres, 15″ gap, 6′ between centres, screw cutting.
Emery Stone. Two wheels 1′ dia.
Emery Stone. Two wheels 1′ dia
Saw, Metal. 1′ blade.
Slotting Machine. 14″ stroke.
Planing Machine. 36″ stroke.
Screwing Machine. 1¼″ bolts, 2″ pipes.
Screwing Machine. 1¼″ bolts, 2″ pipes.
Lathe. 8″ centres, 13″ gap, 5′ between centres, screw cutting.
Vertical Drill. Table 16″ dia.
Vertical Drill. Table 13″ dia.
Vertical Drill. Table 16″ dia.
Sheer, Punching and Angle Iron Cutting Machine. Cut $\frac{5}{16}$″ plate
    or angle irons.
Milling Machine. 6″ centres.
Saw, Metal. 16″ blade, 6″ stroke.
Saw, Wood (Circular), with travelling bogies. Saw 21″ dia.
Saw Grinders.
Fan Blower. 18″ dia.
" Robey " Semi-Diesel Engine, for shop power. Compressed air
    starter run on kerosene oil. 5-k.w. Dynamo (Westinghouse),
    D.C. compound wound, 230 volts, 1100 revs.
Portable Engine, with boiler coal consumption (spare for shop
    power).
10-k.w. Dynamo, D.C. compound wound, 200 volts, 50 amps.,
    650 revs. Direct coupled to single-cylinder steam engine.

DYNAMOS :

    1 Machine by Electro-motor Ltd. Output 20 k.w.

INTERNAL COMBUSTION ENGINES :

    1 Single-cylinder, by Petters, Yeovil. 35 b.h.p. Complete.

STEAM PORTABLE ENGINES AND BOILERS :

    1 32-h.p. Engine and Boiler. Over-type, oil-fired. Marshall
    & Co., Gainsborough.

1 16-h.p. Engine and Boiler. Over-type, coal-fired.
Marshall & Co., Gainsborough.
1 16-h.p. Engine and Boiler. Over-type, coal-fired.
Brown & May.

PUMPS :
1 Rotary Pump. Geared pulley, belt driven.
1 Worthington.
1 Worthington.
1 Air Pump for charging air receiver, $3\frac{1}{4}''$ dia.
1 Fore Pump for boiler testing.

MORTICE MACHINES :
1 Hand Mortice.

GRINDSTONES :
1 Grindstone, belt driven.
1 Grindstone, belt driven.
1 Grindstone, hand power.

Pneumatic Hammer, 2 cwt. blow.
10-k.w. Dynamo, compound wound, 230 volts, 1300 revs.
Direct current, belt driven by single-cylinder engine (horizontal steam).
16-k.w. Dynamo. Direct current, 220 volts, 72·6 amps.,
950 revs. Direct coupled to Keighley's imperial four-cylinder kerosine set. Revs. 850, h.p. 30–33.

INWATER WORKSHOPS, HILLAH

LIST OF MACHINERY

7-h.p. Hornsby Oil Engine.
$7\frac{3}{4}''$ Centre Lathe.
$8''$ Centre Lathe.
$6''$ Centre Lathe.
Small Drilling Machine.
Horizontal Shaping Machine.
Small Blast Fan.
Circular Saw (Wood).
Screwing Machine up to $3''$ gas.

"VULCAN" FLOATING WORKSHOP AT DHIBBAN

LIST OF MACHINERY

1 8-h.p. Stockport Oil Engine.
1 Lighting Set, 3 h.p., 10 amps., 100 volts.
1 Lathe. 7" centre.
1 Lathe. 6" centre.
1 Planing Machine. 6" stroke.
1 Universal Drilling Machine.
1 Fan for forge and cupola.
1 Pump for filling fresh water tanks.

FLOATING WORKSHOP, "NGAWUN"

LIST OF MACHINERY

1 New Kelvin Engine.
1 Lathe. Screw cutting with 2 chucks.
Hand Drilling Machine.

APPENDIX E1

BULK OIL STORAGE AT VARIOUS DEPOTS, DECEMBER, 1918.

Capacities in gallons unless otherwise stated.

Station.	Tank.	Capacity.	Remarks.
Beit Naama	Kerosene	1 1000	E. & M.
New River Front Pump	,,	2 1000	,,
Khora Creek	,,	1 220 tons	I.W.T.
Central Power Station	Fuel oil	1 2000	E. & M.
,, ,,	Kerosene	1 2000	,,
Ashar Supply Depot	Fuel oil	1 3390	S. & T.
,, ,,	Kerosene	1 1000	,,
Khandaq Creek	,,	1 5000	Political.
Tanooma Pumping Plant	,,	1 400	E. & M.
Tanooma Supply	Fuel oil	1 800	S. & T.
,,	Kerosene	1 800	,,
Dockyard	Fuel oil	1 6777	I.W.T.
,,	,,	1 5000	,,
,,	,,	2 490	,,
,,	,,	2 400	,,
Muftieh Oil Depot	,,	2 256,000	,,
,, ,,	,,	1 220 tons	Railways,Makina
,, ,,	,,	1 10 ton	I.W.T.
,, ,,	,,	1 42 ton	,,
I.W.T. Stores, Margil	Kerosene	2 1000	I.W.T.
Filtration, Margil	,,	2 1000	E. & M.
Supply Depot, Margil	Fuel oil	4 1000	I.W.T.
,, ,,	Kerosene	1 1008	,,
Re-erection, Margil	Fuel oil	1 4000	,,

244

Station.	Tank.	Capacity.	Remarks.
Makina Supply	Fuel oil	4 1000	S. & T.
,,	Kerosene	2 1000	,,
Brick Kilns	Fuel oil	1 5120	Other depots.
Nahr Umar	,,	6 400	I.W.T.*
,,	,,	1 35 ton	S. & T.*
Kurna	,,	1 390	S. & T.
,,	,,	4 400	,,
,,	,,	1 350	,,
,,	Kerosene	2 325	Other depots.
,,	,,	1 400	,,
,,	,,	3 840	,,
Ezra's Tomb	,,	1 330	I.W.T.
Narrows	,,	3 330	,,
Qalet Saleh	,,	1 375	,,
,,	,,	2 439	Political.
,,	,,	1 966	,,
Amara	Fuel oil	1 1000 ton	I.W.T.
,,	,,	1 50 ton	,,
,,	,,	1 400	,,
,,	,,	2 400	Dairy farm.
,,	,,	3 200	S. & T.
,,	,,	3 200	,,
,,	,,	1 300	,,
,,	,,	4 191	,,
,,	,,	3 400	,,
,,	,,	4 400	Other departs.
,,	Kerosene	1 1144	Political.
,,	,,	1 346	,,
,,	,,	1 400	,,
,,	,,	1 5292	S. & T.
,,	,,	1 1032	E. & M.
,,	,,	1 5292	,,
Ali Gharbi	,,	1 1200	I.W.T.
,,	,,	1 400	Political.
Kut	Fuel oil	2 18 ton	I.W.T.
,,	,,	6 220 ton	,,
,,	,,	2 905	S. & T.
,,	,,	1 468	,,
,,	,,	3 1037	Dairy farm.
,,	Kerosene	2 800	I.W.T.
,,	,,	1 2400	Political.
,,	,,	1 3927	E. & M.

* To be dispensed with.

R

Station.	Tank.	Capacity.	Remarks.
Kut	Kerosene	1 989	E. & M.
,,	Qualyan	2 742	Political.
Sumar	,,	1 452	Other departs.
Zeur	Fuel oil	1 220 ton	I.W.T.
	O.C. 4 sta	tionary barge	extra storage.
,,	Qualyan	1 2310	Political.
,,	,,	2 1566	,,
Baghailah	—	—	—
Khaniquin	Fuel oil	1 30 ton	I.W.T.
Advanced Base	,,	1 500 ,,	,,
,,	,,	8 30 ,,	,,
,,	,,	3 220 ,,	,,
,,	,,	1 500 ,,	,,
,,	,,	2 800	S. & T.
,,	Qualyan	2 800	,,
,,	,,	1 400	,,
Baghdad	Fuel oil	1 100 ton	I.W.T.
,,	,,	1 220	,,
,,	,,	1 176,293	E. & M.
,,	,,	8 628	,,
,,	,,	8 265	,,
Hiniadi	Petrol	2 2186	I.W.T.
,,	,,	6 2385	,,
,,	,,	2 2269	,,
,,	,,	1 2372	,,
,,	,,	1 2368	,,
,,	,,	1 2235	,,
,,	Fuel oil	1 2177	,,
,,	,,	1 1000 ton	,,
,,	Petrol	1 400 gal.	Other departs.
,,	,,	1 781	,,
Hillah	Fuel oil	1 42 ton	I.W.T.
,,	Qualyan	1 2272	Political.
,,	,,	5 2418	,,
,,	,,	2 2380	,,
EUPHRATES :			
Ur	Fuel oil	1 1000 ton	I.W.T.
,,	,,	1 220 ,,	,,
,,	,,	1 1100 ,,	Removed from Khora Creek.
Nasiriyah	,,	1 220 ,,	I.W.T.
,,	Kerosene	2 4750	Political.

Station.	Tank.	Capacity.	Remarks.
Suk	Kerosene	1 717	Political.
Darraji	Fuel oil	1 400	S. & T.
Samawa	,,	1 50 ton	I.W.T.
Baiji	,,	1 220	,,
,,	,,	1 30	,,
,,	,,	1 1400	Political.
Waar	,,	2 400	S. & T.
Sibil Camp	,,	2 400	,,
Shenafiyah	Kerosene	2 330	Political.
Dewanieh	Fuel oil	1 400 ton	I.W.T.
,,	,,	1 220 ,,	,,
,,	,,	1 450 ,,	Railways. Removed from Ezra's Tomb.
,,	Qualyan	2 781	Political.
Kufa	Kerosene	8 400	,,
Diala	Qualyan	1 5003	,,
Felujah	Kerosene	1 2310	,,
Dhibban	Fuel oil	1 400 ton	I.W.T.
,,	,,	1 220 ,,	,,
,,	,,	4 $11'1'' \times 7'5\frac{1}{2}'' \times 9'11''$	,,
,,	,,	2 $9'10\frac{1}{2}'' \times 7'5\frac{1}{2}'' \times 8'6''$	,,
,,	,,	3 $9' \times 5' \times 5'11''$	,,
Ramadie	,,	4 $11' \times 2'9'' \times 4'$	,,
Hit	,,	6 $11' \times 2'' \times 9'4''$	,,
,,	,,	2 $9'8'' \times 3' \times 5'10''$	,,
,,	,,	2 $8' \times 4' \times 4'$	
Beled	Kerosene	1 2103	Political.

APPENDIX E2

Average monthly consumption of Coal, Oil Fuel, Kerosene and Petrol by all departments during 1918 :

COAL.	OIL FUEL	KEROSENE.		PETROL.	
Tons.	Tons.	In bulk. Tons.	In tins. Gallons.	In bulk. Tons.	In tins and cases Gallons.
25,665	9500	450	150,000	20	470,000

APPENDIX F1

REGULATIONS REGARDING NATIVE CRAFT

SECTION 1.—General.

1. All native craft over 12 tons belonging to natives of occupied territory or persons resident therein, are placed under the control of the Director, Inland Water Transport, and will be managed as a department of the Inland Water Transport by the Controller of Native Craft.

The Controller of Native Craft may requisition at any time such other craft as are required for Government work.

Native craft will be allotted to departments requiring them in accordance with the orders of the Inspector General of Communications.

2. No native craft is to be used by any services or department unless specially allotted by the Controller of Native Craft.

3. Private individuals are forbidden to employ native craft of 12 tons or over except under special sanction from the Controller of Native Craft. Craft below 12 tons are permitted to work for private individuals on passes given by the Controller of Native Craft, showing that the boat is not required for Government work at the time.

4. All passenger bellums will, as at present, be registered by the Commissioner of Police, but such passenger bellums as are required for Government work or have been allotted to departments duly authorised to have them, will now come under the direct control of the Controller of Native Craft.

5. It is an offence for any native craft of 12 tons and over to be on the river without a number allotted to and painted on it, under the authority of the Controller of Native Craft.

SECTION 2.—Registration.

1. All mahailas or bellums of 12 tons and upwards will be numbered as follows :—

(a) Working on the Tigris and Karun ; letters and numbers black, 2 feet high, on the white ground on each side of the bow.
  50 tons and over ; Letter A. and Serial No. (separate series for each letter) :

35 to 49 tons ; Letter B. and Serial No. (separate series for
each letter) :
25 to 34 tons ; Letter C. and Serial No. (separate series for each
letter) :
12 to 24 tons ; Letter D. and Serial No. (separate series for each
letter).
(b) Working on Euphrates ; Serial No. only.
(c) Euphrates bellums, allotted to the XV. Division as transport, will
have the No. XV. painted in front of the Serial No.

2. Boats under 12 tons, permanently employed for Government work, to have the Letter E. in front of the Serial No.

3. Passenger bellums belonging to Government or engaged on Government work will be numbered F. and Serial No.

SECTION 3.—Applications for Boats.

1. Applications for craft for the conveyance of material from place to place in port or up-river will be made as follows :—

(a) "A.," "B." and "C." boats, Ordnance and S. and T. Margil, to
A.T.O. Mahailas, Margil ; other departments to Mahaila Depot
Officer, Muftieh.
(b) For "D.," "E." and "F." boats, to the A.T.O. Mahailas, Small Craft
Office, Ashar Creek.

2. All applications for craft for the conveyance of stores or other material should show the amount required to be carried, in tons.

SECTION 4.—Loading.

1. With the exception of S. and T. and Ordnance, Margil, where special arrangements under mahaila officer are in force, departments to which craft are allotted for loading will return receipts for the craft to the offices from where they have been allotted and will inform the Controller of Native Craft of the date of arrival of the boat and the date on which they have completed loading. Consignors are held responsible that boats are properly loaded. Where possible, boats should not be loaded entirely with bulky material which takes up much space and does not weigh down the boat.

SECTION 5.—Way-bills.

1. Way-bills will in each case be made out by the consignor, showing the total of tons (payment is made on tons carried), and handed to the nakoda of the boat as soon as loading has been completed and before the boat is allowed to depart.

2. Consignees are held responsible that receipted way-bills

arc handed back to the nakoda immediately his vessel is discharged and before she moves off.

3. Deficiencies, if any, will be noted on the back of the way-
bill, together with their value, by the consignee before the way-
bill is returned to the nakoda. No deductions for loss will be
made, or questions regarding shortages entertained, unless these
instructions are complied with.

SECTION 6.—Passes.

1. All craft when allotted for loading will be given passes,
showing the department to which allotted, and destination to
which cargo is to be carried. These passes are on no account to
be taken from the nakodas, and no alteration may be made in
them without previous reference to the Controller of Native
Craft. On being cleared at their destination nakodas will be
given passes to return empty by the mahaila officer concerned.
No craft of under 12 tons, working for private individuals, will
bo permitted to leave the following places without passes signed
by the officer noted against each :—

BASRAH : A.T.O. Mahailas, Small Craft Office, Ashar Creek.
QURNAH : A.T.O. Mahailas, Qurnah.
AMARA : A.T.O. Mahailas, Amara.
NASIRIYAH : R.H.C., Nasiriyah.
AHWAZ : I.W.T. Officer, Ahwaz.

SECTION 7.—Towage.

1. All applications for towage of craft up-river, loaded by
various departments, will be made to the Controller of Native
Craft. No craft are to be despatched up-river, towed or otherwise, without previous intimation to the Controller of Native
Craft.

SECTION 8.—Payments.

1. All payments on account of pay of crews, and hire of native
craft of any description, engaged by, or allotted to different
departments will, in future, be made by the Controller of Native
Craft. No other department should, in future, make any direct
payment whatsoever under this head.

2. When sending boats for payment departments to whom
boats are allotted must give nakodas a certificate showing that
they have worked satisfactorily during the month. Without
such certificates no payments will be made.

3. Any department using boats not already paid for by the

Controller of Native Craft will, when sending nakodas for payment, provide them with a statement showing the authority under which the boat was originally engaged or allotted ; the rate at which the boat and crew were originally engaged and are being paid ; the date up to which the last payment has been made ; lastly, the advances, if any, to be deducted from future payments.

4. The following are the pay centres to which boats may be sent for payments :—

BASRAH	Large Craft, A., B. and C. Class Small Craft, D. Class E. and F. Class	Muftieh, Mahaila Depot Small Craft Office, Ashar Creek, opposite Custom House.
TIGRIS LINE.	A.T.O. Mahailas A.T.O., Mahailas	I.W.T. Office, Qurnah. I.W.T. Office, Amara.
EUPHRATES Line		R.H.C., Nasiriyah.
AHWAZ		I.W.T. Office, Ahwaz.

5. Other pay centres will shortly be established at Sheikh Saad and Ezra's Tomb, of which due notification will be given.

Printed in Great Britain at
The Mayflower Press, Plymouth. William Brendon & Son, Ltd.

APPENDIX G 1.

DIAGRAM ILLUSTRATING TONNAGE CARRIED UP RIVER

BETWEEN SEPT. 1916 AND NOV. 11th 1918.

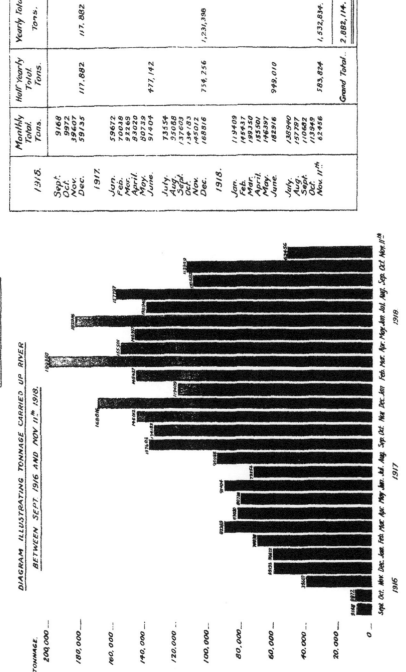

	Monthly Total. Tons.	Half Yearly Total. Tons.	Yearly Total. Tons.
1916.			
Sept.	9168		
Oct.	9972		
Nov.	39607		
Dec.	59135	117,882	117,882
1917.			
Jan.	59672		
Feb.	70048		
Mar.	92269		
April.	83020		
May.	80739		
June.	91404	477,142	
July.	73554		
Aug.	35088		
Sept.	137603		
Oct.	134183		
Nov.	145012		
Dec.	168816	754,256	1,231,398
1918.			
Jan.	119409		
Feb.	145437		
Mar.	199350		
April.	155501		
May.	146397		
June.	182916	949,010	
July.	138940		
Aug.	157797		
Sept.	110682		
Oct.	113949		
Nov. 11th	62456	583,824	1,532,834.
		Grand Total	2,882,114.

Lightning Source UK Ltd.
Milton Keynes UK
UKHW010658170121
377156UK00001B/24